I0825425

Advance Praise for *Cosmic Goodness*

"*Cosmic Goodness* reminds you what I had to learn the hard way: Life gets better the moment you stop trying to control everything, trust the pull inside you, and let yourself become who you're meant to be."

—Mel Robbins, *New York Times* bestselling author and host of *The Mel Robbins Podcast*

"Cassidy Gard doesn't just intellectually understand spiritual principles. She has lived them. She viscerally gets it, aligning the earthy and the divine in a fantastic way. What a heart, what a brain, what a writer. She hits you right between the eyes and you feel blessed."

—Marianne Williamson

"*Cosmic Goodness* is an effervescent coming-of-age memoir that feels intimate yet universally resonant. Rising into her own leading-lady arc, Cassidy's voice shimmers with fearless honesty and radiant spirit."

—Emily Giffin, *New York Times* bestselling author of *Love You More*

"*Cosmic Goodness* is a heartfelt reminder that by trusting the unseen threads of serendipity and choosing conscious healing (and nature) over old stories, we step into our inner guidance and embrace soul-aligned joy and love of the wondrous life we are meant to live."

—Mariel Hemingway

"As my father said, 'The real you is not a puppet which life pushes around. The real, deep down you is the whole universe.' *Cosmic Goodness* is the playful invitation to become your own Big Bang."

—Mark Watts, Alan Watts Org

"Authentic, vulnerable, and beautifully written in a voice that makes you want to be friends with the author, *Cosmic Goodness* is an important, timely read."

—Zibby Owens

"*Cosmic Goodness* is a love letter to every woman who's ever chased success and lost herself in the process. Cassidy writes with the precision of a journalist and the heart of a poet—transforming burnout into breakthrough, loneliness into light."

—Deuxmoi

"Paolo Sorrentino spoke of 'The real, the useless, and the unspeakable kind of love that brings pain, yet also forces you to start again.' If you've had love and heartbreaks and are on the road to rebirth, Cassidy Gard's luminous memoir will accompany and inspire with wit, kindness, honesty, and hard-fought wisdom. Plus all the Tinseltown wildness you could ask for."

—Junot Díaz, Pulitzer Prize-winning author
of *The Brief Wondrous Life of Oscar Wao*

"Cassidy writes with the kind of honesty that makes you laugh through your tears. Her gorgeous story is a roadmap for anyone searching for meaning in the mess of ambition, love, and family."

—Jo Piazza, bestselling author
of *Everyone Is Lying to You*

"*Cosmic Goodness* is a wonderful door to open and look inside a very colorful life. Cassidy and I share some really unique life lessons. Both our parents took us to Grateful Dead shows beginning from our earliest days. We just had different seats. Also, we both did time on *The Bachelor* television show. She was in the field, I was in an editing suite. But we were weaving in and out of the same worlds and Cassidy's book is a great glimpse into her perspective of it all. Her sense of humor carries you through the darker moments and I found I couldn't put down the book once I started the journey."

—Justin Kreutzmann, director
of *Let There Be Drums!*

"In *Cosmic Goodness*, Cassidy Gard trades breaking news for inner stillness, tracing her transformation from burnout to belonging. With the warmth and wisdom of a late-night letter to a friend, she explores ambition, grief, sobriety, and the miracle of divine timing. Gard writes with the heart of a seeker and the clarity of someone who's met her shadows and decided to love them anyway. This sparkling memoir is a reminder that reinvention isn't a deadline, but a divine unfolding. Every page glows with tenderness, humor, and the courage to begin again. It's a book that will leave you with more grace for your past and more hope about what's still to come."

—Mari Andrew, *New York Times* bestselling author and artist of *Am I There Yet?*

"*Cosmic Goodness* is an essential companion for any woman navigating the divine intersection of soul-aligned pursuits and the transformation of becoming a mother—proof that we are the designers of our own lives."

—Liz Tran, founder of Reset and author of *The Karma of Success* and *AQ*

"*Cosmic Goodness* is an illuminating mirror for any woman who's been frozen by perfectionism and is brave enough to drop the heavy mask to be free."

—Amber Rae, bestselling author of *Loveable* and *Choosing Wonder Over Worry*

"I couldn't put this book down. Each page brought forth a nugget of wisdom like a scavenger hunt for the soul. *Cosmic Goodness* takes you right to the heart of womanhood with a raw authenticity we can all relate to. Akin to a timeless poem, I find myself rereading and reciting her words over and over again."

—Carson Meyer, doula and author of *Growing Together*

"*Cosmic Goodness* is a masterclass in what it looks like to stop performing and begin living from within. It traces her own path out of the 'desert of lack and the city of not-enoughness' toward a life rooted in healing, motherhood, and a spiritual homecoming. Cassidy Gard writes with the kind of radical truthfulness that reminds us our mess is not the end of the story—it is the doorway."

—Jennifer Pastiloff, bestselling author of *On Being Human* and *Proof of Life*

"This is work of rare honesty and grace. *Cosmic Goodness* captures the raw, messy, mystical, and magnificent landscape of motherhood—the parts that are too often left unspoken, too taboo to say aloud. This is a book to read slowly, to breathe with, and to feel seen through."

—Aviva Romm, MD, *New York Times* bestselling author of *Hormone Intelligence* and founder of The Mama Pathway

"In a world rushing to hide its wounds, Cassidy Gard slows down to meet hers with light. *Cosmic Goodness* reveals what happens when attention meets truth—when awareness becomes love. A tender, honest reminder of the healing power of being present."

—Mitra Manesh, senior mindfulness educator at UCLA

"In *Cosmic Goodness*, I am grateful to witness the challenges Cassidy encountered. They illuminate how deeply these same forces shape so many women's lives—and they make me appreciate the women in my own life even more."

—Barry Barnes, author of *Everything I Know About Business I Learned from the Grateful Dead*

"It doesn't get better, you get better. What beautiful words to live by, and how Cassidy Gard embodies that and shows us there is a way to crack open our hearts and embrace all the cosmic goodness there is in the world; for every woman who has embraced the pain, got through it, and learned how to come home to herself."

—Jane Green, *New York Times* bestselling author

"For any thirtysomething who has felt lost in the "shoulds" and craved a deeper alignment with their life, but wasn't quite sure how to get there. Cassidy Gard translates her own improbable but true experiences into tangible advice for heeding quiet synchronicities and building a singular path home. A reminder to follow your own wildness into the light."

—Leslie Stephens, author of *You're Safe Here*

"A remarkably assured debut. But what's most surprising about the book are the universal truths. Ms. Gard has the ability to appeal to an incredibly diverse intersection of readers: professionals, day-dreamers, hippies, seekers, and, ultimately, mothers and daughters. She's the kind of person you'd find yourself inexplicably opening up to."

—Drew Fortune, author of *No Encore: Musicians Reveal Their Weirdest, Wildest, Most Embarrassing Gigs*

"Cassidy Gard is here to bring us breaking news. In *Cosmic Goodness*, she shares the most important news for all of us today; that we live in a time of breaking and that through this breaking, we may awaken to our greatest potential. It's the telling of Gard's life story stepping out from the light of newsrooms into the open sun that, through its intimacy, reveals a path for readers toward a higher existence not through rapture, but rupture. The story and structure of *Cosmic Goodness* presents a clever and effective way of utilizing one's own personal experiences and one's relationship to media as a means of interrogating how your inner narratives play out not just in your mind, but in your body and spirit. Gard leads the way through her exercises with her own lived experience, offering herself as a compassionate guide for readers into the underworld of their own psyche to graciously lead back out toward a more truthful light. May her vulnerability in sharing her stories and the practices that she has used to reveal them help you to open yourself up to yours. As she wisely says at the finish, 'you cannot outsource your becoming.' The journey is yours to take, but Cassidy Gard, intrepid and true, is a spiritual journalist shining a light to show you the way into parts unknown in the soul."

—Will Cady, author of *Which Way Is North*
and cofounder of HEAL MVMNT

"I was riveted by *Cosmic Goodness* from page one. Cassidy Gard's memoir—from a frenetic, burnt-out life as a young television producer covering breaking news 24/7 to a spiritual rebirth and motherhood in Montana's Paradise Valley—is a page-turner, a beautifully recounted journey, and, most importantly, an insightful, witty, and prescient guide to life and the power of renewal and reinvention."

—Peter Davis, editor in chief
at *Avenue Magazine*

"In *Cosmic Goodness*, Cassidy does an incredible job of showing how a deep-rooted belief and inner optimism illuminates the right path for us all."

—Peiman Raf, cofounder and
CEO of Madhappy

"Cassidy Gard's quest to follow her bliss rings through these pages. We all have something to learn from this heroic journey and the deep wisdom Cassidy shares from the path."

—Joanna Gardner, PhD, managing director
of the Joseph Campbell Foundation

Cosmic Goodness

Cosmic Goodness

Surrendering the Shadows to Live in the Light

CASSIDY GARD

A POST HILL PRESS BOOK
ISBN: 979-8-89565-507-8
ISBN (eBook): 979-8-89565-508-5

Cosmic Goodness:
Surrendering the Shadows to Live in the Light

Cover design by Elisha Zepeda (based on an idea by Cassidy Gard)
"Rejuvenation #9" original artwork by Karen Lynch
"The Birth of Venus" artwork by Sandro Botticelli

Post Hill Press
New York • Nashville
posthillpress.com

Published in the United States of America
1 2 3 4 5 6 7 8 9 10

Printed in Canada

Dedicated to the constellation I call mine:

My Mom (Mother Earth)

Squirrel (the Big Bang)

Golden (my sun)

and

Indigo (my moon).

I am

grateful

the cosmos

hold

our orbit…

You each

have made my

Universe

infinitely brighter

and the source of my gravity.

I love you, I love you, I love you.

Contents

Part VII: More Will Be Revealed

Foreword

There are books you read, and books that read you. From its very first pages, *Cosmic Goodness: Surrendering the Shadows to Live in the Light* pulled me toward something larger than words on a page. It arrives at a moment when so many of us are quietly asking how to step out of inherited darkness and into lives that feel authentically our own. I know that question intimately.

In my thirties, raising my daughters, I stood at the kitchen window watching them chase their father across the grass. Laughter rose like birds. I should have been smiling, but a wave of sadness pinned me in place. I was jealous of their ease, of his playfulness because I had no idea how to join them. My days were calendars and checklists: feed, teach, protect, perfect. On paper I was the ideal mother. Inside, I was a child who had never learned to play.

Growing up in a family rattled by alcoholism, I made a vow: I would hold everything together. I would fix the chaos, soothe the pain, make the world safe for everyone else. In the process I buried my own childhood under layers of responsibility. That afternoon at the window cracked me open. I saw the cost of carrying those shadows: I had lost the ability to let go, to laugh without agenda, to be present in the ordinary miracle of a summer day.

Surrendering the shadows, for me, began there. It meant naming the shame I carried not just for what happened in our home, but for the ways it shaped me. It meant choosing, day after day, to lay down the role of perpetual caretaker and pick up curiosity instead. Moving to New York at seventeen had been my first act of surrender; no one knew my last name or the stories behind it. I built a life on my own terms. Years later, with my daughters, I learned the harder surrender: allowing mess, allowing joy, allowing myself to be the beginner.

"Surrendering the shadows to live in the light" is a quiet revolution. It reminds us that light is not the absence of shadow but the choice to walk through it. *Cosmic Goodness*, to me, is the invisible thread that stitches those choices together. It is the friend who calls at the exact moment you need to hear you are enough. It is the sunset that stops you mid-stride and whispers, Pay attention. It is the grace that turns a scheduled life into a spontaneous one, a guarded heart into an open one. Sometimes it wears the face of Venus, sometimes the stillness of a redwood grove, sometimes the laughter of children who have no idea they are healing you.

Breaking the generational inheritance of alcoholism is part of this surrender. My family's illness taught me vigilance; sobriety teaches me trust. Conscious sobriety, like Cassidy's and mine, is less about abstinence and more about presence. We notice what we once numbed. We name patterns instead of repeating them. We give our children a different inheritance: the freedom to play, to fail, to feel without apology.

Living in the light also means honoring the divine feminine the wild, complicated, nurturing force that refuses to be tidy. It is the mother who schedules and the mother who dances in the kitchen. It is the woman who grieves and the woman who creates. Embracing that complexity is not indulgence; it is reverence.

When we allow ourselves to be both fierce and tender, we model wholeness for everyone watching.

Cassidy, your story is a lantern. May every reader who opens these pages feel the warmth of their own shadows softening, the promise of their own light growing. And may *Cosmic Goodness* keep surprising us all, one surrendered step at a time.

Mariel Hemingway

"I saw my life branching out before me like the green fig tree in the story. From the tip of every branch, like a fat purple fig, a wonderful future beckoned and winked. One fig was a husband and a happy home and children, and another fig was a famous poet and another fig was a brilliant professor, and another fig was Ee Gee, the amazing editor, and another fig was Europe and Africa and South America, and another fig was Constantin and Socrates and Attila and a pack of other lovers with queer names and offbeat professions, and another fig was an Olympic lady crew champion, and beyond and above these figs were many more figs I couldn't quite make out. I saw myself sitting in the crotch of this fig tree, starving to death, just because I couldn't make up my mind which of the figs I would choose. I wanted each and every one of them, but choosing one meant losing all the rest, and, as I sat there, unable to decide, the figs began to wrinkle and go black, and, one by one, they plopped to the ground at my feet."

—Sylvia Plath, *The Bell Jar*

Prologue

The phrase "last kid left at summer camp" came to me in the middle of the night, somewhere between the police scanner and lukewarm cups of coffee in the newsroom. I was twenty-seven years old working the overnight shift as a breaking news producer on the network's national desk at ABC News, 11:00 p.m. to 7:00 a.m. five nights a week. My dad had died just weeks earlier. Even with our complicated history, his absence clung to me like a shadow. I lived in a kind of twilight world surrounded by flickering monitors, the hum of fluorescent lights, and the steady thrum of anxiety that came with waiting for the worst thing imaginable to happen.

To this day, I can still recite the New York City newsroom number by heart. In Los Angeles, the overnight shift was quiet on the surface. Just one producer in the studio tasked with watching the feed and waiting for something to break. Beneath that stillness was a pulse of constant readiness. Each night, a rotating list of producers stayed on call, bags packed, waiting for the phone to ring. It could be 3:00 a.m. when you'd get the call: a flight had been booked for 6:30 a.m., and a car would be outside in thirty minutes. No questions. Just go.

The newsroom's alert tone was harsh, like a fire drill for your nervous system. The sound was so abrasive that it would startle me every single time it rang. The New York City news director spoke faster than anyone I had ever met. Each time a call came through, I held my breath waiting to find out if it was a standard touch-base call or a tragedy had struck somewhere, and it was all systems go to get field teams on the ground.

That night, on the floor beneath my desk—my unofficial bed for catnaps between global crises—I was hit with the phrase "last kid left at summer camp." It felt like a lightning strike of truth. My isolation from the normal routine of society was a toxic cocktail of loneliness, sheer exhaustion, anxiety, depression, and panic.

"Last kid left at summer camp" wasn't literal. It was a metaphor. Swap out "summer camp" and replace it with any word that captures the creeping feeling of anxiety that bubbles up in your chest. The triggers of our childhood inadequacies are enough to haunt us well into adulthood. That low-grade panic that starts in your chest when it feels like everyone else has moved on, evolved, outpaced you. The fear wasn't just about being alone. It was about being forgotten. It didn't help that I constantly clocked how far everyone else around me was propelling forward.

At twenty-seven, I couldn't stop doing the math. Three years until thirty, that looming milestone that had somehow been inflated into a deadline for everything: love, babies, homeownership, legacy. My career was on fire. My personal life was in ashes.

I was living in reverse. While my peers met partners, planned weddings, and tried on the word "we," I was going gray under newsroom lights and spiraling in "compare and despair" at 4:00 a.m. My schedule was the opposite of the world's. I was single, isolated, and so deeply out of sync with the rhythm of life, I could barely recognize my own.

I lived in a fever dream of night shifts and red-eye exhaustion. You can't build a life when your waking hours begin after dark. You can't fall in love when your weekends are Tuesday mornings. You can't move forward when you're locked inside a cycle of proving your worth every single day just to keep the job.

I had two Emmys by then. But they mocked me. They didn't hold me at night. They didn't text back. They were shiny, hollow symbols of a life I had given everything to, but one that had given me no room to build anything of my own.

Each time the plane touched back down at LAX, fresh from covering another tragedy, a strange mix of pride and emptiness would settle into my chest. I had just produced coverage that millions of people would watch. Stories that mattered. Lives that had changed in an instant. And yet, as the wheels screeched onto the tarmac, and the cabin lights blinked on, a dull ache would rise in me. I would instinctively check my phone. No texts. No "Did you land safely?" No "What should we do for dinner?" Nothing. Just silence. The kind that echoes.

I would come off the biggest, most high-profile projects of my career, and somehow the hardest part was never the pressure or the deadlines or the heartbreak of the stories themselves; it was walking into an empty apartment afterward. Kicking off my boots, putting down my bag, and realizing there was no one to decompress with. No one to make sense of the day with. No one to wrap their arms around me and say, *"I'm so glad you're home."*

I could feel myself grieving something I had never actually had. Mourning a family that didn't exist. A partnership that hadn't yet found me. I wanted it so badly I could taste it. I didn't want to admit that out loud, especially not in a world where women are constantly told to be self-sufficient and grateful. But the truth was, I wasn't ashamed of wanting love. I was just tired of chasing it.

I was on Raya. I was matching with other career-obsessed creatives and sometimes a world-famous celebrity fitting in coffee dates and rooftop drinks at Soho House between breaking news shifts and red-eye flights. But none of it felt real. None of them could hold my attention for more than five minutes. My brain, wired from years of adrenaline and deadlines, couldn't settle long enough to genuinely connect. ADHD makes that harder. It's like trying to hear your own voice in a room that's always buzzing. I could be staring directly at someone across a table and still feel a million miles away.

The problem wasn't that I didn't want intimacy. I craved it. I just didn't know how to slow down enough to let it find me. I was always one foot out the door, half-packed for the next assignment, glued to my phone just in case the New York desk called with a developing headline. And yet, beneath the velocity of it all, I was desperate for something simple. A quiet dinner. A safe place to land.

When I turned thirty in November 2019, I didn't throw a party. I checked into the Serra Retreat Center in Malibu. No cell service. No mirrors. Just silence and the sound of the ocean. My friends joked it sounded like rehab. Technically, it was entitled "Spiritual Renewal and Recovery Retreat." It was hosted by SLAA, Sex and Love Addicts Anonymous. People who aren't familiar with the twelve-step community always widen their eyes with curiosity with those weighted five words.

I wasn't in SLAA because I was a sex addict. I wasn't even necessarily a love addict. My affliction was that my whole world shattered after each break-up. Each potential relationship represented not just the connection with the person in front of me but also my future life. The one that I envisioned with a family, children, and becoming the roles of partner and mother. It's ironic because I never dreamed of a wedding. I didn't have any interest in a giant ceremony and party. I yearned so deeply for a family. I understood on every level that I needed to create a foundation within myself where I learned how to stand solo. I couldn't only know how to exist in the world by leaning on someone.

I kept thinking about that children's book *Are You My Mother?* where a confused baby bird stumbles from cow to bulldozer, asking each one if they're his mom. It became an oddly fitting metaphor for my dating life in Los Angeles. To keep things light, I'd turn it into a running joke with my friends: dating here felt like the millennial woman's sequel *Are You My Husband?*, starring me, wandering through coffee shops, awkward industry networking events, and swiping right on apps asking myself if guys with man buns and commitment issues were "the one."

My relationship with Miles, my boyfriend of a year and a half, unraveled just three months before my thirtieth birthday. It didn't end in a dramatic fight or a single act of betrayal. It dissolved in the quietest way. He was never going to commit, and deep down, my gut had known it long before my heart was ready to surrender. I just didn't want to be the one to walk away. In the end, I pulled the trigger the only way I knew how. I blocked him on everything. It felt harsh and juvenile, but it was the only thing that made the pain subside enough to feel in control again. I couldn't keep feeling my heart leap out of my chest every time I had a new text and hoped it was him, realizing the fear of losing me was bigger than his commitment issues.

What made it so hard to let go wasn't just the love. It was the fantasy. The idea that this could be it. Maybe I had finally found my exit ramp. For two years, we had mapped out timelines and circled imagined milestones. I remember the way it landed in the air between us, like we had claimed something that wasn't real yet but could be.

This man and his airy beach bungalow felt like sunlight on my skin after too many years beneath the glare of newsroom lights. A way out of the chaos and the mental toll of being *on* all the time. Someone to text when the plane landed. The grief wasn't just about losing him. It was about losing what I thought he represented. A life I had been craving in silence.

And still, I kept going. Because I knew somewhere, something else was coming. I didn't know what. But I knew I would not settle for a love that kept me waiting.

When it ended, I came undone. Not in a dramatic way, but in the slow, dull ache of something you know isn't right but still wanted to keep. We were compatible in a way that made everything feel easy until it suddenly wasn't. We talked fast and often, laughing at things that only we were clever enough to understand, making inside jokes out of nothing. Even errands had a rhythm, our own strange version of intimacy. At Whole Foods, he'd swipe a tiny cookie from the self-serve bakery box, crumble it into his mouth in one go, and grin like a guilty five-year-old.

But the core of us was never steady. His attachment style was avoidant. Mine was anxious. A psychological cliché that felt like living in a loop. When I leaned in, he leaned out. When I finally pulled away, he came back with a tenderness that made me question everything. It wasn't sustainable. It wasn't peaceful. But it was magnetic.

There were details that felt weirdly cosmic. We shared the same half-birthday. He was a Gemini. I was a Sagittarius. Opposite signs, perfect mirrors. It made sense, and it didn't. I looked up our chart once and immediately regretted it. It was like reading a recipe for chaos.

More than one person asked me, "Is he on the spectrum?" throughout our relationship. It made him incredibly literal, unexpectedly charming, and funny in a way that was totally unfiltered. He didn't know how to play social games, which made his attention feel sharper, more deliberate. When he looked at you, he really looked. No performative empathy, just the directness of someone who noticed the things most people missed. I admired that.

Looking back, I don't think we were meant to last. We were mirrors, yes, but we kept reflecting each other's instability. Maybe it wasn't a relationship. Maybe it was a lesson disguised as one.

The only thing that helped me heal from the unraveling was a therapist gently suggesting I check out a SLAA meeting. I walked into a room filled with thirty strangers, all in some stage of heartbreak, some freshly cracked open, others already stitching themselves back together. It was the first time I didn't feel completely alone.

That's where I first heard the phrase *"No contact."* Someone explained it like detox. You treat the person like a drug. You don't call. You don't check their Instagram. You don't reread old texts like they're scripture. You let the craving pass. And when it doesn't, you sit still anyway. I held onto that like a lifeline.

As the weeks to the big birthday closed in, all I could think about was that I had officially aged out of *TIME*'s 30 Under 30. It sounds silly now, but at the time, it mattered. I had clung to those milestones like lifeboats. Bright, shiny benchmarks of progress. Proof that I was keeping pace. That I wasn't falling behind. That I was still someone to watch.

But now they felt like glittery lies. Empty promises disguised as ambition. No list could save me from the quiet panic I felt settling into my bones.

I hadn't gotten married.

I hadn't had a child.

I hadn't bought a house.

I had a career.

I didn't have a life.

And then, just three months after my thirtieth birthday, the world stopped. The pandemic rolled in like a tide, slow at first, then all at once. Death tolls climbed. Cities shut down. And the panic that had once centered on my own small, spiraling world turned outward.

There was no time to mourn missed milestones when the world was unraveling in real time.

I had left the overnight breaking news shift by then and moved to Diane Sawyer's Special Units team. I was producing long-form pieces on loss, grief, and resilience. Every day, I reported on lives upended. I covered stories that would end up in history books. My priorities shifted in real time. That became the hinge on which everything turned.

During lockdown, when interest rates hit historic lows, I stopped waiting. I had always imagined I'd buy a house with someone. But I was done postponing my life. I bought a home. Alone. Because it was time. Because I could. It was a thriving vacation rental, and I named it *Cosmic Goodness* to symbolize the quiet power of trusting your own timeline.

An exercise that helped me was to imagine the montage sequences on television. The ones where the starring woman activates the change in her life. She moves cities. A new love interest enters the story. She lands the job that alters her path. There is a surprise pregnancy. A sudden loss. A long-awaited yes. The music swells. Her posture softens. She cuts her hair and moves on. There is no mistaking it. Something is transforming.

That is how it felt for me.

Cosmic Goodness became my saving grace. Beyond the newsroom, I worked the land every single day for six weeks. My arms did not grow strong under the dim lights of a West Hollywood Pilates studio. They formed from clearing brush, splitting wood, and lifting stones. My legs did not strengthen from sprinting through airports to chase breaking news. They thickened from hiking the mountains with bear spray clipped to my hip.

I had to physically remove myself from Los Angeles to find the kind of perspective that offers you a way forward. I kept returning to Elizabeth Gilbert's line from *Eat Pray Love*: "I crossed the street to walk in the sunshine." It became my reference point. A quiet promise to honor what felt good and holy in my life.

My energy discernment spun on its axis. I could finally name what kept me in the shadows and what pulled me toward the light. People. Places. Patterns. I began to see with new eyes.

I had something larger than myself. Six acres of land in Paradise Valley that demanded my presence. It was a humbling paradox to acknowledge that the pandemic, as devastating as it was, had also lifted me out of the fever dream I had been living for seven years as a news producer.

That rupture created clarity. And from that clarity, I found my own mantra.

Surrendering the shadows to live in the light.

Surrendering the shadows to live in the light.

Surrendering the shadows to live in the light.

The beauty of the prayer is that you can replace the word shadows with anything standing in your way. Grief. Trauma.

Silence. Familiar patterns that once kept you safe and now keep you small. Your shadows are not my shadows. My shadows are not yours. But the ache beneath them is the same. We all want to live in the light.

There is no perfect map. No polished recipe for joy. But what I have learned as a journalist and as a woman is that our stories matter. They become our legacy. Our lore.

In the deepest part of me, I believe in what Cosmic Goodness represents. It is the sweet spot of alignment. The place where clarity meets courage. When you are standing in that space, your ability to release what no longer belongs becomes almost immediate. You stop clinging to what never truly served you. You stop offering the most tender parts of yourself to people who have not earned the right to hold them.

This is what I learned by choosing, again and again, to turn my face toward the sun. It is not a single moment. It is a muscle. It is a practice. It is quiet bravery. It is a new way of seeing.

Sylvia Plath once described envisioning her future as a branching tree full of possibilities, each potential life ripening like fruit she couldn't bring herself to choose. She described the paralysis that came with indecision. The figs began to wrinkle. They dropped. She starved from the inability to choose. That passage gutted me. Because I know what it feels like to sit in the shadow of your own fear.

To know that a literary hero could be that brilliant and still suffer from the kind of depression that keeps you in the dark cracked something open in me.

Cosmic Goodness was my fat purple fig.

And by the time I reached for it, I was so starved I took the juiciest bite imaginable.

It fed me. It rooted me.

And it led me to everything.

I wasn't the last one left; I was the one who stayed long enough to rebuild. Healing wasn't sudden. It was slow and uneven. It was learning to sit with the pieces and then choosing which ones were still worth carrying. The vision didn't paint the way I imagined. It unraveled then rewrote itself into something more miraculous. I got to re-invent on a divine timeline as someone new.

I used to be terrified of turning thirty. But what I didn't know then was that thirty would be the release. That the fears that gripped me in my twenties would evaporate the second I crossed the threshold.

I stopped measuring my life by borrowed timelines. I woke up to the truth that divine timing doesn't rush, and I was never behind. I was being prepared to recognize the gifts, so when they finally stood right in front of me, I could say with conviction, "Yes. That's it."

I met him, and we slipped into a beautiful rhythm almost instantly, a shared routine of laughter, late-night talks, and playful ease. Within weeks, we had a nickname for each other: Squirrel. It was lighthearted, but it meant something. Squirrels adapt. They gather, prepare, survive. All it took was a single squirrel emoji over text to say, "Hi. I'm thinking of you." There were no games. No ulterior motives. No manipulation. Just presence. Just us.

I was never the "last kid left at summer camp." I was just the one who needed a little more time to pack her bags, walk herself out, and finally come home to herself rather than wait for someone to invite her into their home.

As Joan Rivers once said, "I wish I could tell you it gets better. But it doesn't get better. You get better." And she was right.

PART I

Florida

1

Cosmic Goodness

"Synchronicity is an ever-present reality
for those who have eyes to see."
—Carl Jung

It took me years to recognize the point wasn't to be accepted by the hypothetical room but to walk in and feel like I belonged to myself.

For so long, I was hypnotized by proximity to power. I thought if I could just get close enough to it, some of it might rub off on me. I thought power meant being the one who didn't have to wait in line because I was on the list. What I hadn't yet learned was that the smallest leap, from fan to insider, from consumer to creator, can be the most spiritually expensive.

If you haven't anchored yourself to something eternal, you'll shape-shift to survive. You'll contort to belong. You'll abandon yourself to stay invited.

That kind of inclusion is not belonging.

It is performance.

It is exile in disguise.

And one day, if you are lucky, the cost of staying split in two will become too high to keep paying.

And that is when you begin to come home to yourself. If you're reading this while quietly unraveling under the weight of the life you built, exhausted, accomplished, and disoriented, you're not broken. You're awakening.

For years, I chased the version of success handed to me like gospel. Earning a college degree. The job title. The apartment with crown molding and just enough exposed brick to feel like I'd made it. But what I hadn't been taught was how to stay rooted inside my own body. How to live a life that *felt good*, not one that just looked good on paper. Cosmic goodness is the universe showing you how luminous life can get when you stop holding space for what dims you.

We are living in a crisis of disconnect, especially among women.

It's not that we're weak. It's that the system is cracked. We were conditioned to push past the whispers of our bodies and emotions in pursuit of accolades that never quite fill us. *Cosmic Goodness: Surrendering the Shadows to Live in the Light* is a reclamation.

Cosmic goodness is the quiet alignment that begins to reveal itself when you stop chasing and start listening. It's the idea that the universe isn't neutral or punishing; it's participatory. It responds to your clarity. When you start choosing what lights you up, even in the smallest ways, you change your frequency. Your energy shifts. And from that shift, new people, opportunities, and insights begin to appear. Not because you're forcing them but because you're finally attuned to them. That's the pulse of cosmic goodness. You don't earn it. You return to it.

It's a field guide for those of us who performed perfection for years and woke up one morning feeling restless and aimless. Two of the most disorienting feelings, especially for someone that thrives on being in control.

There is another version of your life running parallel to this one. A track you can't always see, but you can feel. Joseph Campbell once wrote,

> "Follow your bliss. If you do follow your bliss,
> you put yourself on a kind of track that has been
> there all the while waiting for you...."

When I first read that line, I dismissed it as poetic optimism. It wasn't until I broke, until I sobbed on the floor of a newsroom bathroom stall, that I began to understand what he meant. Bliss isn't a bubble bath or a vacation. Bliss is the place inside you that still glows despite the burnout. It is not an escape. It is a sacred homecoming.

Start here: when your heart feels heavy, when you've forgotten what joy feels like, write down seven small things that make your nervous system exhale.

Always seven. Not five. Not ten. Seven is the seeker. The bridge between logic and longing. In numerology, it's the number of introspection and truth. It's where the sacred lives.

Here were mine on a recent Tuesday:

1. Morning light slanting across the hardwood floor
2. The first bite of watermelon with lime and sea salt
3. Nina Simone's voice curling around the first line of "Feeling Good"
4. Walking through New York City and people watching with nowhere to be by a certain time

5. The sound of my dog Hazel's paws tapping across the room before she curls into my ribcage
6. Singing along to a live concert from the front row making eye contact with the artist who wrote the lyrics
7. The exhilaration I felt when I gave birth to my son, and the first time he was placed on my chest

These are not aesthetic joys. They are anchors. Markers of aliveness. As you start paying attention to them, you begin to come home to yourself, not as a project to fix but as a presence to feel.

We were never meant to white-knuckle our way through life. We were meant to feel it. Fully. Fiercely. Without apology.

You are not too much. You are not too late. You aren't being left behind. The timing isn't punishing you. It's preparing you.

2

Shakedown Street

"It is not a sign of health to be
well-adjusted to a profoundly sick society."
—Jiddu Krishnamurti

If you grow up inside the storm, it becomes just part of the daily forecast. The damage doesn't reveal itself until much later when you're crawling from the wreckage, blinking in the sunlight, trying to understand what just happened, and who you've become because of it. All you know is the debris. Sharp, chaotic, spinning so fast you can't tell what's sky and what's ground. That's what my childhood felt like: a permanent state of disorientation, where survival came before clarity. Only now, with distance and years behind me, do I understand: my nervous system wasn't broken. It was responding exactly as it should to a world that never taught it safety. I didn't lack peace; I lacked a compass.

My father was an alcoholic. What I lived through was messy. Loud. Volatile. For a long time, I didn't know it wasn't normal. I didn't know it was *fucked up* for a child to witness the things I saw. I just knew that innocence wasn't something I ever had the luxury of growing out of. Sometimes, even now, a wave of anger swells inside me not just at what happened, but at what *never* did. With my dad's addiction, childhood slipped through my fingers, never mine to hold, never mine to savor.

The stand-up comedian George Carlin once said, "If you take the country and shake it up, all the loose ends end up in Florida." My dad was one of those loose ends.

He was a die-hard fan of the Grateful Dead. He was religious about it in the way some people are about God or football. When he found their music, he didn't just find a soundtrack; he found a new identity. With it came the full suite of chemical companions: LSD, ecstasy, mushrooms, marijuana. I have box after box of photos of him on the lot at a Dead show, smiling in that glassy-eyed, lost-in-the-universe way, a balloon of laughing gas in one hand and a beer in the other. Every detail was spot-on: the Stealie bolt cap, tie-dye shirt stretched over a sunburned beer belly, red sweatpants that sagged at the knees, and the same black Birkenstocks. Held together by stubbornness and duct tape for fifteen straight years. His cheeks were always bright red and covered in broken blood vessels from all his drinking.

He was the kind of man who could quote Jerry Garcia like scripture, who lived with the reckless freedom of someone who believed rules were for other people. He was also the biological father of three children, none of whom shared a mother or much else.

There was Marcus, my oldest brother, ten years ahead of me and raised in Alabama. Then there was Cole, the secret child. Conceived during a one-night stand in Virginia three years before I was born; his existence was a whispered footnote I didn't learn about until long after the fact. And then there was me.

Three children. Three mothers. One man orbiting in and out of our lives like a comet. A catastrophic force of charm and chaos, always on his own timeline.

One of the very few times my dad showed up to one of my soccer games, he made sure it was unforgettable for all the wrong reasons.

He brought a beach chair. Unfolded it like he was poolside, stripped off his shirt, and stretched out in the tightest, teal swim trunks you could imagine. Then came the brown paper bag. He drank and tanned while the rest of the parents sat quietly on the sidelines.

No one had ever seen him before, so the whispers started immediately, *Who's that guy?* At some point, clearly drunk, he started shouting my name again and again across the field. I remember the faces of the other six-year-olds, wide-eyed and confused, whispering, *It's her dad.*

That moment etched itself into me, not just the hot stifling shame but the quiet realization that whatever *normal* was, this wasn't it. That kind of humiliation doesn't just sting; it settles. It embeds itself into your nervous system. I wanted the kind of Steve Martin dad I saw in *Father of the Bride*. Khaki pants. Asics sneakers. The kind of man who would show up to lunch at the Four Seasons in a baseball cap not because he was a Deadhead but because he had come straight from playing doubles.

Even as an adult, standing in A-list rooms, brushing shoulders with producers and celebrities, my sneaky self-esteem would whisper, *They all know you're not from this world.* If you grew up splitting your time between a trailer park and a quiet longing for a Nancy Meyers aesthetic—hardwood floors, giant vases of hydrangeas, the warm glow of stability even years later—a memory like your dad bringing a forty-ounce beer to your soccer game still finds a way to follow you in. You can be in a kitchen with white subway tile and glass jars of quinoa and still feel like an impostor.

So how do we disentangle from that? How do we build a life so rooted in self-worth that the ghosts don't get to set the tone?

You start with the truth. You name what was. You grieve what wasn't. And then, brick by brick, you build what never existed for you. Not to prove something. Not even to heal something. But because you are worthy of that kind of beauty. You do it for yourself first. And if one day, a partner or a child gets to live inside that softness with you, that's not the point; that's the miracle.

The way some Christians hang a portrait of Jesus above the fireplace, my dad had a giant photo of Jerry Garcia on the wall. For the longest time, I thought Jerry was a relative; his face was nestled among family photos like an uncle we didn't see often. I must've been around four when I first asked about him. I just remember thinking his cascade of curls looked soft and kind, like someone who might play guitar at a family reunion.

To him, it was communion.

To me, it was noise.

I *hated* the Grateful Dead as a kid. Despised the droning guitars, the meandering jams, the aimless quality that so many people found spiritual but to me felt like being trapped in a dream I didn't ask for. Worse yet, I was *named* after one of their songs. *Cassidy.* And just to make sure I could never outrun it, my parents threw in a middle name for good measure: *Rainforest.*

Cassidy Rainforest.

Born in 1989, the year the Dead launched a campaign to "Save the Rainforest," fundraising at their shows and selling t-shirts with slogans like "Jam for the Jungle." It was supposed to be meaningful. Cosmic, even. But try telling that to a second grader sitting in a public school classroom, face burning with humiliation when the teacher took roll for the first time:

"Cassidy...Rainforest?"

A pause. A raised eyebrow. Sometimes even a chuckle.

One girl turned to the kid next to her and whispered, loud enough for me to hear, "Her parents are *hippies*."

She said it like an insult.

My dad was an English teacher, the kind who bounced from school to school, fired every few years for reasons I was too young to fully understand: disagreements with the principal, missed days, something about being "inappropriate." It always felt vague, slippery, and it always ended the same: unemployment.

My mom, too, was a teacher, special education, working with children on the autism spectrum. She was steady, devoted, exhausted. She did what she could to keep us afloat. But with my dad unreliable and mostly absent financially, we were poor. Not always in the dramatic, food-stamp-commercial kind of way. I don't remember going hungry. But I remember the quiet humiliations; the ones that stay with you.

Like the time in second grade when the vice principal left a giant black trash bag at the front door of my classroom. Inside were hand-me-down clothes, her daughter's old things, bundled together for me to take home. On the outside was a piece of white paper, taped to the bag. In thick marker, it read: "For Cassidy to bring home."

There's a particular silence that follows something like that. The kind that tightens the air in the room. Kids may be young, but they're perceptive in the cruelest ways. A dozen little heads turned toward me. One girl said what they were all thinking:

"Oh. It's because she's poor."

That was my first taste of self-loathing, the kind that doesn't just sting, but *boils.* It spreads through your chest like heat and makes you want to shrink until you disappear completely. I didn't even want to cry. I just wanted to stop existing for a minute. To vanish.

At home, I could hide. I could fold myself into the chaos and pretend I was invisible. But when my private reality crept into school, I had nowhere to run. No mask thick enough to cover what was now obvious.

3

Gimme Some Truth

"To survive childhood without love is to carry
a ghost on your back for the rest of your life."
—Clarissa Pinkola Estés

We all carry ghosts from our childhood. Some loud and obvious, others quiet and carefully disguised. Not all wounds bleed. Some look like hyper-independence. Some look like people-pleasing. Some look like perfectionism, rage, numbness, or the inability to sit still in silence.

What we call "personality" is often just protection. What we call "normal" is often the trauma we've normalized.

If you grew up in a home where love was inconsistent, where the rules changed depending on someone's mood, or where your emotional needs were too heavy for the room, you may have never learned what nervous system regulation feels like. You may have adapted in brilliant, resilient ways. But adaptation isn't healing. It's just survival wearing a mask.

This chapter is an invitation. To pause. To ask:

What was stolen from me?

What did I *not* get that I needed?

What parts of me have been shaped around absence, instability, or silence?

This is where *Cosmic Goodness: Surrendering the Shadows to Live in the Light* begins to do its deeper work. Not just naming the pain but untangling the story. We don't do this to blame our parents or dwell in the past. We do this to reclaim the life we *were* meant to live. One rooted in clarity, not confusion. In truth, not coping.

If you never got to be a kid, if your innocence was interrupted, or your worth was left unspoken, you're not alone. And you're not broken.

You were shaped by your storm.

But you were never meant to stay inside of it.

Practice: "The Truth Mapping Exercise"

Purpose: To untangle inherited beliefs, emotional patterns, and identity distortions from your upbringing and begin to reclaim your truth.

Step 1: Draw Two Columns

Label them:

- **"What I Was Told (Directly or Indirectly)"**
- **"What I Now Know to Be True"**

Take your time here. This doesn't need to be dramatic. Subtle messages are often the most powerful. Examples might be:

What I Was Told	What I Now Know to Be True
My needs are too much	My needs are valid and worthy of care
Love is earned through obedience	I deserve love just by being
Anger is dangerous	Anger is a signal. Not a shameful emotion
I had to take care of everyone	I am not responsible for other people's chaos

Step 2: Feel Into the Body

After each truth you write, pause.

Ask yourself:

- "Where do I feel this belief in my body?"

- "How long have I carried it?"
- "Am I ready to let it go?"

Use breath. Use stillness. Let it *move through* you, not just live on the page.

Step 3: Create a "Soul Truth Statement"

Write a single sentence from your reclaimed truth. Something you *didn't hear enough* as a child but needed to. This becomes a healing mantra.

Examples:

- "I am safe now."
- "I am allowed to have needs."
- "I am no longer in the storm."
- "I am whole, even if no one taught me how to be."

Repeat it daily. Put it on your mirror, phone, altar—anywhere your soul will see it.

4

Made to Fade

"You're not the same as you were before.
You were much more…muchier.
You've lost your muchness."
—The Mad Hatter,
Alice in Wonderland

The wild thing about growing up in an unconventional household is that it rewires you in ways you don't even recognize until you're standing in the ruins of your own relationships, asking yourself, *why do I disappear when I most want to be seen?*

I didn't hear the word *trigger* until I was in my twenties, perched on the couch in a therapist's office. I had spent most of my life mistaking emotional landmines for love. I thought anxiety was chemistry. I thought disappearing was polite. I thought silence meant I was finally being "good."

There were so many moments—quiet, forgettable to the outside world—that told me I was *too much.* Too loud. Too emotional. Too needy. The message never screamed, but it was clear.

I remember weekends at my father's house where time was divvied out like rations. I was allowed ten-minute intervals with him once an hour, like a scheduled visitation inside a life that should've been mine. At noon, I could enter the room and sit with him. At 12:10, I had to leave. Fifty minutes of invisibility. Then another ten-minute dose of fatherhood. And repeat. For two full days.

No shared meals. No board games or bike rides or bedtime stories. Just a stopwatch and a child learning to shrink herself to fit into someone else's limitations.

In a strange detail I've never been able to shake, there were times he performed as the most hands-on, present, funny, and engaged father. It was usually when he was using me to meet up with women.

I remember once, he took me to the house of a woman he was dating. I sat on her couch, looking around, thinking, *who are you?* He talked to me more in that one hour than he sometimes did over an entire weekend. He laughed at my jokes. Asked questions. Played the role.

At one point, I accidentally knocked over a bowl of blueberries on the kitchen table, and they scattered across the floor in every direction. She snapped. Screamed at me about the mess like I had broken something irreplaceable. Behind her, on the refrigerator, I saw a school photo of me.

I registered, "This is all so fake."

I've met you once. You're yelling at me. My dad is pretending. And I don't want to be here. I was paraded around at his convenience, shown off only when there was a woman he wanted to charm.

Before we left, I slipped the photo off her fridge and tucked it into my pocket. It felt strange that someone who barely knew me would pretend to care enough to display my picture. Stranger still that I was expected to believe any of this was real.

By the time I started dating in my twenties, I had already absorbed the belief that presence was a burden. That I needed permission to exist. That if I stayed too long, I would be resented for it. Every time I was in someone's house—of someone I liked, someone I loved—I felt the familiar whisper rise: *You should go now.*

That was the deepest root of my healing journey: *not learning how to leave*, but learning how to stay. How to hold eye contact. How to feel discomfort and remain anyway. How to believe that I am not an interruption, not a mistake, not too much.

This wound isn't just about dysfunctional parenting or broken love stories, it's about what it means to belong to yourself again. To trace back the places where you were emotionally rationed and say: *No more.* I am not here on borrowed time. I am not here on an hourly pass. I am here. And I am allowed to take up space.

For so many of us, this is the untold cost of growing up in dysfunction: we inherit the blueprint of absence. We are conditioned to disappear before we inconvenience anyone. To ghost ourselves before anyone else gets the chance.

But healing is about reclaiming your seat at the table. It is about understanding that you belong not because you perform perfectly, not because you calculate your presence like clockwork, but because you exist. That alone is enough.

I started small. I stayed ten minutes longer than I wanted to. I spoke my needs aloud. I didn't apologize for asking to be held. I reminded myself, again and again, that love is not measured in minutes or in tolerance, but in presence. Real presence. Whole presence.

And every time I stayed—with myself, with the discomfort, with the moment—I rewrote a story that never should have been written in the first place.

5

Edge of Seventeen

"And the day came when the risk to
remain tight in a bud was more painful
than the risk it took to blossom."
—Anaïs Nin

This was the moment my story shifted. It stopped being chaotic and started to feel calculated. By thirteen, something in me clicked awake. My brain was still growing, still unfinished in places, but one thing had become clear: my father wasn't misunderstood. He was deeply broken, and I no longer felt the need to earn his attention in ten-minute increments.

That realization was its own kind of freedom. I started counting down. Not towards anything specific yet but knowing I was getting closer to flying the coop. Away from the chaos, the shame, the quiet rage of pretending it was all okay. I didn't know what healing was yet, but I was learning how to extract myself. I had begun the arduous and invisible process of emotional disassociation. The contortion of shrinking and shapeshifting into someone who could survive. My physical body stayed in the room. My spirit started packing its bags.

Not long after, my father left the country. He had fallen in love with a Ukrainian mail-order bride. But instead of bringing her here, he flew to Kiev to meet her. He would go on to drift around Ukraine for many more years. I distinctly remember she was twenty-five, just twelve years older than me. By then, my own mom was fifty-three.

When he left, I felt relieved. I prayed he would stay gone. That he would lose interest in pretending he wanted to be a father. And he did.

By then, I was living full-time with my mom. The only way to describe my mom's house was a mini, seven-hundred-square-foot version of *Grey Gardens*. Built in 1923 and never once renovated, it felt less like a home and more like a forgotten structure someone had given up on halfway through. There was no heat or air conditioning. We were cold in the winter and hot in the summer with no real transition in between. A family of roaches lived in the walls. We could never get rid of them. I learned that if I got up to go to the bathroom in the middle of the night, that there would be dozens scampering across the floor the moment the light came on.

The ceiling had collapsed in places. When I looked up, I could see wooden beams through the gaps where plaster should have been. Slivers of sunlight snuck through cracks in the roof. There were no closets, so everything that didn't have a place to be tucked away, like clothes, papers, old holiday decorations, and unopened mail, was piled high on chairs and tables. The couches had long since been lost under the weight of what couldn't be put away. I didn't know the word for it back then, but when I came across the reality show *Hoarders* many years later, I recognized it instantly. That was our house. There was nowhere to sit. Nowhere to rest. Nowhere to breathe.

Looking back, I have a tremendous amount of compassion for the girl trying to hide and conceal what my home looked like; I didn't want anyone to know. Sometimes, I've felt anger toward my mother for not creating a beautiful, clean home for me. I deserved that. There were maggots in the refrigerator. The clutter never seemed to bother her. I believe now that it was generational habits more than anything. Patterns passed down like heirlooms not out of malice but out of muscle memory. My mother did what she knew. What she had seen. What had been modeled for her. And while that doesn't excuse the neglect, it does explain the silence, the mess, the instability. It wasn't personal. It was inherited. And now, it's mine to interrupt.

Her parents' house looked almost exactly the same. They came of age during the Great Depression, and I think they believed you had to hold onto everything in case the worst happened again. Those rooms were overflowing. Not just with things but with tension. I remember the feeling of claustrophobia, like the walls were pressing in. Like I was being buried by what no one had the energy to let go of.

As a single mother, she did what she could. That house was what we could afford. She rented it, and I don't think she ever felt much ownership over the space. There was no energy left for gutting it or fixing what had already started to collapse. The landlord refused to make repairs, and she didn't have the extra money to take it on herself. It was the best we could manage at the time.

When I discovered minimalism in adulthood, it felt less like a trend and more like a belief system that had been waiting for me. I didn't ease into it. I sprinted in the opposite direction of everything I had known. Empty counters felt sacred. Drawers with space in them felt like relief.

A few times a year, I fill large bags with anything that no longer serves a purpose. If it doesn't belong, it goes. I clear the clutter the way you open a window after a long, stale winter, to let the air move again, to bring the room back to life.

For years, *The Life-Changing Magic of Tidying Up* lived on my nightstand like a sacred text. I read it slowly, deliberately. I picked things up, thanked them for what they gave me, and let them go. It wasn't about organizing. It was about release. It was about learning how to stop carrying what I never chose to hold.

It has never been about tidiness. It has always been about weight. I know what it feels like to drown in things that were supposed to make life easier.

Between thirteen and fifteen, there were two moments that changed the trajectory of my life. I hesitate to call them turning points. They weren't dramatic or cinematic. They arrived quietly, without announcement and almost slipped past me unnoticed. But they cracked something open.

I wish I could say it was literature that changed me, or philosophy. That it was a brilliant conversation or a profound book that found me at the right time. But that's not what happened.

What happened was this: two deeply ordinary, deeply Millennial moments collided with just the right amount of longing inside me. And they gave me a glimpse of something I had never seen before.

In eighth grade, I made a friend. His name was Blake. He was quiet and nerdy with two oversized front teeth and thick, black glasses. Some of the meaner kids called him a chipmunk, mocking the way his teeth rested against his lower lip. But he was kind.

I don't remember why he made me a CD. But one day, he handed it to me like it was nothing. On the front, in black marker, he had written: John Mayer—*Room for Squares.*

At the time, I only owned a handful of CDs. And no boy had ever made me one before. I took it home, slipped it into my portable Walkman, and lay on my bed with the volume turned up. From the first few lines, I was somewhere else. The lyrics transported me directly out of that house onto another planet; I was practically levitating.

It was the first time music felt like mine. Not just something playing in the background of my parents' lives. At home, it was always The Grateful Dead, Van Morrison, Tom Petty, The Beatles, Bob Dylan. Now, as an adult, I can see they had incredible taste. But back then, I wanted something different. I wanted something that spoke to where I was, not where they had been.

I was not just listening to music. I was building a world. John Mayer's voice wasn't famous yet. He still felt small enough to belong to me. I listened to his lyrics like they were coordinates for escape. Every song gave me a language for feelings I hadn't yet said out loud.

These lyrics hit me like a prophecy:

I'd like to think the best of me
Is still hiding up my sleeve
They love to tell you "Stay inside the lines"
But something's better on the other side

I clung to that line like it was fact. Like it was an instruction. There was a world beyond what I knew, and it was for me to discover.

By the time *Heavier Things* was released, I was completely submerged. That album reached places in me that *Room for Squares* had only begun to touch. It carried a quieter ache, something more reflective, more lived-in. It felt like he had been through something and came back changed, carrying the weight of it in his voice. Each lyric resonated in such a deeply profound way.

Around the same time, I discovered his fan forums Local 83 and MyStupidMouth.com and slipped quietly into them, studying how others traded bootlegs from his shows. I learned to unzip files, to convert audio, to load entire sets onto my iPod like a personal archive. Thanks to the handful of tapers who uploaded recordings after every concert, I could download the entire show from the night before, wake up early, and carry it with me through the day.

Mornings began on the bus, alone in the back.

So what, so I've got a smile on
It's hiding the quiet superstitions in my head.

That lyric felt like my headspace in the school hallway. I smiled. I said hello. But I was somewhere else entirely. I was immersed in the music. In the voice that didn't flinch when it named the ache, I was still learning to recognize in myself.

There was one more line I kept tucked into my chest. A line I didn't fully understand at the time, but that stirred something sharp and ancient inside me.

Check your pulse
It's proof that you're not listening to
The call your life's been issuing you
The rhythm of a line of idle days

It felt like permission. Not just to listen, but to move towards creating dreams bigger than my reality. Believing that wanting more did not make me ungrateful. It woke me up.

I never told anyone about this ritual. It was too sacred. Too personal. I had never had anything that was entirely mine. A secret path back to myself. The music didn't just give me a way out. It gave me a reason to stay tethered to who I really was even when everything around me demanded that I disappear.

This wasn't about becoming someone new. It was about remembering someone I hadn't yet had the chance to be. I had fallen in love with an imaginary world painted by the lyrics of these songs.

Then came Blockbuster.

One afternoon, while scanning the shelves for a DVD, I saw them. All the *Sex and the City* seasons lined up like rows of candy. The spines were neon and feminine and unmissable. I don't remember if my mom asked if it was appropriate for a fifteen-year-old to watch.

From the first episode, I was gone. Transported. The backdrop of New York City lit something up in me that I didn't know had been waiting. There was a magic to it. A wildness. A sense that anything was possible in a place where the sidewalks never emptied, and no one ever seemed to apologize for being too much. Carrie. Miranda. Charlotte. Samantha. They were messy and chaotic and self-centered and complicated and magnetic. They were everything I had been taught to suppress.

They talked about their lives like they mattered. They dressed like they were the main character in their own stories. They failed. They recovered. They demanded things. They left when they weren't satisfied. They took up space without explaining themselves. I had never seen women do that before. Not in Florida. Not in my family. Not in real life.

John Mayer gave me something to cling to day-to-day. He gave me comfort in the in-between, when high school felt like a holding cell and home felt like a trap. But *Sex and the City* gave me direction. It gave me a destination. I had never once thought about New York before. It wasn't even on my radar. But now, suddenly, I had a place. A fixed point to aim toward.

It wasn't just that I wanted to leave Florida. That had always been true. It was that now I knew *where*. New York City. I could picture it. I could see the version of myself that didn't flinch, didn't shrink, didn't try to make herself smaller to survive. That changed everything. Wanting to leave is one thing. Having a place to go is another.

6

Spark Map

"The universe buries strange jewels
deep within us all, and then stands
back to see if we can find them."
—Elizabeth Gilbert, *Big Magic*

A personal excavation of the moments, people, places, and ideas that have ever stirred something awake in you.

This is not about setting goals or naming accomplishments. This is about identifying the *feeling of ignition*, the times you felt something shift in your chest, catch in your breath, or ring like a tuning fork in your body. The sparks.

Those moments are not random. They are breadcrumbs. They reveal who you are beneath what you were taught to be.

Step One: The Inventory of Aliveness

Without overthinking, write down moments where you felt *drawn*, *lit up*, *curious*, *charged*, or *unshakably pulled.* These can be small or large, specific or vague. Use sensory detail and memory.

Prompts:

- A song that made you feel like your heart remembered something
- A scene in a movie you wanted to live inside
- A quote or line of dialogue you underlined and couldn't forget
- A place that made you feel like you belonged
- A person whose energy felt magnetic
- A smell, color, or object that felt inexplicably holy

Example (for inspiration):

- The way Van Morrison's "Into the Mystic" made the ordinary feel enchanted.
- Liv Tyler in *Stealing Beauty*. A girl on the brink of becoming a woman, unapologetically tender and wild.
- Michelle Pfeiffer in *One Fine Day*. A single mother, late for everything, building a career and a life, radiating intelligence and sensuality even in chaos. I love the end scene when she is in a t-shirt and a ponytail, and as a kid, I saw that as the epitome of beauty.
- Tom Petty's discography, a soundtrack stitched into the fabric of my geography. Gainesville, Florida (our shared hometown) taught him how to ache; Los Angeles taught him how to outrun it. Later, he would sign my ticket after a show at the Fonda in 2013.
- My childhood obsession with *Erin Brockovich*; I thought she was the most badass woman I had ever seen in my life. As a ten-year-old, I appreciated it was a true story.
- The first time I heard Abraham Hicks, something ignited in me. Her words felt like flight. *The Law of*

Attraction spoken with such clarity, it made me feel high on possibility.

- Cheryl Strayed's grit on the Pacific Crest Trail struck something in me so deep that when the world shut down during the pandemic, I laced up my boots and began snippets of the trail. Reese Witherspoon's portrayal of her in the movie *Wild* was heart wrenching.
- The romance of the lyrics of "When I get my Hands on You" by The New Basement Tapes helped me envision the type of love that I wanted to find.
- Sandra Bullock and Nicole Kidman in *Practical Magic.* Whimsical. Wild. Untamed. Women who carry magic in their bones, who move through the world barefoot and brave. Confident without trying, luminous without makeup, magnetic without apology. They are the kind of women who laugh freely and light up a room without effort. Rooted in nature, ruled by instinct, radiant in their authenticity.
- Kate Hudson's Andie Anderson in *How to Lose a Guy in 10 Days* showed me that being a journalist was a career path; it planted a seed.

Step Two: Find the Thread

Now go back through what you wrote and begin to trace patterns. Ask:

- What kinds of people spark something in me?
- What kind of aesthetics, places, and atmospheres feel like home?

- What emotional tones do I return to again and again: tenderness, rebellion, mystery, power, devotion?
- What am I always chasing, even unconsciously?
- What am I drawn to that I've never given myself permission to claim?

Underline or circle the ones that *still* stir something in you.

Step Three: Write This Sentence

"I am someone who comes alive when..."

Write this line **over and over,** filling in the blank each time with a new insight from your Spark Map.

Examples:

- I am someone who comes alive when I have a stimulating conversation with a stranger.
- I am someone who comes alive when I do something out of spontaneity, not obligation.
- I am someone who comes alive when I hear lyrics that capture what I can't put into words.
- I am someone who comes alive when I am in nature, off the grid.
- I am someone who comes alive when I am completely unknown in a brand-new city.

This is your map. Not to where you're going but to who you are when you are most *you.*

7

The Reckoning

"Some women fear the fire. Some
women simply become it."
—R.H. Sin

It is heartbreaking to tell the truth about your mother when a part of you still wants to protect her. Still, I owe my healing more than I owe anyone's comfort. The truth, however tangled, is worth more than silence. I have felt guilt tighten in my throat each time I tried to name the parts of her that hurt me. Not because it is untrue, but because I know she was doing what she thought was her best. And sometimes, a person's best is shaped by what they never had.

Through years of therapy, I began to see something I could not understand as a child. My mother never moved past the age she was when her father began to break her. She stayed there, emotionally marooned. A girl frozen in survival mode, dressed in the body of a woman. She grew up in a house ruled by fear. It was the 1950s. Her father's rage was the wallpaper of her life.

No one questioned a man's fists back then. Women and children just braced for them.

She went to Catholic school with welts beneath her sleeves. She told me the same stories over and over. The nuns who looked away. The neighbors who stayed silent. No one stepped in. That kind of neglect teaches you not to expect anything. No one showed up to protect her, so she struggled to protect me. She never learned how to advocate for herself, which meant she couldn't always see the danger when it was right in front of me. She missed the red flags that should have safeguarded my innocence. I have spent years untangling the generational trauma she carried and passed down. I am making sure the pattern dies in my hands.

Her trauma was physical. Mine was not. My injuries left no bruises. They lived in the quiet spaces. My father measured my words by the clock and treated my voice like it was his to control. I learned to shrink what I needed to say into the time fragments he allowed. They grew in the silences that followed my needs. They taught me how to question my instincts and mistrust my own heart.

My mom went to therapy once. One appointment. Near the end, the therapist gently let her know their time was up. My mother never returned. She told the story often, as if it explained everything. "They cut you off. I don't like how rushed it feels. I found her rude."

That became her shield. It was easier to dismiss the help than to risk being seen. She never imagined that there could be another therapist, another kind of support, another path that she would click with more. She operated in extremes. There was no middle ground, only overreaction or silence. She could never consider that maybe the interruption was not rejection but structure. That maybe healing would ask her to stay exactly where she was most uncomfortable.

She clung to her version of the story. It kept her safe from the unknown. But it also kept her emotionally stunted.

I began therapy at eighteen. I walked in not knowing what I would say. I only knew that I needed to be heard by someone who was not in the story with me. My first therapist was named Sandy. She listened with a calmness that I had never known. She did not interrupt. She did not try to fix anything. She simply held space while I unraveled. That in itself was medicine.

With her, I learned how to look directly at my childhood without flinching. Naming the pain didn't erase it, but it stripped it of its power to own me.

The difference between my mother and me is not strength. It is direction. She turned inward and shut the door. I turned inward and opened one.

She taught me how to survive by disappearing. Therapy taught me how to return to myself. She learned to protect herself by staying small. I am learning that growth requires taking up space. Even when it makes people uncomfortable. Especially then.

There is a moment that comes without ceremony because you don't recognize it at first. You just stop waiting. You stop hoping she will become the mother you needed. And instead, you begin to become that person for yourself. That is when the fire stops being the threat and starts becoming the torch. She did not give me what I needed. But she gave me the map of what I would never do.

I carried a grief I didn't know how to name. Not just for what my father did but for what my mother allowed.

She never stood between us. Never put her body or her voice in the way of his destruction. If it were me, I know exactly what

I would have done. I would have told him he could not see his child until he got sober. I would have drawn a line so clearly it could never be mistaken. But she did not do that. She kept dropping me off into the burning building, and because I had learned to hide the emotional burns, she convinced herself there was no collateral damage.

I remember overhearing her tell a friend how nice it was to have a break when I was at his house. A break. While I was tiptoeing around his shifting moods, never knowing which version of him would show up. While I was locking the door and climbing out the window just to escape his volatile outbursts. A break, at the expense of my sanity, my stability, and the childhood innocence I'll never get back.

She grew up with a father who exploded often and without warning. She absorbed his rage and passed it down in quieter, more controlled ways. I only remember her hitting me once. We were in the middle of a grocery store. I was in kindergarten, overwhelmed by feelings I didn't yet know how to name. I was crying loudly, openly, and she slapped me across the face. Right there in front of strangers. My cheek burned, but what stayed with me longer was the humiliation. I remember thinking, even then, that something about this was deeply wrong. That a mother's love should never land like that.

She never hit me again. Instead, when I upset her, she would retreat. She would slam her bedroom door and tell me to leave her alone. I would sit in the hallway, waiting. There were no siblings to distract me, no other parent to turn to. Just a quiet house and a locked door. Sometimes I would write apologies on scraps of paper and slide them under the crack. I was too young to realize that she should have been the one apologizing. That I was a child. That I had been left to parent the silence.

This is why, even now, I shut down when someone raises their voice. Not out of weakness but muscle memory. The moment volume fills the air; I am no longer in the room. I am back on the hallway floor, scanning every moment for what I did to cause the storm even when the weather had nothing to do with me.

My mother never taught me how to calm myself because she never learned how to calm herself. There were no emotional tools in the house.

She continued sending me to my father's house even as his addiction worsened. I do not remember her checking in. I do not remember her asking if I felt safe. She knew he was drinking. She warned him not to drive drunk as if that was enough to keep me alive. He drove drunk anyway dozens of times. I was in the passenger seat, holding my breath, begging him to put the cigarette out while he turned up the Grateful Dead.

He sang along like the words belonged to him. And I sat there, a child in the wreckage of his choices, bracing for whichever version of him the next turn would reveal.

He smoked constantly in the car with the windows rolled up while I begged him to let me crack one open. I knew the scent of marijuana before I knew how to spell it. I had no doubt what any of the substances were. His drawers were lined with pill bottles as ordinary as socks or spare change. DARE had already taught me what secondhand smoke could do. I knew it could kill you. I knew I was breathing it in anyway. What enraged me most was that he did not care. Not about my lungs. Not about my body. Not about what I would carry because of him. I was just one side effect of his disease.

I would come home reeking. My hair smelled like ash. My clothes held the stench of his addiction. The taste of it stayed on my tongue. I felt invaded. My skin never felt clean. I told her this. She wrinkled her nose and said he should not be doing that. Then she sent me back again the next week.

There was no fight in her. No line she was willing to draw. No moment when she looked at my face and saw a child in need of rescue.

What stayed with me is not just what he did. It is what she didn't do.

Somewhat ironically, in fifth grade, there was a district-wide speech competition for the DARE program. It was part of a statewide convention in Florida, packed with police officers, school officials, and corporate donors applauding children who promised to stay clean. Out of the entire state, they chose three students to deliver their speeches onstage. I was one of them.

I didn't win because I understood the message. I won because I was already surviving it. The dangers of addiction. The importance of saying no. I didn't learn those lessons in school. I learned them in my father's house.

Everything I stood onstage condemning was still waiting for me that weekend.

The applause didn't mean anything. It never followed me home.

The biggest tipping point came in the form of a man who bagged groceries at Publix. He was in his fifties, borderline intrusive, always smiling a little too wide. He remembered our names. He made small talk that stretched too long. I do not know if my mother was lonely or just tired of being invisible, but she started to warm up to him. I watched them exchange numbers by the checkout line. My stomach dropped.

Even at seven, I could feel that he was *off.* Something about him unsettled me. My body tensed without warning, like it was trying to repel him before my brain could catch up. I didn't want him to have our number. I didn't want him to know where we lived.

He had a second job delivering Chinese food for a local restaurant, and before long, he started showing up at our front door. I remember feeling a jolt of alarm that he knew where we lived the first time his car pulled into the driveway. Why was the man from the grocery store at our house?

He knocked, and my mother opened the door like it was nothing. He smiled, too eager, and said he had an idea. Maybe I'd want to ride along on deliveries. He said it would be fun to jump out and leave the food on doorsteps. He told me he'd give me fifty cents for every house we stopped at. Like it was a game.

I remember leaning in close to my mother and whispering that I didn't want to go.

She brushed it off with a lightness that still makes my blood boil. Said it would be good for me. That I could get some air. Earn a little money. She said it like he was a neighbor offering to let me walk his dog. Like it was wholesome. Like I hadn't just told her no.

She didn't ask why I was uncomfortable. She didn't pause. She didn't look at me long enough to see the unease on my face. As if my instincts were an inconvenience. As if my discomfort could be reasoned away with a few quarters and a drive around town.

That man was a stranger. She didn't know where he lived, who he was outside of a checkout lane, or why he suddenly wanted time alone with her child.

And still, she let me go.

I remember climbing into the front seat of his car, heat rising under my skin like a warning. I had said no. She could have made up anything. Said I had practice. Said we had plans. Said no for me when I couldn't make it loud enough. Instead, she told me to get some fresh air even as the panic pressed so hard against my chest I could barely breathe.

He was large. Sweaty. His size filled the space in a way that made me feel smaller than I had ever felt. I was a wiry string bean of a child. I stared out the window and told myself that if he ever tried anything, I would open the door and jump. I planned escape routes. If I had to get out at one of the houses, and something went wrong, I would ring the bell and beg whoever answered to call the police.

He never touched me. He never said anything overtly threatening. But that does not mean it was safe. My body was in full alarm the entire time. The fact that nothing happened does not erase the fact that something could have.

And that should have been enough. My fear should have been enough.

I made about seven dollars that day. A handful of quarters and a mountain of anxiety. I remember holding the coins in my hand, wanting to throw them across the room. The emotional cost of that ride far outweighed the money.

The idea that I could have been taken haunts me more now than it did then. He could have locked the car doors. He could have driven past every house. He could have kept going, and no one would have known until it was too late. Cell phones did not exist. There was no way to call for help. No GPS tracking. No Find My iPhone. Just silence. Just me and him, and the terrifying truth that he could have done anything, and no one would have been there to stop him.

How did my mother not stop to ask why a middle-aged man wanted to spend time alone with a seven-year-old girl? She had no idea who he really was. She didn't know if he was a predator.

She knew nothing about him, not his last name, not where he lived, not what he wanted.

To this day, I still don't know either.

It's another blurry detail from my childhood that refuses to settle. One of those cracks in the story that no amount of remembering can repair.

Sometimes I ask myself what my mother would have told the police if he never brought me back. That he picked me up and just disappeared? That she let a man she barely knew take her daughter out alone for a ride around town?

She had no plan. No instinct to protect. No willingness to hear the distress in my voice.

And that is what stays with me. Not just the ride. Not just the man.

The betrayal of the one person who was supposed to say no. The mother who was supposed to stand between me and potential danger.

When I was thirty-five, after a therapy session that left me shaken, I called one of my mother's oldest friends, someone who had known me since the day I was born. I told her I was starting to process parts of my childhood. I mentioned how filthy and chaotic our home had been and how I had grown up in clutter and neglect and a constant sense of instability.

She didn't try to soften it. She didn't say I was imagining things. Instead, she confirmed it. She said she had always felt a deep sense of shock and sympathy that no one had created better conditions for me. She remembered the floor rotting around our toilet, how it leaked every time it flushed. You could see straight through to the ground below. It stayed that way for years. She said it was a miracle the toilet never collapsed through the floor. She remembered the maggots in the refrigerator. The piles of junk that swallowed the furniture. How there was no place to sit on the couch because it was buried under clutter.

And then, without any prompting, she said something I'll never forget.

"Cass," she told me, "the thing that shocked me most was when your mother said she let that man from the grocery store take you on rides in his car. You were in second grade. I couldn't believe she would let a middle-aged man take her daughter out alone. It made me sick to think about what he might have wanted from you."

I spent most of my life carrying the weight quietly. The hard parts. The unanswered questions. The memories I wasn't sure I was allowed to name. I learned early that silence kept things calm. So, I kept the peace by keeping it all inside.

But silence doesn't dissolve grief. It stores it. In your jaw. In your stomach. In your shoulders. I thought I was strong for holding it together, but the truth is, my body was doing the holding, and it was breaking under the weight.

What saved me wasn't forgetting. It was speaking. Letting the truth move through me. Out of my mouth. Into the air. Away from the places it had lived for too long.

And when I started sharing it, not all at once but piece by piece, I realized I wasn't the only one. Some of us grew up in houses where we had to wear armor just to feel safe. We learned to survive the sharp edges without reacting. But survival has a cost. The wounds don't vanish just because we got good at hiding them. They stay quiet until the same pain keeps showing up in different forms, and we get too tired to carry it any longer. As they say in Twelve-Step programs, "You get sick and tired of being sick and tired." When we tell the truth, we don't just unburden ourselves. We find each other. And that connection, that moment of being seen, is the very thing shame cannot survive.

Even now, if I sense toxicity or unpredictability in a room, my body wants to bolt. I still hate carpooling. I want to leave when I want, how I want, without having to rely on anyone. I never let a guy pick me up for a date. I always drove myself. It was not a preference. It was a survival reflex. I know exactly where it started. I was seven years old, in a car with a man I did not trust, begging not to go, and no one listened.

In the midst of everything, a few quiet comforts held me together. Our four cats became my lifeline. They were constant and comforting in a world that was not. I slept beside them. I fed them and loved them like they were mine alone. One of them, a black and white cat I named Abbey after Abbey Road before I realized he was a boy, was especially devoted. He would wait for me every day and run to greet me when I got home from school. They were outdoor cats. We never trained them to stay inside because my mom hated dealing with litter boxes.

One September, during hurricane season, the weather turned. The warnings were clear. It was supposed to be a big one. While the wind picked up, and the sky darkened, my mom put all the cats outside and shut the door. I begged her to let them stay in. I pleaded with her to at least let them on the porch, somewhere with shelter. She refused. She said they would be fine. That they would go under the house.

I spent two days crying, terrified they were gone. She told me they were under the crawlspace. That she had put bowls of food under there. When the storm passed, three of them came back. Abbey never did.

I was gutted. I made signs by hand and taped them to street poles all over the neighborhood. Every day after school I rushed home and hit play on the answering machine hoping someone had called. No one ever did.

He had given me something my parents could not. Comfort. Loyalty. Devotion. And she let him disappear into the storm.

Now, as an adult, I think of my dog. I have had her for fourteen years. She is part of my family. My son is infatuated with her. Every morning, he asks where she is. I already dread the day she dies. I know it will break him. I will have to hold his heartbreak.

And I will. I will hold it all. I will not shut a door and tell him it is fine when it is not.

I don't know what was missing in my mother that made her unable to protect me from that type of heartbreak over and over again. But whatever it was, I had to grow around it.

Eventually I learned that what I once called independence was actually hyper-vigilance. A symptom of children who grow up in chaos. It shaped me. It robbed me of ease. Of innocence.

And it lit a fire in me that still burns.

8

Line Drawn in the Sand

"I will not stay, not ever again—in a room
or conversation or relationship or institution
that requires me to abandon myself."
—Glennon Doyle, *Untamed*

We are told to move on. To be grateful. To forgive. But what if the wound hasn't even been acknowledged? What if the harm was never named, never spoken aloud, never validated, not even by the one who lived it?

This is where healing begins: not with forgiveness, but with truth.

For daughters of mothers who couldn't protect them, who couldn't see them, who turned away when it mattered most, there is a quiet kind of grief. Not loud or cinematic. It is the grief of not being believed. The grief of doubting your own memory. The grief of being shaped by something everyone else said wasn't real.

Naming is the first act of reclaiming. When you name something, you give it shape. You stop it from disappearing into the blur of "it wasn't that bad," or "she did her best."

You are not doing this to hurt her. You are doing this to find yourself.

Because somewhere in your body lives a younger version of you who remembers it all. She remembers the things that were said, and the things that weren't. The slammed doors. The silence. The way you learned not to ask twice.

She does not need you to make excuses for anyone. She needs you to write it down.

This practice focuses on the act of reclaiming oneself after a legacy of trauma, silence, or emotional neglect. Healing is presented not as perfection or resolution but as a homecoming. It can include themes of:

- Rebuilding trust with your own instincts
- Relearning softness without fear
- Letting go of generational shame
- Recognizing that healing does not erase the past, but reclaims the present

Practice: The Unedited List

Find a quiet place. Take out a notebook or open a blank document. Begin a sentence with:

"I remember…"

And do not stop.

Let it be messy. Let it be unfiltered. Let it be full of contradictions.

Do not explain or apologize. Do not skip over the parts you think are too small to matter. This is not a courtroom. This is a reckoning.

Your only job is to let the truth land on paper.

Write until your hands hurt. Write until you feel something shift. You are not making a list of complaints. You are making a record of what shaped you.

You are naming what was never named.

And that is the beginning of healing.

9

Guardian Angels

"You don't have a right to the cards you believe you should have been dealt. You have an obligation to play the hell out of the ones you're holding."
—Cheryl Strayed, *Tiny Beautiful Things*

There are different versions of this lesson, and they meet us at different times in life. There is the version you live through in real time, the season when you are still in the thick of it, searching for meaning in the connections forming around you. You are trying to figure out who matters, who will last, who might shift your direction in some unseen but important way. It is a period of intuition, of instinct. You say *yes* to something, and you do not know why, only to look back years later and see how that yes rerouted your life.

And then there is the version that comes later. The postmortem. The one where you sit in your favorite sunlit corner of the house, sometimes laughing, sometimes shaking your head, and trace the invisible strings of your life backward. You realize that ten or fifteen years ago, a throwaway moment—a coffee shop conversation, a missed flight, a party you didn't want to go to—became a hinge that swung a whole new door open. You begin to understand that not all fate is loud. Some of it whispers. Some of it looks like coincidence.

My favorite origins are the ones that start with a single, seemingly inconsequential choice. That is how fate hides. It does not always arrive in grand gestures.

I started noticing these patterns more after watching the Gwyneth Paltrow film *Sliding Doors*. In it, the story splits into two realities, one in which the main character catches a train, and one in which she misses it. From that moment, her life takes two entirely different paths. It is the same woman, the same world, but two timelines. And that movie haunted me. Not in a scary way but in a truth-telling way. It revealed what we already know in our bones: that life hinges on the smallest moments. That everything can change because of a single delay, a quick decision, a stranger's kindness, a coincidence that no one else would recognize as divine but you.

When it comes to the path that pulled me out of Florida, a place I once thought I might never escape and dropped me into a life that felt closer to something out of *Sex and the City* than anything I had ever known, I have one person to thank.

Gus. Short for August.

He was the first openly gay person I had ever met, and at fifteen, that alone made him feel like a force of nature. We rode the bus together, and everything about him stood out. He had a rat-tail mullet because he liked the look of it. He wore tie-dye t-shirts, bright red Crocs, and handmade ankle bracelets that clashed with everything. He was magnetic. Mysterious. He told stories that felt like folklore. Gus made me feel like a bigger life was out there. He was as disenchanted with Ocala, Florida as I was. Suddenly, I had a friend on the bus who understood. We started talking because he asked what I was listening to on my iPod. I told him it was a bootleg of a live John Mayer concert. He smiled and said, "Rad."

Over time, I felt more and more comfortable with him. Since he was only romantically interested in guys, our friendship felt pure. There were no ulterior motives. He was a safe person, and I began to look forward to our daily hangs. When I look back, I wonder how different my life would have unfolded if we hadn't been on the same bus route.

Only because of him did I learn that our school had quietly begun offering a new option for students: online classes. He was going to do his entire senior year online during his junior year. By the end of it, he would have enough credits to graduate. He would be free.

That one conversation changed everything for me.

The reels in my head began to spin immediately. He and I went to different high schools, but our bus route was shared across the district. That very same morning, I marched into my guidance counselor's office and requested a meeting. I felt lit up with possibility. For the first time, I saw an escape hatch.

When I sat down across from her and explained what I had learned, she looked at me as if I had completely misunderstood the system. She said online classes were not designed for that. They were intended to free up space in a student's schedule. One or two courses to accommodate sports or electives. But not to accelerate. Not to graduate a year early. That was not the point.

I could feel the shift in the room. It was the first time I realized that adults in power will often say *no* simply because no one has ever asked them to say *yes*. It was not about rules. It was about familiarity. It was about keeping kids in line and on track even if that track leads nowhere.

I pressed her. Why not just call the other school? Why not ask how it was structured? If another student in our district had done it, why couldn't I? She offered no real explanation. Just silence and dismissal.

But I had already seen the map. Gus had drawn it for me. That knowledge emboldened me. It chipped away at the myth I had always believed, that if you followed the rules and stayed polite, the adults in charge would help you. For years, I had worked hard to be the agreeable kid. I knew I came from less. Everyone knew it. My clothes. My free lunch. The smell of smoke on my backpack. If I could not disguise where I came from, I could at least be charming. I could be likable. I could be the student the teachers rooted for.

That was the day I stopped being the agreeable girl. The rule follower. The teacher's pet who tried to soften my poverty with politeness. I stopped trying to make myself small and acceptable and easy to supervise. I started trying to get out.

But that day in the guidance counselor's office, I saw the truth. No matter how pleasant I was, she was not going to help me. She had already made up her mind. The answer was no. She was not interested in hearing how another school in the same district had already made an exception. She was not interested in making anything easier for me.

Hearing no over something that felt so thrilling, so full of possibility, was the first time any goodwill I had built with her went straight out the window. She wasn't curious. She wasn't flexible. She didn't even pretend to consider it. She just sat there, unmoved.

I pressed on.

I don't think it's fair that another student in this district is being allowed to finish school early using the same system, and I'm being denied just because it wasn't designed that way.

This is the first year online courses are even available. How can you control how kids use a resource that no one even told us existed?

I could hardly believe how defiant I sounded. How confident. I had never advocated for myself like this before. I didn't flinch. I didn't apologize.

The next day, she told me it had been approved.

This remains one of the most pivotal moments of my life.

I had a plan. A way out. Something different from every other kid at my school. My escape hatch had just been cut in half. If I could pull it off, I would be seventeen years old with a high school diploma. I could leave.

And right then, I made a choice.

I told no one.

Not my mom. Not my friends. Only Gus knew.

I didn't want to be talked out of it. I didn't want anyone planting seeds of doubt in my mind or trying to slow me down. I wanted to stay focused. I wanted to protect this tiny, powerful spark of hope before anyone could dim it.

I knew what I was doing. I was getting out.

That August, I took my journal and mapped out an entire plan. Month by month, I wrote down which classes I needed to finish to make sure I could graduate by May.

Around the same time, a family friend was clearing out a 1989 Buick Century that had been sitting for years. The car was silver, streaked with rust along the sides, and made a sharp screeching sound every time it started. He planned to junk it, but since it still technically ran, he offered it to me before it got impounded. I didn't care how it looked or sounded. It felt like fate. I had a way out and a way to move.

I got a job as a hostess at a local restaurant. My days started at 7:00 a.m. I went to school until three, then rushed to work from four to nine. I would get home just after nine, log into our painfully slow AOL dial-up, and start my homework. I had to complete assignments for both my in-person classes and my online coursework, often working until one or two in the morning. I was only getting five hours of sleep a night, but I didn't care. I was chasing something.

Both financially and physically, I was preparing to extract myself from an environment that had always felt stifling and claustrophobic.

As my bank account slowly grew, so did my confidence. It was exhilarating to experience financial independence. I had something that belonged only to me. A quiet pride started to build. I knew how shocked everyone was going to be.

By May, I had completed every required senior-level credit. I had earned eight thousand dollars.

I didn't tell my mother until the very end of the school year. When I finally did, it hit her like a bomb. The look on her face was a mix of disbelief and devastation. I understand now how frightening that must have been for her. But I told her plainly: I would be graduating in two weeks, and I was moving out.

The tension between us was unbearable. She was fifty-eight, staring down the reality of becoming an empty nester a full year earlier than expected. I was seventeen, simmering with unspoken grief, and bubbling anger over everything I had just begun to realize was not normal.

But now I had a dream to hold onto. I was ready to leap, and I knew New York City would be the one to catch me.

10

Seen

"I wish I could show you when you are
lonely or in darkness the astonishing
light of your own being."
—Hafiz

I believe in momentum. The quiet but undeniable force that builds when you start moving away from a life that no longer fits. At first, it feels like restlessness. A slow tug from the inside. A quiet voice that wonders if maybe, just maybe, there is something more.

And then, without even realizing it, you start to shift. You stretch past the roles you used to play. You grow out of the self that once helped you survive but now feels too tight against your skin.

That kind of change can feel disorienting. But it is also a miracle.

I think about the caterpillar. How strange it must be to wake up one day and realize your body is no longer what it was. To crawl into yourself not knowing that what waits on the other side is flight. It does not ask permission. It just happens. A transformation that begins quietly and ends in the sky.

And that is what healing feels like. One small, steady movement after another, until you look around and barely recognize the ground you used to crawl on.

When the healed version of yourself begins to show up, everything starts to shift. Doors you never even noticed begin to creak open. Invitations appear where there used to be silence. You become available in a new way. Available to possibility. Available to wonder. Available to life.

For me, what happened next felt sacred. It was so personal, so precisely timed, that I've kept it close for years. At the very same moment I was daydreaming and scheming my way out of Florida, one of my guideposts appeared. That is the only word that feels right. Calling him an icon is too surface. He was something deeper. A mirror. A compass. A spark.

John Mayer was releasing a live album, *Try!*, with the John Mayer Trio.

I remember the email like a lightning bolt. A fall tour. Small venues. No stadiums. No fanfare. Just standing-room-only shows in a handful of cities across the country. Intimate. Raw. Rare. Fall 2005.

I had watched his *Any Given Thursday* concert DVD so many times I could recite entire stretches of his monologues by heart. It played in the background while I powered through online classes. His words, his presence, his sound had become part of the atmosphere of my becoming.

A few short weeks later, I managed to score a ticket to the Orlando House of Blues through his online fan forum, Local 83. There is something universal about the rite of passage that is seeing your favorite artist live for the first time. For some girls, it's glitter and screaming and fainting in waves of Beatlemania. For me, it was quieter. More sacred. I wasn't chasing euphoria. I just wanted to be in the room. In the same orbit as the man whose words had been a lifeline during some of the darkest parts of my childhood.

It wasn't about spectacle. It was about proximity. The quiet ache to feel equally understood by someone who didn't even know I existed.

September 30, 2005. I showed up to the venue eight hours early, determined to be front row. I wasn't going to miss my chance to be as close as possible to the songs that had carried me through so much. The lyrics that had become like scripture to me would be sung just feet away, and I needed to feel that. I needed to feel the vibration of them in my bones.

By the time I got there, maybe a dozen of us were already gathered. Just enough to stretch across the narrow front barricade. It felt almost ceremonial. We weren't there for fanfare. I didn't care about getting a selfie or an autograph. I just wanted a place to stand, something solid to hold onto while I let the music hit me like a wave. A spot to lean against the edge of the stage and feel seen, somehow, by the sound itself.

It was pitch black when he stepped onto the stage. No lights. No buildup. Just the silhouette of a man walking slowly, deliberately, across the floorboards. Then, without warning, the first growling stroke of guitar ripped through the silence, and the lights exploded into life. It sent a current straight through my body.

There is nothing quite like the moment a rock star towers above you, casting his gaze downward, locking eyes without flinching. When he begins to sing lines you've played over and over in your headphones, and somehow, impossibly, he looks right at you as he does, it is not just electrifying. It is disorienting.

It is transcendent. It scrambles your brain and rearranges your molecules. It is intimacy masquerading as performance. It is *unreal* in the most deeply real way.

For two full hours, I was no longer in Florida. I was in a dreamscape. Every chord, every lyric, every story between the songs pulled me deeper into something beyond the physical room. If his music had once been a lifeline through my computer speakers, hearing it live was a kind of spiritual recalibration. It felt like stepping through a portal into the world I had always imagined for myself: one filled with color, feeling, and the freedom to become someone new.

He spoke often between songs back then. Not just quick banter, but winding, vivid stories. That night, he talked about how recording a live blues album had been seen as a risky detour by his label. How he was expected to release another polished studio record, but instead, he trusted his gut. He thanked us, his fans, for following him into unfamiliar territory. For allowing him to grow instead of staying in the neat, commercial box he was expected to live inside.

It was the first time I realized that making art from the gut, even when it intimidated people, wasn't about applause; it was about alignment.

A few fans I met earlier that morning had mentioned that the stage door at House of Blues led straight to the tour bus, and that sometimes, if you were lucky, the artist would come out for a quick hello. After the show, I followed the trickle of people around to the side alley—curiosity guiding me more than expectation. Only about ten of us had gathered, and I quietly slid into the last open space along the barricade just a few feet from the steps to the bus.

When he emerged, he took his time moving down the line. No rush, no pretense, just a quiet presence after an electric show. When he reached me, I didn't gush or freeze or say something rehearsed. I just wanted to reflect the honesty he had shared on stage. Calm and steady, I looked at him and said, "I like the blues stuff. Keep going with it."

He stopped. Really stopped. Looked me square in the eyes and, without a word, gently reached out and touched my forehead with his palm. It wasn't theatrical. It felt like a blessing. A quiet moment passed between us full of gravity and grace. He took my red-bound journal and scrawled across the back cover *To Cassidy! <3 John Mayer 2005.*

And then, just like that, he was gone. But something about the exchange lingered. Like I had been witnessed. Not as a fan. As a person. Considering I would go on to run into him exactly seven times after that, in random, unpredictable places, it felt strangely fitting that he had unknowingly stamped the first chapter.

The high after a show stays with you. It lingers in your chest, in your bloodstream, in the way the world looks a little brighter the next day. This was no different. I floated for weeks. Every time a memory from that night flickered back, a quiet giddiness would swell in me. Then, a month later, another email landed in my inbox. Tower Records in New York City. They were releasing one hundred wristbands at 7:00 a.m. on November 22, 2005 for a special album event. My sixteenth birthday was four days later. I couldn't believe the timing. And then, another announcement: a live show at Bowery Ballroom on November 23.

There are moments when my mother was so deeply kind, so tuned in to what lit me up inside, that it softened the edges of her missteps. Even now, years later, those moments shine brighter than the ones that broke me. As an adult, I can finally see what it took for her to make that trip happen. She saw how much it meant to me. When I showed her the email about the album release and whispered that it was all I wanted for my sixteenth birthday, she paused for a moment and then asked quietly, "Is that what you want to do for your birthday?"

"Yes," I blurted, barely able to contain my hope.

We didn't have extra money for spontaneous trips. Vacations weren't something we did casually. They were planned down to the penny, sometimes a year in advance. But she found a way. We stayed in a hostel in Harlem, bunk beds and peeling paint, but I didn't care. I just wanted to be there.

Those four days felt like lightning in a bottle. It was everything I craved. John Mayer. New York City. The electric possibility of a different life. The morning of the show, I set my alarm for 5:00 a.m., and my mom, half-asleep but still willing, boarded the subway to make our way down to Tower Records. I was one of the first people in line to buy the album and secure a wristband for the release event.

I didn't even have an iPod back then. I tore the plastic off the case and slid the CD into my clunky Discman. Then I hit the Manhattan pavement, headphones on, volume up, heart wide open. I spent the whole day walking the blocks like I was in a coming-of-age film no one had made yet.

And then *"Gravity"* came on.

His voice poured through my headphones, slow and deliberate, like he was offering something holy.

Gravity is working against me.
And gravity wants to bring me down.

It stopped me in my tracks. I stood frozen on a street corner, staring into the blur of taxis and pedestrians; the words curled around something tender inside me.

Oh, twice as much ain't twice as good.
And can't sustain like one half could.

It was the first time I had ever heard someone articulate the ache of wanting so much it hurt. The hunger for more. The fear it would collapse you.

It's wanting more that's gonna send me to my knees.

I must have replayed that line a dozen times that afternoon, looping the part that shattered me every time.

Just keep me where the light is.

It felt like a prayer. Not one I learned in church, but one I had always carried somewhere deep in my bones. A quiet plea that gave shape to everything I had never known how to explain. All those years of feeling less than. Of folding into myself in the shadow of my father's darkness. Of being bullied, overlooked, and returning each day to a house that sagged under the weight of neglect.

I had been reaching for the light long before I ever knew its name. And now I had the words.

Just keep me where the light is.

That evening at Tower Records, I didn't make it to the front. I was maybe four or five rows back, close enough to feel the warmth of the lights but not close enough to reach the barricade. Still, it didn't matter. I got to hear those new songs live, the ones

I had looped all day in my headphones, each lyric burrowing deeper into me with every listen.

I had come to New York with wild anticipation, chasing the high of live music and the promise of a city that pulsed with possibility. And even from where I stood, a few rows back, I could have sworn he was singing directly to me. His gaze swept across the room, but when it landed on mine, it stayed. I stood tall at five foot eight, my head rising just above the sea of shoulders around me. I wore my navy New Balance Classic 574s, the same pair I always laced up for general admission shows.

When the final chord rang out, and the house lights flickered up brought me back to reality, I moved with the crowd toward the exits. Outside, a line had already wrapped around the block for the meet and greet. I slipped quietly into it, somewhere near the end, heart thudding again, not from the music this time but from the knowing that I was about to stand face to face with the man whose voice had once kept me company in the loneliest rooms of my childhood.

The line inched forward, steady but unhurried. After about ten minutes of waiting, a man approached me out of nowhere and handed me a folded piece of paper. Confused, I asked, "What is this?"

"It's for you," he said simply, then turned and disappeared into the crowd before I could say another word. Everyone around me had seen the exchange. A few leaned in, curious.

I didn't answer. Instead, I unfolded the paper carefully, my fingers already trembling. There it was: the unmistakable sprawl of his handwriting. Thick black marker on lined notebook paper. Each song from the show listed out in his hand. The setlist.

I refolded it slowly, almost reverently, and tucked it deep inside my coat. My fingers tingled. It felt like I was holding something holy. Something that had just been passed from him to me. I stood there, stunned, the heat of it burning into my palm.

When I finally climbed the stairs to the second floor, he was seated in front of me at a table. Once again, no fanfare. Just a quiet calm that washed over the room. I didn't need my album signed; the handwritten setlist felt infinitely rarer. I pulled it out of my pocket and handed it to him. I was still trying to make sense of it. Why me? Out of everyone in that packed room, why was I the one holding this?

"Some guy randomly handed this to me," I said.

He looked up from the table, and the faintest smile playing on his lips, though his eyes held the weight of recognition. "It wasn't random," he said. "You're beautiful."

I was stunned and barely had a moment to whisper back thank you before he continued, "I remember you from the Orlando show through the fence." Trust me, when a fifteen-year-old girl who is still learning how to carry herself in a room gets a moment of recognition from a rock star that she might actually be memorable, it is a shot of confidence like no other. I took that compliment and tucked it in my back pocket for every time I would feel the sting of invisibility.

My voice had barely caught up to the moment. But it didn't feel like he was hitting on me. It wasn't that kind of beautiful. I was fifteen. He was twenty-seven. He said it in a room full of people, under fluorescent lights, without even a whisper of secrecy or seduction. It felt pure. Like he was naming something that had lived quiet inside me for a long time, an energy I was only just learning to access.

With just five words, he cast a spell. Not a romantic one but a soulful acknowledgment. A quiet, holy affirmation. He had seen something in me, something light-filled, something bright. Something I had only just begun to glimpse into myself.

I carried that light forward, and it lit a path. Even now, my eyes land on the setlist pinned to my library wall, and I feel fifteen again, days away from my sweet sixteen, wrapped in a strange and tender gratitude. That moment was never about flirtation. It was about being seen. It was intimate without crossing a line. Sacred without being dramatic. It was a before-and-after moment, and I've never forgotten the feeling. I began to believe in my own radiance.

The next night was the Bowery Ballroom show. I got there about an hour before doors opened and still managed to slip to the front, pressed once again against the barricade. To my left stood a videographer live streaming the concert for AOL. As John stepped into the light, the camera moved between him and the crowd, sweeping across the room, sometimes lingering. I could feel it pause on me. Not once or twice, but again and again, like I was a fixed point the lens kept returning to.

To this day, those clips still float to the surface: old videos that show up unexpectedly on my Airplay when I'm playing live shows in the background at home. I'll catch a flash of my fifteen-year-old self, bright blonde hair bobbing in the crowd, face upturned, singing every line like a lifeline.

At the end of the show, just as the final notes hung in the air, he stepped forward and reached down toward the barricade. Without a word, he pressed a guitar pick into my palm and held my gaze. His lips formed a soft "Thanks," then he turned and walked off stage, long limbs moving in rhythm, a scarf loose around his neck.

I stood there with the pick still in my hand; the energy of the moment humming through me. "No," I thought, *"Thank you."*

Because it wasn't just about the show, or the songs, or even the gesture. He had reflected something back to me that I hadn't yet known how to see in myself. A brightness. A strength. A kind of belonging I had never felt in Florida. I needed a mirror to recognize it and somehow, in that moment, he became one.

I floated out onto the New York City night electric with possibility. The night was chilly and pulsing, but my cheeks were flushed. Those two days had shifted something fundamental in me. I knew now what it felt like to be awake. To be seen. To be moved by art so deeply that it rerouted your entire sense of self.

I still get a wave of nostalgia for that time and place when his songs show up in the wild. In waiting rooms, at the grocery store, at restaurants. Each time I hear music from that era, it feels like a quiet nod from the universe. His music became the soundtrack to my coming-of-age story.

PART II

New York City

11

Home

"One belongs to New York instantly, one belongs to it as much in five minutes as in five years."
—Tom Wolfe

My road to New York City began with a detour through the Thousand Islands. We had a family friend my parents had known long before I was born, and he owned a cottage along the river. It was the kind of place we visited now and then over the years, familiar and quiet. When I graduated high school at seventeen, I had already booked a flight and a hostel. I was ready to land in New York and figure things out from there. The hostel cost seventeen dollars a night. I still remember that number. I told myself if I had to live there for a few weeks while I found work and a better place to stay, then that's what I would do. I had no backup plan. I had no fear. I never once believed it would go badly.

The night before I was supposed to leave, my mother threatened to report me to the police as a runaway. She was panicked and didn't know how else to stop me. I sat on the floor of my bedroom, trying to think of how to get out anyway. That's when I came up with a new plan. I told her I'd go visit the family friend instead. It wasn't New York City, but it was something. She agreed, relieved that I wasn't getting on the flight. I didn't argue. I knew I was still heading in the right direction. At least I was getting closer to the state of New York.

I stayed there for just under two weeks. I wrote in my journal. I walked the edges of the small town. I laid by the water and did the math on how to stretch my eight thousand dollars. I thought about everything and nothing. On the tenth day, my brother sent a text saying he'd be in New York City the following week with his wife and kids and asked if I wanted to come meet them. That text was the opening I needed.

I caught the 10:00 p.m. overnight bus. I kept trying to close my eyes, to let sleep pull me under, but my body was wired with adrenaline. I sat in the very first row with a wide, unobstructed view of the road. I pulled out my notebook and wrote to keep my thoughts from spiraling. On and off for seven hours, I journaled whatever I could. At around five in the morning, I looked up just as the sky began to glow. The skyline was approaching, and the city was still shimmering from the night before. The lights were sharp and alive. I took out my pen and wrote in big, bold letters:

"I'M HERE!!! I made it to New York City and I'm never leaving." —June 7, 2007

I always pay attention to dates and numbers.

The last time I had been in the city was the year before, just after I turned sixteen. I had come with my mom on a short trip, wide-eyed and full of questions, still half a child. This time was different. This time I was alone. But I didn't feel scared. I felt clear. I felt ready. There was something about being seventeen with a one-way ticket and a head full of conviction that made the unknown feel like a challenge instead of a threat. I didn't know what was coming, but I wasn't worried. I was bold. I was brave. I trusted myself to figure it out.

On the first day, my brother had meetings all day, and my sister-in-law had a full day of activities planned with my niece and nephew. I saw this as my window. I slipped down into the business center at the hotel and pulled up Craigslist. I was searching and searching with my eye on something that could be a landing spot for the next few weeks, so I could stay longer. Studio apartments way beyond my budget, sublets that I wasn't old enough to rent, roommate situations that sounded chaotic and unpredictable, not right, no, not that.

Then, an ad. Posted by a man named Nico. He was a part time single dad with a two-year-old. He was willing to rent his futon in his kitchen for $250 a month in return for watching his daughter so that he could work. Okay, he was a dad; that put me at ease. The apartment was in the East Village on 10th and 2nd Avenue. I held my breath as I called; he answered. I explained my situation, and he suggested I come over that very same morning to meet and see the space.

I pulled up an NYC subway map and scanned it. From Times Square–42nd Street, take the N train down to a place called Union Square, and then a short ten-minute walk. I ran upstairs to change and headed out. The taste of rebellion was hot on my lips, and my chest was bursting with anticipation. I arrived at a beautiful tree-lined street; this neighborhood looked more like the ones I used to watch on *Sex and the City* with many more true New Yorkers wandering around unlike the cheesiness of Times Square.

The buzzer clicked. Nico let me in. I stood at the base of the stairwell, took a breath, then climbed the four flights. My heart thudded louder with each step. I knew meeting someone on the Internet and going to their apartment was risky. But he was a dad. That detail made me feel safer.

He swung open the door and said a big, boisterous, "Hello!" and I instantly recognized that he was a surfer. There were framed photos of Montauk, and boards leaned against the lofted bed in the room past the kitchen. He was wearing a white-t-shirt, board shorts, flip-flops, a buzzed head, and he had a buoyancy to the way he talked. I scanned the futon behind him and saw it pushed up against the wall to create a narrow walkway between the tiny kitchen and bathroom on the opposite end.

I instantly felt at ease. There was nothing intimidating at all about him. He never asked my age; I think he just absolutely assumed I was eighteen and definitely not a minor. We went over the details, and he seemed totally confident and assured me this would be a great setup. He wouldn't have to hire a babysitter when he had his kid, and I would be paying dirt cheap rent. There was no lease or agreement, only a verbal acknowledgement for the plan, and he said if I could go get the first month's rent, he would have a second key made for me.

Those first few weeks were a blur of giddiness, bliss, and enchanting memories of such a specific time in my life. The dynamic with Nico was effortless. He worked in nightlife as a DJ, so he was out all hours of the night while I slept. When he rolled in at early dawn, I was already showering to get ready for another day of wandering the city. I was incredibly frugal. I only let myself take the subway if I was going somewhere really far; otherwise, I walked miles a day. I hadn't found a job yet, so I had nowhere to be at any certain time.

What I felt was sovereignty. Not just the freedom to move through the world on my own terms, but the rare kind that lives in your bones. It was the feeling of exhaling after holding your breath for years. The city met me with its noise, its urgency, its breathless possibility, and something in me said yes. I belonged here. Not because I had earned it, or because anyone had invited me, but because something unspoken had always been pulling me toward it. The streets felt familiar like I had dreamed of them long before I ever walked them. I gave myself to New York completely, and in return, it wrapped itself around me like a current pulling me into its rhythm. It was not just a place to live. It was a place that recognized me. A place that mirrored back my hunger, my hope, my need to begin again. It was a mutual understanding. I didn't have to prove anything to be here. I just had to arrive and stay.

In New York, no one knew who I was. No one knew about my dad. No one knew about the house I grew up in or the chaos that lived inside it. There were no whispers, no sideways glances, no pity.

And that was freedom.

It felt like the city had wiped the slate clean. A kind of silent blessing from the universe. Something was waiting for me. I didn't know to call it cosmic goodness back then, but that's what it was. A moment of alignment. A doorway that could have been missed if I had chosen to walk just one block in another direction.

12

Gossip Girl

"I was a Goldwyn Girl and a Chesterfield
Girl. I worked as a model, a showgirl,
even a stand-in. I watched everything
and everyone. That's how I learned."
—Lucille Ball

Even though I hadn't named it back then, *cosmic goodness* was always guiding me. Walk down that street. Turn down that alley. My internal compass never shouted. It whispered. And I listened. I always listened. Even in the noise of the city, even in the unfamiliar rush of it all, I could still hear the quiet inside me pointing the way.

I am endlessly grateful I moved to New York at seventeen, in that fleeting window of time before the world tilted toward the internet and never looked back. Social media was just beginning to stretch its legs; Myspace, Facebook, maybe Twitter if you were ahead of the curve were around, but life still lived mostly offline. The instantaneous life casting hadn't started yet.

You couldn't scroll through other people's moments. You had to make your own.

It is sacred now; the memory of what New York City was like just before it became a stage for everyone. Before the backdrop of every block turned into a photoshoot. Before the captions. Before the filters. Back then, you could walk the streets and feel anonymous and infinite at the same time. You weren't thinking about how it looked. You were just inside of it. Living it. Breathing it.

People looked up more. There was more eye contact. More conversations that started with a glance and turned into whole afternoons. It felt like the city was conspiring with you and lining things up just to see if you were paying attention. Everything felt a little bit destined. A little bit enchanted. Now, everyone's noses are just buried deep in a screen watching what everyone else is doing, somewhere else.

One afternoon, a few weeks after I arrived, I was walking down the street and noticed a group of young people gathered together. They looked around my age. Somewhere between eighteen and twenty-two. Holding clipboards, chatting nervously, clearly waiting for something.

I craned my neck around the long line and caught sight of a sign taped to the studio wall: *Gossip Girl* Open Call. I had heard whispers about the new CW show. I had been reading *Variety* and *Hollywood Reporter* like scripture, flipping through pages and scanning the trades not because I had any reason to but because I was curious. Curious about what was being made. What was going into development. Who was getting hired. It made me feel close to something. Like I was circling the edges of a world I wanted to belong to.

An open call meant anyone could go. No agent. No invite. Just show up.

I didn't have a headshot. I didn't have a résumé. I was wearing a white tank top from Urban Outfitters; a pair of faded, oversized jeans; and flip flops. My long blonde hair was pulled into a loose, messy braid down my back. I hadn't dressed for this moment because I didn't know it was coming.

But I was too far from home to go back and change, so I did the only thing I could do: I stayed.

I quietly slipped into the back of the line and watched. The girls in front of me looked like they had been preparing for this for days. Blowouts. Lashes. Sky-high heels. Thick foundation. Knock off Hervé Léger tight dresses from Forever 21. I didn't look like any of them. But I stayed anyway. I didn't feel underdressed. I felt curious. Open. And completely at peace with having nowhere else to be.

That's what New York teaches you. Trust your curiosity. Follow the energy. Everything you're looking for might already be looking for you.

This was before everything was online. You didn't search job boards. You didn't click and apply. I was still flipping through physical copies of *Backstage*, circling open calls with a pen. I didn't have an agent or a reel or even a clear plan. I had instincts. I had nerve. And I had the same dream everyone in that line had: to belong to the world that had raised me from the other side of a movie screen.

Film has always been my portal. It gave me language for feelings I hadn't known how to name. It cracked open doors inside me that I didn't know were closed. I wasn't trying to be famous. I just wanted to be close to the magic. I wanted to live inside the stories that had made me feel seen.

And I needed to make money.

At seventeen, fresh out of high school, chasing modeling jobs felt like the most immediate access point. No one asked for a résumé. They just needed to know you could show up on time and fit into the clothes. It wasn't glamorous, but it was a start. It was forward motion. It was one small foothold in a city where no one knew my name yet, but I already felt like I belonged.

The line moved slowly. I didn't mind. I wasn't rushing toward anything. I was just there, in it. Present. The moment felt big, but it didn't feel pressured.

When I finally made it inside, they took my name, height, and a few quick photos. A little digital camera clicked as I held a sheet of paper with my details scrawled across it. No fuss. No feedback. Just a click, a thank you, and I was out the door.

The next day, my phone rang.

They wanted to book me as a stand-in for Blake Lively.

Apparently, our measurements were identical. I saw her in *The Sisterhood of the Traveling Pants*. I knew exactly who she was. She was luminous. And now, somehow, I was going to stand in her light. Literally.

They needed me the very next morning. Call time: 6:00 a.m. Location: Silvercup Studios in Queens.

It was my first-ever call time. My first job. My first real step into the thing I had dreamed of from across the country, across my childhood.

I was electric with anticipation. I didn't have a laptop. I didn't have internet access. So, I asked Nico to help me map out which subway lines to take to get to set. I wrote it all down on a piece of notebook paper.

Since I was a stand-in, I wouldn't be on camera. They told me I didn't need to pack wardrobe options. No need for hair and makeup. All I had to do was show up.

And I could barely sleep that night just thinking about it.

The next morning, I woke up, and it was still dark outside. That thick, summer heat had already settled over the city—the kind that made everything feel damp and heavy before the sun had even risen. The sidewalks were still asleep. The air buzzed with a low, electric hum.

I was wide awake, pulsing with adrenaline.

I was going to set. A real one. The kind I'd only ever seen in glossy behind-the-scenes clips on *Access Hollywood*, where actors glided through soundstages like they belonged. But this time, I wasn't watching. I was hired. I had a call time. A purpose. I wasn't a fan lingering at the edge; I was part of the production.

When I arrived, I gave my name at the check-in table and was ushered into the wardrobe trailer. Then makeup. The pace was brisk but calm. Professional. Practiced. Precise. No one fussed over me. They just got to work. Blake and I had nearly identical long blonde hair and similar coloring. That was all they needed. My only job was to match her light.

I was just a touch shorter, so they handed me the perfect pair of kitten heels to close the gap. A sapphire blue dress. Light makeup. No frills. No fanfare. My job was simple: stand exactly where she would stand while the camera operators adjusted the lighting, then get escorted back to holding—a quiet limbo where we waited to be summoned again.

Back and forth all day long. And I loved it.

I lived for the voice crackling through the walkie-talkie. "Serena stand-in to set." That meant me. They needed me. I belonged somewhere even if only for a moment.

I was falling in love with the mechanics of television. The quiet choreography of dozens of people doing their jobs at once. Camera operators threading film through their machines. Production assistants whispering cues into walkies. Wardrobe scrambling to piece together ensembles that would later appear in *Cosmopolitan* under headlines like, "How to Recreate This Look." Script supervisors watching every word. I didn't even know what all these roles were yet. But I was watching them work. I was studying the rhythm. And I knew I was exactly where I belonged.

No book could have prepared me for it. I could have read a dozen guides about set etiquette, film production, or union codes, and it still wouldn't have touched what it felt like to actually be there. To feel the hum of creation. To see it all happen in real time.

I kept quiet. I didn't want to draw attention to myself. I was seventeen. I was green. I was trying not to look like the youngest person in the room even though I probably was. I spoke only when spoken to. I paid attention to everything. I had this deep sense that I was getting a private education just by standing still.

And the cast. They were glowing. Like actual CW royalty. Luminous skin, high-shine hair, gleaming teeth, and posture like they'd been trained in some secret school of stardom. Every single one of them looked like they'd been manufactured on the pages of *Seventeen*. The clothes, the heels, the casual way they carried themselves in and out of frame…it all felt like watching a magazine cover walk past me again and again.

I had come from a world where a seven-dollar burrito felt like a splurge. So, when I learned there would be three full-catered meals on shoot days plus this magical thing called craft services, I was stunned. Trays of fresh fruit. Bagels and lox. Salads. Hot food. Coffee. Candy. All free.

But more than the food was the money. At my first job in Florida, I was hostessing at a restaurant for just above minimum wage. And here I was in a union job. Earning actual pay. On my first day, I worked over twelve hours. I didn't even understand what "double time" meant yet, but when they handed me my signed time sheet and told me I had made just over three hundred dollars, my eyes went wide.

One day. One paycheck. My entire month's rent was covered.

At the end of that day, they asked about my availability. I said I was completely free. No conflicts. No other jobs. They put me on hold. Then they called me back. Then they gave me another call time. And another. And another. I kept showing up. The checks started coming in. My name kept showing up on the call sheet. I was booked.

And I had found a job—but not just any job.

I had found the beginning of everything.

I had found myself on a real set surrounded by people who knew what they were doing. And I was learning how to do it too. There were dozens of shows and films shooting in New York every single day. And suddenly I knew how to find them. I knew how to walk onto a lot and belong.

The horizon stretched open like it had been waiting for me. I was working. I was learning. I was paying my rent. I was feeding myself. And I was lit up in a way I had never been before.

If this was what it meant to follow your bliss, I was all in.

I just felt grateful. Lucky even. Every day I stepped on set, I reminded myself not to take it for granted.

There were murmurs about Blake. The kind that buzz quietly through crew corridors and waiting rooms that you overhear enough times that it starts to become a trend. People said she wasn't very friendly. I noticed how, when she arrived on set and swapped places with me, she never acknowledged me. Not even a glance. She brushed past me like I was a prop or a lighting stand. Not a person. Not another seventeen-year-old girl standing where she stood, wearing her dress, holding her place.

Blake and I never exchanged more than a word. Maybe two.

But truthfully, I didn't care. I was on cloud nine. I wasn't there to make friends with stars. I was there to work. I was there to learn. I was there because I had followed my gut and landed in a world I had dreamed of for years. I never took her distance personally. I assumed she was memorizing lines. Maybe staying in character. Maybe, like me, chatting would break her focus.

Years later, when the internet turned on her, when the headlines began stacking up and TikTok started dissecting her interviews, her interactions, her alleged on-set behavior, I felt something unfamiliar rise in my chest. It wasn't bitterness. It wasn't satisfaction. It was clarity. A deep, almost warm knowing that her lack of cordialness back then had never been about me. I had just been nearby. A body standing where she stood. A mirror she didn't want to look into.

She wasn't the only thing I brushed shoulders with that year. On days when we shot on location in Manhattan instead of inside Silvercup Studios, it felt like stepping into a different reality altogether. I never had a trailer. We waited in church basements or rented community rooms labeled "holding." But when we stepped outside, the air shifted.

Crowds would gather. Security would block off sidewalks. Teenage girls would scream from behind barricades. They held up phones and posters. They craned their necks for a glimpse.

Sometimes, walking with a production assistant past the crowd, people would stare at me with wild curiosity. You could feel them asking, "Is she the new cast member? The one they haven't announced yet?"

I wasn't. I was a stand-in. But in those moments, I felt like a star. A quiet one. A hidden one. But a star all the same.

As the paychecks grew, the hunger began to change. Not financial hunger. That was being fed. I was paying rent. I was buying groceries. But the deeper hunger—the hunger for meaning, for belonging, for contribution—started finding nourishment too. The more time I spent on set, the more I realized I didn't just want to be near the story. I wanted to help shape it.

Over time, I found a rhythm. A small tribe of fellow stand-ins, extras, crew members, and production assistants began to form around me. We traded intel like it was currency. Someone would whisper, "No filming Friday, but a feature film is casting girls our age for a scene in Brooklyn." Someone else would mention where to be seen. I'd call my booker at Central Casting and ask to be submitted. If I wasn't on hold, I wanted to be working.

And I was. Every single day. I was showing up. Landing new call times. Logging hours. Collecting checks. Building something I didn't have the language for yet. I was building a work ethic. A life. A way into this magical world of television that I was just beginning to understand.

Set became my happy place. The scent of coffee brewing at craft services. The call of "first team" over the walkie. The shuffle of crew moving lights, hitting marks. It was a world with its own heartbeat, and I was beginning to pulse in time with it.

Everyone else was waiting to be on screen. I just wanted to keep showing up. And somehow, that became its own kind of arrival.

13
Feral

"You were wild once. Don't let them tame you."
—Isadora Duncan

That first year in New York was a magical oasis of movie sets and television soundstages. I was seventeen, working almost every day, making a decent living with no education beyond high school. By November, just five months after I arrived, I turned eighteen.

I have always believed the word *wild* is deeply misunderstood. It is often lumped in with party girls chasing attention or temporary highs in all the wrong places. But to me, wild was never about recklessness or losing control. It was about trusting your own current. Wild meant moving from instinct, not impulse.

I love what wild represents, but less in the world of nightclubs and more in the way a gushing stream tumbles over rocks shaped by the earth and pulled by gravity, carving its own path without asking permission. That kind of wild does not need validation. It just *is.* It crashes and flows and adapts. It does not force its way forward, but it never stops moving. It is messy, untamed, and absolutely alive.

That, to me, is the kind of wild worth aspiring to. Not the kind that burns out by sunrise, but the kind that runs deep, guided by something older and quieter than rebellion. A kind of wild rooted in nature, intuition, and truth. My dad had been wild too, but in a different way. He was the kind of wild that burned hot and fast, always chasing the next high, the next escape, the next excuse. His life flared and collapsed in cycles. There was no flow to it—only combustion. I did not want that. I wanted to be a stream: steady, alive, always moving forward. A force shaped by the landscape, yes, but never stopped by it. I wanted a kind of wild that lasted. A wild with no end.

I had built a reputation on set for being reliable, always on time, never disruptive, and able to blend into the background without pulling focus. It was a subtle kind of professionalism, the kind that matters in an ecosystem like film sets where everyone is quietly watching. I wasn't the star, but I was essential. I was booked almost five days a week for that entire first year.

I did meet people around my age; other young wanderers pulled to the city by something they couldn't quite name. Many of them didn't have a clear direction. They would say things like, "I'm not sure what I want to do yet," and I understood the uncertainty, but it always made me want to hand them a flashlight. I remember thinking, just plant yourself in something you love. Anything. Art. Music. Movies. Whatever lights you up. Find the people who are drawn to the same fire and let that be enough for now.

Because when you place yourself inside that energy, when you root yourself in joy or curiosity or something that stirs your spirit, I believe you join a current that will carry you. Whether you call it the universe or cosmic goodness or angel guides or God or Jesus, to me it has always been about aligning with something larger than life. Something greater than your own doubt. Something that wants to move you forward if you let it.

What I began to understand was the value of placement, of being in the right place at the right time. I felt a quiet kind of awe that I had a front-row seat to something other people paid to witness.

14

Hunter

"Colleges are places where pebbles are
polished and diamonds are dimmed."
—Robert G. Ingersoll

Although I had found myself in a steady rhythm, I knew I did not want to spend the next three to five years as a stand-in. It was a valuable entry point, but it also stirred something deeper in me. I wanted to move from participant to creator, from being placed into scenes to understanding how they were built. I was not content to simply be on set. I wanted to know how the story was shaped, who made the decisions, and how the entire machine moved from idea to execution. It was no longer enough to be in the room. I wanted to understand the inner workings, the quiet mechanics behind the scenes that only the people in charge seemed to know. That was what lit me up. I had a front-row seat to the magic but no map to how it was made.

Curiosity has always been my compass. My mother, as always, saw this in me from the outside. She kept reminding me that while the real-world experience I was gaining was rich and worthwhile, I might one day need something more. Not more as in better. More as in deeper.

I resisted her at times. I thought she wanted to pull me backward, to box me back into the systems I had just begun to escape. But she wasn't trying to limit me. She was trying to show me that growth can come from every angle. That education, when chosen freely, can expand us. She wanted me to grow not just in what I was doing but in how I was thinking. Not just on camera or on set but in the blueprint of my own life.

Because real curiosity doesn't settle for proximity to brilliance. It wants to understand how it was made.

That season was my initiation. It showed me that being close to something powerful is not the same as learning how to wield it. It taught me that being invited in is not the same as taking ownership. It taught me that growth does not always mean chasing new roles. Sometimes it means stepping back, asking better questions, and preparing to build something entirely your own.

One thing it pays to be in New York is scrappy. When I started looking at colleges, the numbers were staggering. Even in 2008, tuition felt like a luxury item. I remember scrolling through school websites and feeling the absurdity of it all. The cost of tuition was staggering, and any flicker of excitement was quickly eclipsed by the looming weight of potential debt. I didn't want the pressure of a "real job" just to keep up with repayment. I wanted freedom, not a finish line shaped by monthly bills.

But then, a quiet technicality worked in my favor. Because I had lived in the city the year before, I qualified for in-state tuition at a CUNY school. City University of New York. It was one of those details that could have gone unnoticed but changed everything. I chose Hunter College. It was affordable.

It was near Central Park. It felt close to the pulse of the life I was already living.

I have always believed there is more than one way into any building you dream of entering. When an opportunity feels guarded by clipboards and velvet ropes, it does not mean it is out of reach. Sometimes it just means you have to get creative. Take the alley. Find the service door. Slip in through the side and make your way to the same room. The music will still be playing. The party will still be yours to step into.

What matters more than how you got in is what you do once you are there. How you show up. How you listen. How you connect. That is the part that sticks. I have always looked at those moments not as obstacles but as puzzles waiting to be solved. And the more you do it, the better you get. Each room leads to another room. Each face you remember becomes part of a larger map. Your network starts to take shape, first as a lifeline, then as a living, breathing ecosystem of possibility.

What no one tells you is that the most powerful part of building those connections is when you begin to offer the same thing to others. I believe deeply in the quiet karma of generosity. The more doors you open for someone else, the more often you will find one opening for you. Not always right away and not always how you expect. But the return always finds its way back.

I was not someone who had longed for college. It had never been part of the vision. After spending a year working in television, earning my own money, managing my own time, the thought of returning to classrooms and being told what to do by a professor felt like a regression. I had carved out a life with instinct and momentum. School, on paper, did not match that energy.

I started at Hunter College in the fall of 2008. I registered for a handful of media classes. I had no roadmap or five-year plan. But I did have a pulse on something shifting. The world was changing, and I could feel it. It was a moment of extraordinary quiet before the cultural storm. Social media was still emerging. Tumblr was just beginning to take off. YouTube was no longer a novelty. The idea that you could write something, post it, and reach thousands of people without anyone's permission felt quietly revolutionary. We were standing at the edge of a new kind of authorship.

We didn't call it "personal branding" yet, but that's exactly what we were doing, offering up our voices before they'd been approved. We were Millennial pioneers uploading dreams in real time, no gatekeepers or green lights required. The power was shifting. And somewhere in those pixelated videos and late-night blog posts, we were reshaping the entire landscape of how stories could begin.

I wasn't musically inclined, but I was paying attention. I noticed how artists were no longer waiting for record deals. They were uploading full albums from their bedrooms and hoping the right stranger would stumble across their sound. It felt radical. Democratic. Alive. And I started to believe the same could be true for storytelling, for film, for writing, for all of it. If you had something to say, maybe you didn't have to wait to be chosen.

At the same time, the iPhone was putting video capabilities directly into our hands. Suddenly, we could document anything. We could tell our stories in real time. We could build something with no crew, budget, or permission. That shift cannot be overstated. For people like me—young, hungry, unsure where to begin—it changed everything. What mattered most was no longer who you knew. It was what you created.

Being in that classroom with one foot in the academic world and the other in the emerging digital frontier felt like straddling two eras at once. On one side was the traditional path. The gatekeepers. The résumés. The rules. On the other was something raw and electric, forming right in front of us.

It was wilder. Less polished. More feral and self-made. And I felt the pull of both. One offered stability. The other offered fire.

Hunter gave me a foothold in both.

It reminded me that formal education and creative risk are not at odds. They are twin tools, and if you are lucky, you learn how to use both. Glennon Doyle said it best in *Untamed*: "I've stopped asking people for directions to places they've never been."

15

Media Pass

"The universe is made of stories, not of atoms."
—Muriel Rukeyser

I have YouTube to thank for my entry point into journalism. Not in the way people thank a platform for launching a career or making them famous. I mean it in the scrappier sense. I studied it. Obsessed over it. Treated it like a portal, a crash course, a classroom that never closed. Every night, after class or work or whatever odd distraction the day held, I logged on and watched red carpet interviews. Back-to-back clips of actors spinning through press lines. Reporters volleying questions under velvet ropes.

There was one channel in particular that uploaded nearly every day. I didn't just watch. I tracked it. Memorized the tone of the interviewers' voices, the angles they used, the difference between someone asking a generic, dead-end question like, "How fun was it shooting this movie?" made me cringe versus a prepared journalist with a detailed inquisitive question. I noted which actors lit up when asked a witty question. I was piecing together a language I hadn't yet learned how to speak professionally but instinctively understood. The celebrity interviews weren't fluff to me. They were a blueprint.

In a moment of quiet boldness, I sent a direct message to the YouTube channel that had become my unofficial syllabus. I didn't have a reel. I didn't have a single clip to prove I belonged. But I had something that mattered more in that moment. Willingness. I told them I was a student at Hunter studying media. I asked for their best contact email, so I could send my résumé.

They responded.

And I sent it.

I didn't overthink it. There weren't many rules back then. Maybe none at all. This was before formal internships were filtered through portals and gatekeepers. Before everyone had a polished social media presence and a personal brand. I didn't have that. I had initiative. And a Gmail draft with my résumé attached.

I offered to cover red carpets for free and declared I was completely available.

It's easy to look back now and dissect the transaction. What I gave away. What I could have charged. The labor of it all. But at the time it wasn't about strategy. It was about access. My classes were during the day. The premieres were at night. I could make it work. And more importantly: I wanted to.

The discourse around unpaid work and hustle culture has become a cornerstone of Gen-Z's values and rightfully so. I admire their ability to advocate and negotiate for amounts that they should earn. But for me, at that age, in that city, with a schedule full of possibility and nothing yet owed, I didn't feel exploited. I felt empowered. Like I had found a crack in the wall and slipped through it before it closed.

This wasn't a dream. It was a decision.

I was no longer just consuming the story. I was beginning to shape it.

Within a week, they called and asked if I could cover the *My Sister's Keeper* premiere starring Cameron Diaz. Just like that. No formal audition, no gatekeeping committee. One day I was a college student watching red carpet interviews on my laptop, and the next I was invited to cover one. It was one of those moments where your internal voice just yells, "*Wheeeeeee!*" A full-body jolt of disbelief and elation. I was over the moon. That kind of thrill doesn't just rush through you; it rewires something. It's a chemical, electric, unforgettable high.

I went to Crossroads Trading Post and bought a dress for the premiere. I learned that "press screenings" were a thing. Entire theaters reserved just for journalists before the film opened to the public. Reporters casually taking notes in the dark. I showed up early, walked up to the check-in table, and gave them my name. When they found me on the list and handed me a wristband, I nearly floated into the lobby. It was such a small gesture, but to me it felt enormous. I had never been given access like that before. I had never been on a list other than being a stand-in or background performer for a production.

The next night was the premiere. A real one. Red carpet, velvet ropes, dozens of photographers, talent handlers, fans screaming from barricades. I had seen these events from the other side. I had been background. I had been crew. I stood on cold sidewalks, outside the action. But now I had a credential. A microphone. A reason to be there. A reason to speak.

Being a member of the media was different than being a fan. They needed us. They needed the coverage, the promotion, the story. It wasn't charity. It was a collaboration. This was an energy exchange, not a favor. And that mutuality changed something in me. It shifted the way I saw myself. I was not lucky to be there. I was allowed to be there. Because I had something to offer.

The video was uploaded to YouTube that night. By morning, it had thousands of views. Fans had left comments about the questions I had asked. I logged in, heart pounding, and watched it back over and over again. Not because I was obsessed with how I looked but because I could see, for the first time, what it meant to contribute something real. I had provided value. And that made me feel valuable.

One premiere turned into dozens more. I felt a deep sense of gratitude for the steady stream of opportunity though in hindsight I think the production company was probably just thrilled to have someone willing to work for free. It meant they could stretch their budget elsewhere. I didn't care. I had found the door, and I had no intention of closing it.

By day, I was taking classes with generic titles like "Introduction to News Reporting" and "Journalism 101." The kind of courses that gave you grammar drills and AP style quizzes but rarely touched the pulse of what the work actually felt like.

At night, I was dressing in what I thought a journalist should wear and slipping into an alternate life. A double life. I would take the train downtown, clutching a list of questions in my bag like it was sacred. I was learning not just how to interview but how to *be* someone. How to hold space. How to stay still in the eye of the frenzy.

Eventually, I started editing the interviews together. I created a reel. A reel was what I needed. A résumé in motion. Proof that I could show up, ask questions, hold my own, deliver. As the reel grew, so did my confidence. With each new cut, I watched myself evolve. It wasn't just what I was doing; it was who I was becoming.

Within a month or two, I leveled up. Red carpets were exciting but chaotic. One or two minutes with a star if you were lucky. You had to hit hard and fast. Ask something memorable and pray they didn't walk away before finishing the sentence. But then I got the call to do my first real press junket.

It was for *Zombieland.* The cast included Woody Harrelson, Emma Stone, Jesse Eisenberg, Abigail Breslin, and the one and only Bill Murray.

This was a different format entirely. A quiet hotel suite instead of a crowded red carpet. Four minutes with each pairing of actors. No screaming fans. No publicists yanking shoulders. Just time. Enough time to ask real questions and actually hear the answers. I was no longer just trying to get the quote. I was learning how to guide a conversation not just for soundbites or headlines, but to offer the viewer something real. A surprising detail from set. A candid moment that caught an actor off guard in the best way. A glimpse behind the polished facade. It was about crafting something textured and memorable even in a span of three or four minutes.

What I hadn't expected was how much of it came down to instinct. These interviews required quick thinking, fast pivots, and micro-decisions in real time. If something interesting surfaced in the first answer or two, I had to let go of my prepared questions and follow the thread. That was the work. Not clutching to the cue cards but letting a moment expand into something unscripted and alive. If I was too focused on getting to the next question, I risked missing the thing that could have made the interview special. Maybe even viral. The magic was never in the plan. It was in deviation from it.

Celebrities sit through interviews all day. Most of them are bored out of their minds. I knew that. I kept asking myself, how do I surprise and delight? What does that look like in a format designed to be predictable? How do I break the rhythm without breaking the trust? I started to think of myself less as a journalist and more as a scene partner. Not performing but creating the conditions for something unexpected to happen. That became the goal. Make it feel less like a media obligation and more like a moment worth having.

Interviewing Bill Murray was exactly what I hoped it would be. Our conversation was alive. It had movement and breath. He was open, quick, and surprising. We talked like people, not personas. I left that room with my heart buzzing, knowing something inside me had shifted. When you speak to someone who sees the world in a particular way, and they meet you where you are without condescension or dismissal, it does something. It rewires your sense of what is possible.

A week later, I was walking down Park Avenue after leaving a late afternoon class. It was just beginning to turn dark. The light in the sky was soft and dusty; the kind that signals the day is ending but not quite done. I had stopped into a bodega to grab a water and a power bar when I heard someone call my name.

"Cassidy," he said.

I looked up, and it was him. Bill Murray. Standing in the same bodega as me holding a newspaper and a coffee, looking completely unbothered by the world.

He asked how I was. Told me he was walking downtown to catch the subway. Asked if I wanted to walk with him.

I stepped out into the street beside him. There were maybe four people nearby who recognized him, but for the most part, it was just us. Two people walking south on Park Avenue in early evening light. No cameras. No handlers. No rush. Just that strange, surreal intimacy that can only exist between two people who met once in a professional context and found a flicker of human recognition.

To be seen. Remembered. Recognized. Not just by a prolific actor, but by anyone really. To have your name recalled and spoken aloud. It is an extraordinary thing. A small moment that leaves a lasting mark. We walked a few blocks in step, and although I can't recall everything we said, I remember how I felt.

I belonged.

Not because I had faked it well enough. But because something in me had finally settled into itself. I was no longer the girl sneaking into possibility. I was already inside.

I am not proud of it. It was a quiet violation of trust. But I knew I would want to hold onto every single thing he said. I slipped my iPhone into the palm of my hand and hit record. I was already becoming an investigative journalist not to extract anything but to preserve it. I knew I would want to dissect the conversation later, to relive the cadence of it, to understand what had made it feel so alive. He is notoriously private, which only made the moment feel more fragile. I worried that asking to formalize it in any way would rupture the spell. I didn't want to shatter something real by making it feel transactional. I didn't want him to look at me and see a fan.

He was so perfectly kind. Thoughtful. Curious. Like a long-lost uncle catching up with his niece. I wasn't trying to sell the footage or post it anywhere. I wasn't planning to do anything with it really. I just didn't want to forget. I still have the video saved in the far corner of my archives, a little digital time capsule no one else has ever seen but me.

From time to time, I would play it back. Not out of ego but reverence. It felt like listening to a podcast. His voice is calm and measured. His questions are slow and intentional. It made me think, *this is what every celebrity interview should be.* Not staged. Not rushed. Not squeezed into four-minute slots with handlers checking their watches. Just two people walking down the street. No fanfare. No gushing. No flashing bulbs. A celebrity inviting you to join them on a walk.

Press junkets ran during the day. Premieres were always at night. As my calendar filled with screenings, interviews, and events, the collisions with my class schedule started to pile up. I was technically still a student. But I had started building a real-world résumé that didn't care about letter grades. Professors grew impatient with my absences. Some were supportive. Others rolled their eyes. I just knew I was learning more in one press suite than I had in months of lectures.

I was not sleepwalking through college. I was forging something. Quietly. Without permission. And in real time.

I was missing a lot of classes.

At first, it was manageable. A few skipped lectures here and there. But as the interviews multiplied, and the invitations kept coming, the professors noticed. I was keeping up with my workload, but I just wasn't present for their lectures. Their tone shifted. What had once been amused support turned to eye rolls and thinly veiled irritation. Finally, one of them pulled me aside and said, "If you miss one more class, I will fail you for the entire semester."

I was stunned. Not just by the threat but by the complete lack of acknowledgment for what I was actually doing. I was thriving. Not hypothetically, not in some imagined future. I was already doing the work we were supposed to be learning how to do. It felt maddening. I understood that attendance mattered. But I couldn't wrap my head around the idea that I might fail for pursuing exactly what the degree was supposed to prepare me for.

I walked straight into the academic office and asked to speak to someone in charge. I told them everything. I explained that I was doing real work in the field, not skipping class to party or sleep through life. That guidance counselor changed everything. She listened. She believed me. And then she moved mountains.

She sat down with my transcript and said, "Let's get you out of here as soon as possible." Most students were taking thirteen credits a semester. She bumped me to twenty-one. She mapped out a plan that included summer school and early registration and course substitutions. She filed paperwork to count my red-carpet work as internship credit. She gave my chaos a structure. And I will never forget that. I have her to thank for getting me to the finish line.

I graduated two years early. I'm not sure if Hunter would move mountains like that for other students today. Maybe I caught someone on the right day. Maybe I was lucky. But it felt like one of those rare moments when luck met preparation and collided with just enough audacity to force a way through.

Of course, the professors felt the shift. They knew I had gone over their heads. I felt the tension. But I didn't care.

At that time in my life, that was what wild meant to me.

Wild wasn't backpacking across Europe or quitting everything to chase a feeling. Wild was breaking the unspoken rules. Rewriting the fine print. Deciding I was allowed to shape my life and then doing it.

There is a certain boldness that comes from learning how to advocate for yourself. Unfortunately, in this era, that boldness often gets mislabeled as entitlement. Or privilege. Words that carry sharp, flattening connotations.

But I wasn't trying to cheat the system. I was just refusing to let the system cheat me. I do believe you have to be willing to advocate for yourself. Even when you are young. Even when you are terrified of hearing no. When I found myself wanting to bend a rule or ask for something I hadn't technically earned yet, I would always preface it with a line I had carried with me since Florida. A preface: "You can totally say no, but it never hurts to ask!" said brightly to set the stage for the "ask."

The proverb "You catch more flies with honey than with vinegar" became my guiding principle. You cannot force someone to say yes. But you can be brave enough to ask. That tiny bit of boldness is often the only difference between a locked door and an open one.

What I didn't realize then was that this quality, this quiet persistence, would become the most essential part of my career. Not my voice. Not how I tried to create a personal style. Not even my résumé. But my ability to ask. My willingness to figure out how to get into rooms that were not designed for me. To gather facts, research thoroughly, and find the one email address no one else could find. That instinct became the foundation of my work. I was not just becoming just an entertainment reporter. I was becoming an investigative journalist.

School revealed something else to me too. Something that reshaped how I saw the world. I signed up for a class outside of my major almost by accident, but it consumed me.

Women and Gender Studies.

It cracked my mind wide open in unimaginable ways, devouring fresh perspectives that I had never even considered. We read bell hooks. Judith Butler. Audre Lorde. We unpacked the invisible systems behind everyday interactions. I learned the words for feelings I had carried without language for years. Words like *patriarchy. Internalized misogyny. Male gaze.* Suddenly I had a vocabulary for the friction I had felt as a young woman in New

York City, especially in journalism. I had always known how to smile and nod. But now I could also name the undercurrent. The way power moved through a room. The structure beneath the culture.

We unpacked the invisible systems behind everyday interactions, the ways power, race, class, and gender shape everything even in spaces that claim to be neutral. It was like slipping a sword into my back pocket. I could still play the game, but now I knew exactly what game I was playing.

I graduated the following year with a Bachelor of Arts. A double major in Media Studies and Women and Gender Studies. My reel was packed with interviews from every major film release that year. I had stopped doing background work. I didn't want to be a stand-in anymore. I didn't want to wait around hoping for proximity. I had found something better.

I was a journalist with a press pass. And that, to me, was the golden ticket.

I turned my attention to where I was busiest. Where the calls were coming in. I was an entertainment reporter now. It no longer felt like a side hustle or a temporary role. I had carved out something real.

Los Angeles called me. I had grown up watching Giuliana Rancic on E! and studying every segment like it was gospel. It seemed like the next step. I also hated New York winters. As a Florida girl, I had never made peace with slush and gray sidewalks. I graduated at twenty years old. It was December. The timing could not have been more perfect.

I went on Craigslist the same way I had done each time I had previously relocated. Every single apartment I had lived in post-Florida I found there. And there it was again. A dream listing. A two-bedroom apartment in the heart of West Hollywood.

The photos showed enormous black and white prints of rock stars on the walls. It looked cinematic. Lived in. A little chaotic in the best way.

The man renting it was a rock-and-roll photographer and videographer who toured with bands shooting concert DVDs. He would be on the road often, joining these bands on tours, which meant I'd have the space mostly to myself. As someone enamored with live music, it felt like a wildly unique setup. Maybe, just maybe, proximity would open another door. Maybe I would get access again—this time as a roommate whose bud was crew.

We connected while I was still in New York. I wired him $650 for the first month's rent plus a security deposit. I had a new set of keys that unlocked a whole new coastline.

This time, they opened the door to Los Angeles.

PART III

Los Angeles

16

Gold Dust Woman

"A place belongs forever to whoever claims it
hardest, remembers it most obsessively, wrenches
it from itself, shapes it, renders it, loves it so
radically that he remakes it in his image."
—Joan Didion

Los Angeles and New York were my first love affairs. Long before I cared about any dusty man stealing my precious reservoir of energy, it was the cities that kept me enamored. New York had been my first crush, the heady, fast-talking kind that always kept me on my toes. It gave me an edge. It made me efficient and ambitious. I woke up with purpose and sprinted toward something even when I wasn't sure what that something was. In New York, I felt a deep need to achieve and accomplish. But I rarely made time to do the things that softened me. I didn't stop to lay on a beach and read a novel for hours. I didn't wander into a farmer's market and fill my arms with fruit that had just been picked from a farm north of the city.

The City of Angels taught me to slow down. It gave me permission to move through my days with less urgency and more presence. I learned to savor a moment instead of racing through it. The sunshine did something to my nervous system. I began to understand the value of quality not just quantity. I fell into rituals that nourished me. Driving down the coast. Reading on the sand. Picking up bundles of wild herbs and sweet peaches from small stands off Pacific Coast Highway. Los Angeles was soft, warm, and golden. It gave me back the parts of myself that New York had asked me to set aside.

If New York was a three-year hot love affair, Los Angeles became a long marriage. One that spanned more than a decade and asked me to shape and shift and shed old versions of myself again and again. I didn't just live in Los Angeles. I evolved in it. Over time, I came to see that loving a place could be just as formative as loving a person. Maybe even more so. A city will not mirror you back or mold itself to your fears. It stays steady while you change. And that consistency became its own kind of compass.

I was enamored with the lifestyle, the rhythm, the language of it. There was something about the women a few years older than me in Topanga Canyon with unbrushed hair, sun-washed, and wrapped in linen and eucalyptus. If New York thrived on stilettos and pencil skirts, I was far more drawn to the witchy women who looked like they had been raised on Stevie Nicks and sea salt. They were radiant without trying. Unstoppable without performing.

Some artists don't just fill the background. They imprint themselves on a time. In Los Angeles, during those first few months of learning the city and unlearning everything else, it was Tom Petty and the Heartbreakers.

My car only had a CD player. No Bluetooth. No aux cord. I didn't even know what Spotify was. Just a pile of jewel cases sliding across the seat beside me. I went to Amoeba Records in Hollywood and left with a stack of his albums: *Into the Great Wide Open, Wildflowers, Full Moon Fever, Damn the Torpedoes.* I felt limitless, like anything was possible, and everything was just beginning. There was an energy in the air I couldn't explain, only recognize. I was living inside my own soundtrack and scoring the first scenes of my own coming-of-age story.

We were both from Gainesville, Florida. That detail alone tethered me to him in a way I couldn't fully explain. He had made it out. He had carved something sacred out of smallness. And I was trying to do the same. I knew the streets he came from. The suffocating humidity. The way ambition echoes louder when it has nowhere to go only to feel stunted in a small Florida town. There was recognition in his voice. Like we had grown from the same soil and headed west in search of something more.

At twenty-one, I was learning how to navigate everything—career, money, identity, energy—all without a safety net. I was sharp and resourceful. I had momentum. But beneath that was something else. I had grown used to chasing opportunities, using my masculine energy to push things into place, and making things happen. But I was also beginning to understand how to pull back. To soften. To listen instead of force. To stop gripping the outcome so tightly. That's when I started playing "Walls" on repeat.

It was the only song that captured the full emotional range of what I was experiencing. It felt like it was written for the exact crossroads I was standing in. I wasn't broken. I was opening. I wasn't failing. I was learning how to hold both ambition and surrender at the same time. His lyrics gave me language for it:

Some days are diamonds
Some days are rocks
Some doors are open
Some roads are blocked
Sundowns are golden
Then fade away
And if I never do nothin'
I'll get you back some day
'Cause you got a heart so big
It could crush this town
And I can't hold out forever
Even walls fall down
And all around your island
There's a barricade
It keeps out the danger
It holds in the pain
And sometimes you're happy
Sometimes you cry
Half of me is ocean
Half of me is sky
But you've got a heart so big
It could crush this town
And I can't hold out forever
Even walls fall down

That one line *"Half of me is ocean, half of me is sky"* stopped me in my tracks. It felt like someone had named what I had been trying to live. That I could be expansive. That I could show up to every space as the whole ecosystem, unapologetic, layered, elemental. I didn't have to shrink into one version of myself to be taken seriously. I didn't have to pick a lane.

On the days that felt heavy, I clung to another line, *"Some days are diamonds, some days are rocks."* It gave me permission to loosen my grip on the big dreams. To let them breathe instead of suffocating them with urgency. To stop holding everything so precious that I became afraid of losing it. That one lyric allowed me to rest inside the reality that not every day had to shine.

That song reminded me, every time, not to grip too tightly. Not to confuse control with safety. Even the strongest walls fall down. And sometimes, that's when the most beautiful part of your life begins.

Laurel Canyon. Malibu. The Brentwood Country Mart. Topanga. The Palisades. Silver Lake. Echo Park. These places became my playground, my syllabus, my slow education in beauty, place, and belonging. I wasn't just passing through. I wanted to be a local. I wanted to know the shortcuts, the quiet corners, the way the light moved through each neighborhood at different times of day.

In New York, everything was tight and fast. I survived it. But the pace had nearly swallowed me. Most of the time I was sprinting between obligations with two boys in tow as a nanny or rushing to make it from a screening to class without being counted absent. I rarely got to enjoy the city outside of work and school.

The New York production company I had been doing interviews for didn't have anyone based on the West Coast. There was no one else to call. I became the natural choice. The obvious pick. I hit the ground running.

My roommate at the time had a close friend who owned a boutique dispensary in the Valley right on Ventura Boulevard, just beneath the cluster of studios. NBC, Warner Bros., CBS. He offered me the weekend shift to work at the front desk checking people in. I could keep my weekdays open for press junkets and red carpets. I accepted immediately. The irony was not lost on me. I didn't even smoke weed. I had tried it once or twice before, but it never really stuck.

The dispensary was minimal and polished. It looked more like a Scandinavian design showroom than a place to buy weed. This was long before dispensaries became the sleek wellness empires they are now. Everything was curated. Clean lines. Soft lighting. A steady playlist humming in the background. You had to buzz in to enter. Customers arrived with medical marijuana cards though there was nothing clinical about the space. Technically they were "patients," but it operated more like a boutique than a pharmacy. I found the whole system fascinating. Especially the people.

A lot of them were executives from the studios nearby. Producers. Agents. Engineers. I started recognizing names from movie credits. Men who worked at Warner Bros. during the week would wander in on Saturday afternoons with sunglasses and baseball caps. Musicians recording at Sound City made the quick fifteen-minute drive from Van Nuys to stock up before their sessions. It was an entirely different layer of the industry I hadn't encountered yet. Casual. Understated. Behind the scenes in every sense.

And somehow, I landed there. In proximity again.

Over time, I began to understand why bartenders always say their regulars start to feel like family. These weren't just customers. They were characters in my new world orbiting the same creative ecosystem I was trying to break into. I asked questions. I remembered names. I learned their orders and, more importantly, built a rapport with these powerful players even if I was just the marijuana shop girl.

At 4:20 every day, the owner would pass around a joint for all the employees, a ritual that never failed to make everyone laugh or loosen up. I always declined, and they would chuckle, teasing me about how I ended up working there when I didn't even smoke. Truthfully, it was just comfortable. I liked the rhythm of it. I liked talking to these powerful people in a casual environment that didn't feel as structured or performative as a red carpet or press junket. It felt like a different kind of access, one that offered something rare in Los Angeles, a real conversation.

17

Chateau Marmont

"But they all gravitated toward the Chateau for the same reasons the rest of us do. They wanted something more earthbound. They wanted to keep it real. The Chateau Marmont is the pure essence of what Hollywood is. It has an authenticity to it and an aura unlike any other place you can think of."
—Griffin Dunne

After a few months in Los Angeles, I found my footing. The city started to feel more tangible as I made real connections that felt like actual friendships.

One of my first buddies was Charles. He was nearly ten years older than me, Jewish, and a little awkward in that charming, Adam Brody kind of way. A whip-smart TV writer and a regular at the dispensary, he carried himself with the kind of ease that made him feel grounded and entirely approachable. We started talking one day and never really stopped. He was deep into indie music and got me hooked on LA's underground scene and checking out small shows at Hotel Café. He turned me onto bands and artists like Wilco, Band of Horses, and Iron & Wine.

He would pick me up on a Saturday morning in his Volvo station wagon to wander Silver Lake flea markets, browse used bookstores, and talk a mile a minute. It never turned romantic, but he became a built-in best friend.

As an LA native, he knew all the backroads. The hidden beaches that looked private but weren't. The hole-in-the-wall restaurants like Malibu's Reel In or Topanga Living Cafe. He gave the city a whole other layer of texture. Our friendship felt pure. At twenty-one, that kind of camaraderie is a gift.

One night, Charles texted me to ask if I wanted to join him and a few of the writers from the show at the Chateau Marmont for an after-party. I had, of course, read about it in gossip magazines, always portrayed as a velvet-roped fantasy. But I had never been. I threw on a pair of jeans, ballet flats, and one of those going-out tops every girl owned in the early 2000s. I curled my hair into loose beach waves and headed out.

When I arrived, Charles met me at the door and walked me in.

The Chateau Marmont.

It was a place steeped in mythology. Cinematic in a way that made you question what decade you had stepped into. A quiet sense of old Hollywood hung in the air. The space was scented with Tocca Bianca, a clean and bright fragrance that smelled like white tea and citrus with a hint of something intimate and magnetic. The lobby was dimly lit, glowing with the warmth of table lamps and wall sconces that illuminated corners like secrets waiting to be told.

Chris Robinson from The Black Crowes was leaning against the piano while someone played "Come Together." A small crowd had gathered, singing along without hesitation, like it was the unofficial soundtrack of the night. I had goosebumps. What was this place? A private concert with rock royalty unfolding in the middle of the lobby, as if impromptu jam sessions with rock legends were part of the nightly turndown service.

It felt like the most dimly lit, seductive summer camp imaginable. Only instead of camp counselors, there was a casual bingo card of celebrities scattered across the room. I didn't want to gawk, so I glanced then looked away, trying to play it cool while memorizing every detail. The whole scene was a blur of candlelight and perfume, and I remember thinking, *What is this vortex I've stepped into?*

The courtyard was dotted with dozens of tables, but people drifted between them like it was one long, unbroken dinner party. No one stayed in their seat for long. Someone might slide into the chair beside you with a wide smile and ask, "How's your night?" or pick up a conversation two tables over without missing a beat.

Instagram had only just launched six months earlier, so it wasn't yet a part of the cultural landscape. There were no phones hovering over martinis for content, no one angling for a picture in the perfect light. I've gone back to the Chateau in the years since, but the magic is not the same. Celebrities back then didn't have to worry that their every move might be secretly filmed and end up on TMZ by morning. The place felt sacred. Trusted. It held a kind of unwritten agreement that what happened there would stay there.

Soho House had only just opened, and the Chateau was still the spot. The epicenter. The heartbeat of a certain version of West Hollywood nightlife. I discovered it in a sliver of time that doesn't exist anymore. I don't think it ever will again. There was an openness to the people, a willingness to connect without calculation, that felt rare even then and has since disappeared entirely.

It didn't feel like a press junket. It didn't feel like work. It felt easy. Undone. Natural.

Earlier that year, I signed up for an acting class. At the time, everything felt possible, so I figured I might as well dip my toes into every corner of the industry.

I had just booked a small role in an indie film called *The Oranges* directed by Julian Farino and signed with a manager. I played Adam Brody's girlfriend. Think *500 Days of Summer*, the final scene when Joseph Gordon-Levitt meets Minka Kelly's character, Autumn, a quiet button at the end of the movie to signal the start of something new. It was a similar circumstance. My character appeared just as he was rediscovering the possibility of love.

I filmed a scene with Hugh Laurie and Adam Brody, a "meet the parents" introduction between our characters. The rest of the day, we shot a series of montages of the couple falling in love. I knew Adam from *The O.C.*, the series created by Josh Schwartz, that first introduced me to California. Through its iconic mixtape CDs, it handed me a teenage handbook on indie singer-songwriters.

Funny enough, the casting director had called me in off a headshot I'd mailed into their office all the way back in 2007. It had apparently been sitting on their desk for four years. A little wink from the universe to keep going.

Ultimately, all of our scenes were cut, leaving his character's ending a mystery. But for a brief moment, I was part of the story, and spending a day on set as one of the love interests was its own kind of magic.

That night at the Chateau, I spotted a girl from acting class working as the hostess. I walked over to reintroduce myself. Later, she circled back and told me she had added me to the VIP list. I could call anytime for a reservation.

It was those small glimmers, those quiet gestures of goodwill, that made Los Angeles feel accessible. Not exclusive. They stitched the city together in a way that felt like belonging. That night, I also met a girl named Kaitlin. She was from Florida too, just a month ahead of me in her move. We clicked right away.

I leaned over that first night and whispered that a friend had put me on the reservation list at the Chateau. It meant I could come back anytime I wanted. From then on, it became our spot. We started going three nights a week on Tuesdays, Thursdays, and then either Friday or Saturday. The place felt like a choose-your-own adventure novel. Every night, a different set of characters. Conversations stretched long and languid. We lingered.

That spring, I got two things that would stay with me for the next thirteen years. The first was a top floor, corner unit studio in a 1920s building: sun drenched, rent controlled, and mine for $960 a month. I was twenty-one. I would live there until I was thirty-three. Every single thing that came next—every love, every heartbreak, every pivot, every reinvention I would go through—could be traced back to that apartment. It was the root system of the life I was quietly building in Los Angeles. I held onto it not just because it was practical but because it became my sanctuary in a city that could be chaotic and unpredictable. No matter what was happening out there, I could always return to those four walls, regroup, and find my center.

Even as other people advanced in their careers and moved into bigger, shinier places, I stayed. I had everything I needed. The apartment gave me a sense of peace I had never known. I didn't need to upgrade. With such low living costs and rent control in place, I was able to build a real savings account alongside a sense of financial freedom I had never felt before.

Then, a few days later, I found a listing in the PennySaver for a tricolor Maltipoo puppy down in San Diego. The photo showed the most adorable puppy I had ever seen. Black, tan, and white. Under the photo, it simply said, "Girl."

I called. They said if I could be there by that night, she was mine.

My mental health skyrocketed after I got her. Suddenly, I had a companion on all my little day trips to the beach, to the farmer's market, to nowhere in particular. What I didn't expect was how much easier it became to connect with people. Strangers stopped to ask her name. They wanted to pet her. Conversations sparked without effort.

Hazel.

Now she's fourteen and still my sidekick through every major life event. We've grown up together in every sense of the word. She's still buoyant at the door each time I come home.

I had an apartment. No roommates. A dog I was madly in love with. A small circle of friends. I was building a life. Los Angeles was becoming home.

The apartment held me when I needed it most. I often wondered about the women who had lived there before me and those who would come after. I always wanted to take the original crystal doorknob from the closet as a memento. But it felt like stealing someone's diamond ring. It belonged to her even if I needed a small piece of that place to carry with me.

At the end of that summer, a director named Rebecca Thomas, whom I had done a few short films with during her time at Columbia University, called me. She had written her first feature-length script and wanted to know if I would be interested in one of the roles. The film was ultra-low budget and scheduled to shoot in Las Vegas that September. She offered me the role of Snow, a nightclub dancer. It was called *Electrick Children*, spelled with a "k" because the traditional domain name was already taken.

I said yes immediately. A week later, Rebecca called again, this time her voice buzzing with disbelief. The film had been raising money on Kickstarter with a goal of $100,000 when an investor from New York emailed her asking to read the full script. The next day he called and said he wanted to fund it for one million. His father had invented the Rolodex, and he had always dreamed of getting into filmmaking. Just like that, our tiny, shoestring project transformed into a bona fide indie.

Julia Garner was cast in one of her first major roles. Rory Culkin joined the cast along with Billy Zane and Liam Aiken. Suddenly I found myself on set with actors who had real careers. Esteemed. On the rise. I was in scenes with people I had admired from afar. We had the time of our lives filming. I was so deliriously happy I barely needed sleep. That little film would go on to premiere at South by Southwest, the Berlin International Film Festival, and Deauville American Film Festival.

I traveled to Deauville for the premiere. I did my first press conference as talent, not as a journalist. I kept auditioning. I signed with a big, fancy manager for pilot season and went out for every show that aired the following year. There were no streaming platforms yet. You still ordered DVDs from Netflix in the mail.

By the end of that pilot season, the big fancy manager dropped me. I hadn't booked a single thing. When he told me over the phone, I stayed calm. I said I understood. And I did. In my gut, I knew the auditions hadn't been great. I had psyched myself out. I was being sent out for lead roles that were miles ahead of where I was. Parts that would later go to women like Margot Robbie in *Pan Am*. I was auditioning for *Snow White*, for God's sake—a role that ended up going to Lily Collins. I didn't need to be the star headlining the whole project. I just wanted a guest star role. A memorable day player. A stepping stone. Something to build on.

I said, "Okay," with a steady voice. Waited until I heard the click of the call disconnecting. Then I burst into tears.

I was inside my car at the drive-through car wash, windows up, engine off, as the soap began to pour down. Water thundered in sheets against the roof and windshield. It felt poetic, almost orchestrated, the way the world outside was weeping too. I sat motionless as the blue and green brushes spun past my windows, letting the tears come. They streamed down my face in time with the rinse cycle. Not because I loved acting more than anything but because rejection has a way of cutting right through your center. I had been dropped. Discarded. And it stung.

But in that strange silence, surrounded by suds and whirring machinery and the scent of soap, I made a decision. I was done chasing something that wasn't choosing me back. I would take all of that energy, all of that ambition, and pour it into journalism. That was where the doors were opening. That was where I felt respected. I didn't want to keep begging for a seat at the table.

That moment marked the end of one dream. But it was also the beginning of something far more aligned. The decision marked the beginning of a more intentional relationship with the universe. I was no longer flailing. I had chosen. I did not falter. I think it is a lesson for anyone. If you choose a direction, if you pour all your energy into it, the world will start to move in your favor.

Yes, I felt like a failure for being dropped. But I still had access to the industry just in a different way. I was in the room even if not on the call sheet. I just loved storytelling no matter the medium. There was something about saying I was an aspiring actress that always felt flimsy. Too common. Too expected. But saying I was a journalist felt solid. That felt like pride.

I despised the look people gave me the second I said I was an actress. The eye rolls just behind their smile. But "journalist" piqued curiosity. It opened doors instead of closing them. People leaned in. They asked questions. They saw access instead of ambition, credibility instead of cliché.

I learned early which details propelled my narrative forward and which ones diluted it. The mythos matters. And the truth I chose to tell was still the truth. I was a journalist. I was working. I was building something.

Rejection will try to convince you that you've hit a dead end, but more often it's just a cosmic redirection. A gentle but firm hand saying, "Not this way. *This* way." The people who keep going are not the ones who never get told no. They are the ones who learn to let the no slide off their skin like water and keep walking anyway. You cannot afford to internalize every closed door as a character flaw.

The secret is flexibility. That holy, underrated art of reinvention. If you can stay open, you can always find a way forward. Rigidity is what keeps people stuck. But flexibility creates movement. Momentum. Possibility. Reinvention is letting the dream evolve. Let it shapeshift. Let it teach you. The universe is always offering you a new assignment if you're willing to receive it. That is the essence of cosmic goodness: a faith that something better is always forming even when you can't yet see its shape.

By the end of that summer, I had become a regular at Chateau Marmont. It was probably my twentieth visit. Kaitlin and I were tucked into one of the two-top tables near the garden, a familiar spot that always seemed to be waiting for us. We had a standing order. The burger was eighteen dollars with fries. A glass of Malbec was ten dollars. Only thirty dollars each plus tip. In my mind, it was a modest toll to pay for the kind of night that felt like it could rearrange your life. I learned how to move through opulent spaces without going broke trying to belong.

That night, I was on the edge of something. I was leaving in a few days to shoot my first film, *Electrick Children.* One of the Culkin brothers was cast as my co-star. It felt like the world was starting to recognize what I had sensed quietly for years. I was being invited forward.

My whole philosophy at that time was simple. "Universe, show me how good it gets." I had written it in my journal so many times it had become a mantra. I didn't want to predict anything. I wanted to be surprised.

I hadn't noticed him at first. He sat a few tables away surrounded by three or four men. But once our eyes met, it became a quiet exchange. His gaze didn't let go. John Mayer.

Six years earlier, he had called me "beautiful" inside Tower Records in NYC. I was fifteen then. I was twenty-one now with his eyes meeting mine. My confidence had finally caught up to that moment.

I would never approach his table. That wasn't my style. My friend, who was the hostess, had once told me they kept a rap sheet of "good guests" and "bad guests" at the Chateau. I always figured my name stayed on the good list because I was kind. Respectful. Quiet. I tipped well. I didn't want to disturb someone who was there for privacy.

About twenty minutes into the meal, I got up to use the restroom, fully aware that I would pass his table. I walked with intention but didn't glance back. On the return, I had no choice but to face him. His eyes met mine and stayed there. He leaned forward and said just one word.

"Hey."

My pulse skipped as his gaze caught mine. The fifteen-year-old inside me wanted to thank him for the light he'd once illuminated into my dark corner of Florida. How could I say that two minutes in his orbit had cracked something open in me, revealing the horizon beyond survival? I smiled instead, laughing at the inside joke of crossing paths again, as if guided by the same invisible thread.

"Hi," I said warmly.

He tilted his head with a smile, "Would you like to join us?"

I was intoxicated by the tension, the steady eye contact, the unspoken current between us. It felt pure and almost divine, something beyond being hit on. It was two people drawn toward each other by a magnetism first sparked years ago, an unexplainable exchange of energy that felt both fated and familiar.

I waved Kaitlin over. She picked up her Malbec. We joined his table. The conversation unfolded the way great ones do. Naturally. Gently. Without a trace of performance.

We talked about the difference between New York and Los Angeles, about how everyone was clawing to be seen on Sunset Boulevard, but the real magic happened on Fountain. He said it like a secret. Like something you were supposed to discover on your own. And I never forgot it.

Years later, during COVID, I would be sitting at a red light at Fountain and Crescent Heights listening to *Sob Rock* when he pulled up right next to me. His car. His music. Our street we had talked about a decade before. The universe would wink again.

That night at Chateau, he told me about a place in Montana called Paradise Valley. He said it casually like it was no big deal. But I tucked it away. Later, that place would become an album. And later still, it would become the exact valley where I would rediscover my own power.

Ripples like that are easy to miss if you're not paying attention. But I was. I had made a quiet agreement with the universe. *Surprise me.* And it did.

What I remember most was the gentleness of it all. There was nothing chaotic or loud about the exchange. It was calm. Present. Whole. I left that night not with a story but with a sense of affirmation. That my path was mine to walk. That people who had once seemed unreachable were suddenly across the table. That life could be surprising and still grounded in integrity.

John would reappear many times in my life. Always in moments of transition. Once at a red carpet for a Bob Saget tribute film. He walked over to me and said, "I know your face. Where do I know you from?"

How do you explain it all? Through his music, I metabolized heartbreak and transformation. That I had stood in concert halls and cracked open under the weight of lyrics that said what I hadn't yet been brave enough to say myself. That I had met people, had jobs, changed cities, and found meaning all to a soundtrack he had written that scored my invisible milestones.

But somehow, he remembered me. And that felt like enough.

I don't believe in idolizing anyone. But I do believe the universe sends us reminders when we need them. People. Lyrics. Coincidences. A street name like Fountain whispered at the exact right time.

That moment marked something. A before and after. Not because I met a rock star but because I met a mirror. Someone who showed me what could happen if you committed to the long game. If you kept saying yes to your own life.

You don't always have to barrel down the freeway chasing something that looks like success. You can take the side road. The scenic one. The quiet, unglamorous one. The one you are building for yourself. That's where the magic lives.

You don't have to scream for it. You just have to be listening.

And when it calls, you get up from the table and say yes. Watch how the path will unfold and rearrange to support you.

Let the spotlight chasers try to outrun traffic lights on flashy sunset boulevard while you intuitively reroute to Fountain, still parallel to the momentum but with more space to meander and still arrive home, just on time.

18

Good Morning America

"Don't be satisfied with stories, how things have gone with others. Unfold your own myth."
—Rumi, *The Essential Rumi*

When I try to describe the events that led to *Good Morning America*, it almost feels like recounting the beginning of a love story. The kind where everything had to fall into place just so, and you couldn't have made it up if you tried.

It started with a red carpet. Not for the company I usually worked for, but for a now-defunct Los Angeles magazine. With my usual gig, I would just upload the footage to Dropbox or overnight the memory cards. No questions, no real connection. But this time, they didn't have an in-house editor. They asked if I could drop the footage off to an editor in Brentwood.

So, I drove out there and met him in the parking lot of a tidy post-production building. We started talking.

"You want to do this full-time?" he asked, glancing down at the labeled memory cards I handed him.

"Whenever I can," I said. "But I work weekends at a dispensary."

He raised an eyebrow, curious. "No kidding?"

I shrugged. "Pays the bills. But I like it. You meet the most interesting people."

He paused, holding the footage in one hand and looking at me like he had just remembered something.

"My best friend works at a show," he said.

I smiled, "What show?"

He looked at me and said it like it was nothing, like it didn't hold the weight of my entire dream life in its syllables.

"*Good Morning America*."

Time stilled. My breath caught; my heart kicked. I tried not to show how completely unhinged my insides felt.

"Oh wow," I said, too casually, like my twenty-three-year-old self wasn't melting into a puddle of hope and adrenaline. "That's incredible."

"I'll connect you," he said. "I'll send an email. What's your number?"

He typed it into his phone right there. I got in my car and sat still for a second. Just long enough to say a quiet, private prayer to the universe. This was it. A breadcrumb. A door.

And I was ready to walk through it.

I left with my skin tingling, not knowing if this was a real opportunity or just another spark that would fizzle out and slip through the cracks. But when the email came through, I held my breath. There's something about divine timing; it moves fast when it's orchestrated to unfold in your favor.

She invited me to come into her office the next day.

"Bring your ID," she wrote. "You'll be on the list at the Disney gate for the ABC newsroom."

That night, I stood in front of my tiny closet for an hour. I wanted to look like I belonged, like I had already made it. I chose a black pencil skirt, a polka-dot sleeveless blouse with a big flippy bow at the neck, and modest black peep-toe heels. I gave myself a blowout with the round brush I had no idea how to use properly, smoothed every stray hair, and reminded myself to breathe.

The next morning, I parked outside the lot, my heart galloping. I had fallen in love with journalism and celebrity interviews. But until now, I was making maybe a hundred dollars an event. The thrill of seeing my interviews posted online was real, but this? *This* was different. This was national television. *Good Morning America.* The number one show in the country. The show I had watched my entire life.

I made my way through the lot, through security, and finally into her office. Simone.

She was on the phone when I arrived, speaking fast and clipped in "newsroom" shorthand. "What's up? No, the booking is solid. Airtime is 6:00 a.m. tomorrow."

She motioned for me to sit and didn't miss a beat. Her desk was stacked with call sheets, legal pads, and color-coded folders. The air felt kinetic, like something was always about to happen.

She hung up the phone and turned to me.

"Okay. So, we don't have any full-time salaried positions available right now," she said. "But we need a freelance booker. Someone quick. Scrappy. Reliable."

Then she tilted her head.

"You're not married? No kids?"

I shook my head.

"Good. You have open availability?"

"Yes."

"Sometimes we need someone to jump on a flight last-minute. Mostly domestic. Could you do that?"

"Yes."

"The rate is $350 a day. I'll send you a time sheet. Just fill it out and email it to Disney finance each week."

She spoke like she didn't have time to repeat herself. Fast. Efficient. She told me she was a single mom now and couldn't travel the way she used to. That's why she needed someone on the ground. Someone to get the guests. Someone to be her eyes and ears.

She had me save the newsroom line and her direct extension.

"We'll call when something comes up."

We shook hands.

And that was it. I walked out of the building having no idea when or even if I'd hear from her again. Freelance is funny like that. But I had this feeling. Like something had cracked open. And if they did call, it wouldn't just change my work life.

It would change *everything*.

Days later, I got the call. Amanda Bynes had been arrested.

The assignment was simple on paper, but to me, it felt monumental. Monumental and terrifying and electric. They wanted me to swing by the newsroom and pick up a letter, an official booking request printed on thick, creamy, embossed ABC News stationery, and hand deliver it to an address in Thousand Oaks.

It was her parents' house.

I was instructed to knock on their door. Not to mail the letter. Not to call in advance. Just show up and explain that we wanted to invite them onto *Good Morning America* to speak about their daughter's well-being.

There was something so surreal about it. A celebrity name I had grown up seeing on television. Now it was on the call sheet. Amanda Bynes. Thousand Oaks. Letter in hand. Door knock.

When I arrived at the house, I pulled up quietly and parked across the street. The street was calm and lined with palm trees and modest two-story homes. You wouldn't know this address was suddenly being watched by the entire entertainment news cycle. I sat there for a moment before getting out of the car, running the lines in my head like an actor. What would I say? How should I stand? What if someone yelled at me? What if no one came to the door?

I finally worked up the courage, crossed the lawn, and rang the doorbell.

Nothing.

I stood there for a few minutes in the California sun, shifting my weight from foot to foot. I called the newsroom. "No answer," I said. "Should I just leave the letter at the door?"

"No," they told me. "Stay."

I was too green to realize what was happening. This wasn't a handoff. It was a stakeout. My very first. I had heard of them. I had seen them in movies. But I never thought I would be the one behind the wheel tasked with delivering something that might change a story.

I waited.

An hour passed. Then another. Still nothing. The sun began to dip behind the hills, and the front porch filled with shadows. I called in again. They officially "good-nighted" me, a term I'd come to learn meant the newsroom was done with the assignment for the day. I was told to return first thing in the morning.

I did the math in my head. Another $350. A grand total of $700. To wait. I tucked the letter into the visor to keep it perfectly intact.

The next morning, I was parked in the same spot by 7:00 a.m., an iced coffee in hand. The sun rose behind the neighborhood, and I watched joggers and dog walkers pass by. I watched a sprinkling system sputter to life. I watched the hours slip by. Then, sometime in the early afternoon, a car pulled into the driveway.

It was them.

My pulse jumped. My mouth went dry. I stepped out of the car. This was it. My first real booking attempt. Not a call. Not an email. A face-to-face ask. No script. Just me, twenty-three years old, a freshly-printed press pass in my back pocket, and a letter in hand.

They stepped out of the car cautiously, their eyes flicking toward me with quiet suspicion. I could see it immediately: the exhaustion etched into their faces. Trauma has a way of rearranging a person. It folds the shoulders inward. It dims the light behind the eyes. They looked like two people who had just returned from war.

I walked toward them, slowly and carefully.

"I'm truly sorry to bother you at your home," I said softly. "May I please just hand you a letter from *Good Morning America*? We wanted to give your family a chance to tell your side of the story, in your own words, if you'd ever want to."

They looked at me like they didn't know what to make of me. Not quite "the media." Not quite a threat. Just a girl with a note. Her mother didn't speak. She simply nodded, a quiet, tired nod. I handed her the letter. That was all. I didn't push. I didn't linger.

I turned, walked back to my car, and sat down in the driver's seat with my heart pounding in my ears. I called the newsroom and told them the letter had been delivered hand to hand, not a missed connection. Not a message in a bottle. The assignment was complete. They thanked me and told me I could sign off for the day.

My first real *Good Morning America* assignment. My first stakeout. My first brush with that sacred line between press and privacy. I didn't lead with force. I carried the quiet recognition that even when a camera crew waited in the van, looking for the nod to set up, someone's life was in a crisis on the other side of that door. You cannot forget that.

19

Anchor

"I don't want to repeat my innocence. I
want the pleasure of losing it again."
—F. Scott Fitzgerald

There is nothing I love more than live performances. I keep an ongoing list of the ones that send me to my knees. They are not just moments in time, they are transmissions, emotional frequencies that reach directly into the heart. Of all the arcs in storytelling, it's love that hits me hardest, every time.

Stevie Nicks's 1997 live performance of "Silver Springs" on the MTV reunion special is a masterclass in tension and longing. The way she sings to Lindsey Buckingham, gazing straight into him and never breaking eye contact, is spellbinding. She paces the lyrics like a slow burn as if she is casting a final, aching spell. Her voice shakes at just the right moments, and the restrained fury beneath her beauty is unforgettable. It is not just performance; it is reckoning. It's what it looks like when a woman refuses to be erased.

There have been times in my own life when I got carried away with the idea of that kind of tension. I loved the thrill of not knowing. The delicious uncertainty of the question, "Will they, or won't they?" The dramatic pull of romance not yet settled. It mirrored the way I lived in Los Angeles, wrapped in stories and fantasies, where reality often blurred with cinematic desire. I was intoxicated by the storylines of my own life. I would narrate them in my head, imagining that the most difficult moments were merely the setup before the redemption.

I met Arda on my last night of being twenty-two years old. A few friends and I had gone to The Hudson in West Hollywood to celebrate my birthday, which was the following day. It was a quiet Sunday night, nothing flashy—just a small group of neighborhood twenty-somethings lingering over drinks. I was standing at the bar when the door opened and a gust of wind swept in behind him.

He wore a gray James Perse t-shirt, perfectly tailored jeans, and navy-blue New Balances. His hair was sloppily pulled into a man bun paired with a perfectly grown-in beard. He was my exact type: artistic but not in a tie-dye and Birkenstocks kind of way. I felt a jolt move through my body. If I had to paint the blueprint of my attraction, at least aesthetically, it would have looked exactly like him. I had a rule about not approaching men. I believed that if they were meant to talk to me, they would find a way. I kept stealing glances, and eventually he walked over to the bar to grab a drink for a friend. Then he turned to the bartender, and, like we had shared a thousand conversations before, he said, "And whatever she's having."

It felt so natural, my nerves melted instantly. We fell into an easy rhythm; conversation flowing effortlessly. We traded details about where we lived and where we were from. I learned he was born and raised in Istanbul but had been in Los Angeles since college. He was thirty-one to my twenty-two. Old enough to have lived a decade before me but still young enough that our worlds overlapped. I told him it was my birthday the next day.

At the time, he spared me one detail, but I would later learn that his ex of seven years and I shared the same birthday. He must have quietly chuckled in that moment, feeling the strange wave of recognition. It's funny how astrology works, how two of the women he would spend the most serious stretches of his life with were not only Sagittarius but born on the exact same day. The universe has a wicked sense of humor like that.

He was an environmental engineer, grounded and far removed from the industry that I was swimming in every day. It was refreshing. He was proper, protective, and made me feel safe at a time when I was navigating a sea of chaos.

He lived just outside Santa Monica, and almost without noticing, our lives started to fold into each other. We spent lazy afternoons biking to Venice, stopping at tucked-away cafés where we'd sit for hours, swapping stories and laughing until our sides hurt. That's always been the thing for me, humor. It's the throughline with every man I've loved. With him, it was a slow burn. He took three months to even kiss me, but when we finally did, he asked me to be his girlfriend within a week.

In a city of constant invitation and temptation, he offered clarity and steadiness. But our tension lived in the gap between our expectations. He wanted a woman who would cook, clean, and care for the home, just like the devoted Turkish mother who had shaped his sense of love and duty. He would joke, "I'm just trying to domesticate you." I resisted. I didn't want to fade into a household that wasn't mine at just twenty-three. I needed to become someone before I belonged to someone.

It was during that very season that an acquaintance told me about Marianne Williamson, a spiritual thought leader giving Monday night lectures at the Saban Theatre in Beverly Hills. I looked her up and found her book *A Return to Love*, which was based on the metaphysical text *A Course in Miracles*. I had never read anything like it. It wasn't religion in the traditional sense; it was a spiritual framework that invited you to choose love over fear, again and again, and to see every relationship as a kind of soul assignment placed in your path to show you where you're still unhealed.

A Course in Miracles is a thick, blue book with gold lettering. If you've ever walked through a yoga studio, spiritual bookstore, or your more enlightened friend's apartment, chances are you've seen it floating around. But owning it and studying it are two very different things. The *Course* is more than a book; it's a year-long self-study program in spiritual transformation, broken into 365 lessons, one for each day. It's poetic, symbolic, and not always easy to digest. But for those who stick with it, there's an almost secret language. A kind of invisible community of people who share a belief system on forgiveness, perception, and love.

The Saban Theatre holds just over 1,900 seats, and every Monday night it was nearly full. Sometimes I'd get there early to find a place up front; other times I'd scan the rows for the last empty seat. It was always electric. It wasn't just Marianne. It was the time. Agape's Sacred Order with Michael Beckwith was thriving. *The Secret* had exploded into pop culture. There was this spiritual undercurrent moving through Los Angeles, and I had tapped into it. It was warm, charged, and deeply alive. Holy ground.

I had found a kind of family in those Monday nights. A room full of people who were asking bigger questions guided by an interior compass that aligned with my own. They were seekers of meaning, connection, and something that felt true. And once I had felt the shift of swimming beyond the shallow end, I couldn't return to the surface-level conversations that had once defined life in LA. My standard for what stirred me had leapt forward.

Marianne made *A Course in Miracles* feel accessible. She took the lofty metaphysics and grounded them in everyday life. She talked about romantic relationships as sacred laboratories, places where our deepest insecurities and wounds rise to the surface, not to punish us, but to heal us. She would say things like, "If someone really hurts you, pray for their happiness every day for thirty days. By the end of the month, one of two things will have happened. You will either have forgiven them, or you won't care anymore," or, "If someone upsets you in the moment, say quietly to yourself, 'I forgive you and release you to the Holy Spirit.'" I wrote those words down and returned to them often. They shifted something in me. They became a framework for how to navigate tension without letting it poison me.

I was simultaneously falling in love for the first time and anchoring with a spiritual practice during the first expansive chapter of my becoming. I felt this surge of gratitude that I had found a guide, a kind of sacred manual for how to be in a relationship without abandoning my becoming. I started going every single Monday night. It became a ritual, a recalibration.

It stirred things in me I hadn't yet named. Things I was only beginning to trace back to my childhood. That was the first time I learned the word *trigger*. The first time I understood that not every reaction was about the present moment. Sometimes it's the past echoing through the now.

Years later, when Marianne Williamson announced her candidacy for president of the United States, I was a booking producer at ABC News. I pitched her as a story, and our team at *Nightline* ran a feature. It felt like a full-circle moment, proof that all the goodness we put into the world, all the teachers who shape us, all the spiritual seeds we plant, eventually return. Maybe not in the ways we expect, but always tenfold.

Seeing her on a national stage was surreal. She had once felt like my private treasure, a voice that had quietly rearranged the architecture of my life. When memes began to circulate online, painting her as some kind of eccentric aunt, I felt an almost primal protectiveness. They didn't know. They hadn't been cracked open by her words. But I had. And I would never be the same.

At twenty-three, I couldn't have imagined that I'd one day have the power to pitch national news stories or that someone who'd shaped my spiritual life so profoundly would become the subject of one. Back then, I was being stretched and expanded in every direction, falling in love, working nonstop, and discovering a spiritual path for the first time. It was intoxicating. The drive. The purpose. My bank account was flourishing. I was thriving professionally. And being with someone nine years older, someone so established, who owned a home, ran a thriving business, lit a fire under me.

The thing is, I didn't want to build those things with him, I wanted to build them for myself. I didn't want to be handed a life, no matter how beautiful or secure it looked from the outside. I needed to know that I could craft it with my own hands, on my own terms, from the foundation up. Because real belonging, the kind that lasts, doesn't come from moving into someone else's dream. It comes from making your own. I still carry a quiet guilt for borrowing nearly four years of his life while secretly craving a life of my own. But I couldn't walk away, not then. I loved him. And sometimes love doesn't illuminate the path forward; it blurs the exit signs.

Arda took me to Turkey. We traveled through Istanbul, Çeşme, and İzmir. His family welcomed me with open arms. And though I adored them, I knew in my bones I could never live there permanently. That trip carried the quiet undertone of a question: "*Here's Turkey. I'd like to move back one day. Could you see yourself here forever?*"

Even then, I knew we wanted different futures. We couldn't even agree on where we'd live. But the gravity between us was stronger than logic. The magnetism was real. It was bigger than both of us.

And all it took was one phone call to mark the line between before and after.

20

Dead Dads Club

"Letting go of him wasn't a betrayal.
It was a return to myself."
—Yung Pueblo

Pre-Diagnosis

Discovering Marianne's teachings did not come gently or beautifully packaged in tidy spiritual epiphanies. They ripped through my subconscious, dredging up memories I had buried so far beneath the surface I nearly forgot they were my own. Awakening spiritually was not blissful. It was messy, complicated, and painful in ways I had not anticipated.

It felt as though my mind had waited for me to find some kind of stability, waited for me to feel secure enough to fall in love, before unleashing memories that shattered that stability entirely. Just as I was finally feeling safe, memories clawed their way back from the hidden corners of my past. Raw, fragmented scenes returned to me with sharpness and clarity that made them impossible to ignore.

I had believed I left those shadows behind when I moved to New York City, and later to Los Angeles. In those bustling cities, I was someone new, someone unburdened by family dysfunction and childhood shame. I felt free in a way that almost convinced me my past was something I had invented, just stories, exaggerations. Maybe I had misunderstood it all.

But now, as I traveled relentlessly for work, those memories began to follow me. In hotels, at airports, on airplanes in the liminal space between departures and arrivals, the visions returned with sudden, violent clarity. I would find myself mid-flight, staring at clouds, when suddenly a memory arrived, visceral and vivid, like lightning jolting through my nervous system.

These trips were nothing like the glossy, upbeat celebrity features others imagined when they heard I was a journalist at *Good Morning America.* I was not flying to glamorous events or red carpets. Instead, I was boarding flights toward scenes of mass violence, toward tragedies that defied comprehension. I was landing in towns whose names were newly synonymous with nightmares, armed only with a notebook, camera crews, and questions I barely knew how to ask.

I would step off the plane, heart heavy and hands shaking slightly, and head straight to neighborhoods where lives had just been shattered. My job was to knock on strangers' doors and gently ask them to relive the unimaginable. Doors that swung open to people whose eyes reflected a shock still too fresh to fully register, survivors who had seen a gunman raise a weapon and aim it into a crowd of innocents, felt terror pulse through their veins, and had run for their lives and somehow escaped death.

There was no room for my personal chaos, no space for the memories clawing their way to my surface. These moments were not about my trauma, yet my trauma was always there, waiting, patient, unrelenting.

Quietly, privately, I was wading through a storm of my own PTSD, memories that surged at the most inconvenient moments, jolting me awake in dark hotel rooms, making my hands shake over lukewarm coffee, reminding me how thin the line was between holding it together and falling apart. And all the while, I was tasked with reaching gently into the grief of others, coaxing out their stories, honoring their pain while burying my own.

These assignments forced me to navigate a heartbreaking paradox: I was barely clinging to my own sanity, yet I was responsible for holding space for strangers in the depths of their most devastating losses.

Journalism is often romanticized as heroic, fearless, and exhilarating. But the truth I found in those months was much messier and far more complicated. It required me to be strong even when I felt weak, clear when my mind was clouded, and compassionate when I was hurting deeply myself. It demanded I learn how to hold two opposing truths simultaneously: my own pain and theirs, side by side, interwoven and inseparable.

I carried those stories with me long after I left. Somewhere beneath that heaviness, quietly stirring, was a sense of purpose. A sense that I was doing something that mattered, something essential, even as it threatened to break me.

Later, a therapist would identify what I hadn't been able to name: I was carrying my own PTSD, not from being a direct victim, but from standing so close to the wreckage for so long. That bearing witness to destruction can scorch you too. I was stunned. I had extended so much empathy to everyone else that I hadn't saved any for myself.

These assignments—painful, complex, emotionally wrenching—were also profoundly human. They reminded me again and again how fragile we are, how resilient we can become, and how powerful it is to bear witness even as we are bearing our own wounds.

"Did that really happen?" I would wonder to myself, heart pounding, throat tightening with shame and confusion. "That seems really fucked up for a twelve-year-old girl to do."

Those memories were not tidy. They didn't fit neatly into the life I had carefully constructed. Instead, they shattered illusions I didn't even realize I'd held. The shame returned fiercely, achingly familiar, deep in my bones. It felt raw and vulnerable and exposed, like the truth itself had torn away a layer of skin I didn't know I had been hiding behind all these years.

Awakening spiritually was not simply about finding love and light. It meant reclaiming my darkest shadows. It meant confronting truths I'd spent a lifetime running from.

Arda, who had fallen in love with the bright-eyed, fearless woman determined to carve out a destiny, now stood at the edge of someone he could barely recognize. He was trying (my God, how he was trying), but every kindness felt insufficient against the tidal wave crashing within me. Where there once had been playful conversations and effortless exchanges, silence—dense, thickened only by the quiet sobs I could no longer contain—now filled the space between us.

I didn't want to be comforted. I didn't want solutions or platitudes. I wanted to scream with such raw force that the earth would split open and swallow the history I wished desperately to erase.

I saw myself at twelve years old, the summer before my father moved to Ukraine. His sudden, intense attention felt like rain after a long drought. Attention was so scarce in my childhood that even the smallest gesture felt like salvation. He began taking me shopping, offering approval in tangible ways: swimsuits, dozens at a time, a strange excess I did not yet comprehend. "You could be a model," he told me, something in his voice not paternal but possessive, unnerving even then.

He bought a digital camera, saying he would help me get discovered with "Modeling agents." There were photoshoots at home, staged casually enough that my naïve mind mistook them for normal. Bite your lip. Let your bathing suit strap fall down, far down. Implied nudity. "Look up towards the camera." I posed obediently, craving approval, mistaking his attention for affection, his exploitation for fatherly presence.

I trusted him. I thought this was what "modeling" was. He created a website—the domain name, I have no idea. He made it a locked site where men would have to pay a submission to access the photos. He started getting paid. Lots of money. How much I don't know. I never saw the money. He said I was going to be a very famous model. I was elated, never understanding that my "fans" were sexual predators that got off on looking at a pre-teen pose seductively. To this day, it makes me sick to my stomach.

I remembered my mother screaming one night into the phone, a memory I'd never truly processed. Her sister accused my father of something unimaginable, something sickeningly specific, "Cassidy is doing *soft-core porn.*" My mother's denial had been swift, frantic, aggressive. Not because the accusations were false but because to accept them as truth would dismantle the fragile architecture of the life she'd built. Denial was her survival, too.

For years, that memory hovered at the edge of consciousness, blurred enough to dismiss as fiction. But it was back now, unmistakably clear.

There are a thousand ways to shatter a girl, but my father had chosen perhaps the cruelest. He took from me something I never understood I had until it was gone: the right to innocence, the right to safety, the right to trust those who were supposed to protect me from the very types of men who he was processing credit card payments from.

One afternoon, Arda called simply to say hi. The phone buzzed softly, and I answered, already submerged in grief and anger, my words strangled. Immediately, concern flooded his voice, asking what had happened, imagining the worst.

"I'm remembering," I could barely choke the words out, scraping against the inside of my throat, rough with the raw ache of memories that had waited a decade to find their voice.

Without a word. Without hesitation. He got in his car and started driving toward my apartment. I had no idea. I stayed frozen in place, still clutching the phone like it might steady me, like it might explain what was happening.

Twenty minutes later, there was a knock at the door. It startled me.

Arda stood in the doorway, his dark, gentle eyes meeting mine, holding a pint of Ben & Jerry's as though he could sweeten this new and terrible awakening. His love was steady, earnest, a lighthouse in a storm of memories that made landfall daily.

But love, I was beginning to understand, was no shield against shame.

Now, as I read Marianne Williamson's teachings, trying desperately to embody forgiveness, to extend compassion even toward the man who'd wounded me deepest, I couldn't. Every fiber of my being screamed in protest, demanding estrangement, distance, survival.

One ordinary day in the mundane glow of an IKEA parking garage in Burbank, with shoppers obliviously loading boxed furniture into their cars, I opened my phone and wrote an email. Calm, clear, deliberate. I addressed it to every member of my family except one: him.

My father.

Bobby.

Daddy Bob.

The self-proclaimed black sheep, a title he wore proudly, as though dysfunction was a badge of honor rather than a wound.

I typed carefully: "I no longer wish to receive updates about him. Please honor this boundary."

My fingers hovered for a long moment, heart racing, breath shallow, and then pressed send.

The effect was immediate. Powerful. Revolutionary.

For the first time, I wasn't passively waiting for him to change. Silence is not weakness; silence is power. Silence was the reclamation of autonomy stolen from me as a child.

Predictably, my father noticed immediately. Narcissists always do. Emails began to arrive, subject lines demanding answers, wondering why I'd vanished. I did not open them. I could not. Those messages remain unread, buried deep in my inbox beneath the healthier conversations of a life moving forward.

I thought silence would carry me indefinitely, protecting me. Until one afternoon, nearly a year after I pressed send on that email, my phone rang unexpectedly.

I saw my uncle's name on the screen and picked up hesitantly.

His voice was somber, heavy with reluctance. "There's been a family debate," he began slowly. "Everyone else agreed to respect your wishes, but I strongly felt you deserved to know. Your father has Stage IV colon cancer. The tumor is inoperable. Doctors give him about a year."

The line clicked before I could say a word.

I stood there, numbness overtaking the initial rush of shock. All the strength I had constructed, all the careful distance and protective silence, felt suddenly fragile, painfully insufficient.

Cancer. Terminal. A year.

I sank slowly onto my apartment floor, the walls narrowing around me. Grief surged forward, bitter, confused, and overwhelming, not for the man himself, but for everything he had failed to become. Guilt flooded in after, bone-deep and suffocating. Anger quickly followed, twisting into the messy tangle of emotions already filling me, rendering me helplessly overwhelmed.

Arda was already on his way to pick me up, driving across West Hollywood traffic toward my apartment. We had planned an evening at The Grove to meet up with his friends for dinner. I didn't want to flake on him even though my world had just been tilted on its axis. So, when he called minutes later, cheerfully telling me he was downstairs, I pulled myself up off the floor, steadied my breath, and slid quietly out the door into his waiting car.

The Grove was exactly the wrong place to be after receiving news that shatters you. A sprawling, meticulously landscaped open-air shopping center at the heart of Los Angeles, it always seemed aggressively cheerful. The Grove was loud, overwhelming, carefully curated to project a fantasy world of fakery.

As we parked and walked toward the restaurant, Frank Sinatra's *That's Life* played through the loudspeakers, smooth and rich, almost tauntingly upbeat. Each note felt like a mockery of the numbness I was trying to conceal, a reminder that the world was still spinning while mine had quietly come undone. I forced a brittle smile onto my face, smoothing the corners of my mouth upward in a careful imitation of happiness. I felt wooden; my movements stiff, artificial, and my mouth was dry. Arda's friends greeted us warmly; laughter and conversation swirling effortlessly around the table, but I existed somewhere outside my own body.

My cheeks ached from the effort of smiling, pretending to listen to cheerful small talk, nodding politely through casual conversation about movies, weekend plans, and the appetizers on our table. But inside I was fractured, numb, and raw all at once, replaying the words my uncle had just delivered, words that held more gravity than any twenty-five-year-old could shoulder.

I had carefully built barriers, walls I believed impenetrable. But now they blurred, dissolved in the face of his impending death. Estrangement, I realized painfully, was not tidy or simple. It was complicated and messy, woven together with threads of grief and love and guilt and rage.

This truth pressed upon me with crushing weight:

My father was dying.

And despite every boundary I had set, every choice made to reclaim myself from his toxicity, I did not know how I was supposed to feel about this revelation.

Post-Diagnosis

Discovery

Right after I found out, my uncle gave me a foreign number. It felt strange to dial my father's home; I hadn't spoken to him on the phone since I was fifteen years old. I held the paper between trembling fingers, studying the Chinese number. Finally, I took a deep breath and called him.

The phone rang twice before his voice answered. It was thinner than I remembered, edged with a weariness I'd never associated with him.

"Cass?" he said, a mixture of disbelief and relief woven through the single syllable of my name.

"It's me," I replied quietly, uncertain how to hold this conversation, how to inhabit this strange new territory we had suddenly found ourselves in.

"Did they tell you?" he asked, voice cracking slightly.

"Yes," I whispered, feeling suddenly small and vulnerable, surprised at how quickly anger and estrangement could soften into sorrow.

He paused, gathering himself. "Cass, something strange happened. Something unbelievable. Nana died three months ago...."

"I know," I interrupted softly, feeling a pang of guilt for never reaching out, for distancing myself so completely that even my beloved grandmother's passing hadn't broken through my wall of silence.

He continued, undeterred. "You won't believe this, but I'm a millionaire now. Nana left each of her children exactly one million dollars." His voice was filled with something complicated and almost childlike. Wonder, regret, disbelief. "All my life, that's all I ever wanted. To say I was a millionaire. And now...I finally have it, and now I'm dying."

His laugh was bitter, edged with irony. The cruel symmetry of fate wasn't lost on either of us. I was silent, stunned by the surreal quality of this revelation. It felt painfully fitting. My father, whose entire existence had revolved around hustling, chasing dreams of easy wealth, finally holding a million dollars precisely when money had become meaningless.

Before I could speak, he plunged ahead, his voice softer now, almost fragile. "Cass, listen, something even weirder happened. About a month after Nana died, I had this dream, clear as day. Nana called me from heaven. It was her voice, unmistakable. She just said, 'Bobby, come home.' That's it. Just those three words. 'Bobby, come home.' I woke up covered in chills; I couldn't shake it."

He paused again, and I imagined him there, sitting alone with his thoughts, puzzling over dreams that felt more like visitations.

"That same week, I finally went to the doctor," he continued quietly, more reflective now. "I'd ignored my health for a long time, Cass. A really long time. I knew something was wrong. But after that dream, I couldn't ignore it anymore."

Later, my brother would fill in the gaps my father left unspoken, telling me our dad had been seeing blood in his stool for a full year before finally seeking medical attention. One year of denial, of silent fear, of stubborn avoidance. One year he'd spent bargaining with his own mortality, ignoring symptoms until the illness had silently spread, inoperable and relentless.

I listened to his voice on the phone, frail and distant. He had always lived his life on the edges of possibility, on the reckless belief that rules and reality never quite applied to him. Now, faced with his own death, he seemed almost bewildered to realize that the laws of life and time were not negotiable after all.

"I'm sorry," was all I could whisper, unsure what else there was to say. Not sorry for what he'd done to me, not sorry for the distance I'd placed between us, but sorry for the way life had twisted his fate, sorry for how unprepared we both were for this reckoning.

The silence between us stretched heavy and strangely tender. In that moment, I understood something painful and necessary: no matter how far I'd run, how thoroughly I'd removed myself from his orbit, he was still my father. He was still human. Still profoundly flawed, but deeply, heartbreakingly mortal.

He continued, "Cass, I don't have anywhere to go. Bing Yu said she won't help take care of me." I had heard he had married a Chinese Mail Order Bride, but that was the extent of what I knew. He sounded so dejected that I actually started to feel bad for him.

Pity

No one else in the family wanted to take care of him. My brother, my mom, and my relatives all kept their distance, nursing grievances and justified anger. But I felt a burden so heavy that I couldn't breathe properly unless I did something. I felt the weight of obligation pressing urgently against my heart. He had nowhere else to go and no one else willing. So, I made space. Literally and figuratively.

I moved him into my tiny West Hollywood studio apartment, the place I'd so carefully designed as my sanctuary filled with books, fresh flowers, sunlight filtering through gauzy curtains, and a plush, oat-colored couch I'd saved up to splurge on, a symbol of adulthood and comfort. Curating my apartment into the home I never had as a child became a ritual of healing and an act of self-respect. A way to say, "You deserve this."

Looking back, I still don't understand why he didn't take his million dollars and rent his own apartment. He could have. He should have. But he was always frugal in a way that bordered on pathological. A million dollars meant freedom, but he clung to old patterns instead. He moved into my apartment like it was inevitable, as if my space, my hard-earned sanctuary, was the only logical option.

What I didn't yet grasp was that I wasn't just taking care of a dying man. I was stepping into a role I had been unconsciously rehearsing my entire life. I was about to face the emotional wreckage of an "Al-Anon." The quiet, obedient counterpart to the addict. The one who cleans up the mess, absorbs the impact, pretends it's not that bad.

People talk about addiction like it's the only sickness in the room. But Al-Anons, the ones orbiting around the dysfunction, often carry just as much toxicity. The difference is that ours gets rewarded. We're praised for being dependable, loyal, endlessly forgiving. We're the ones who hold it all together until we can't. Until the rage and the grief and the exhaustion start leaking through the cracks we've spent our whole lives trying to patch.

I didn't know any of this yet. I thought I was doing the right thing. But what I was really doing was reenacting a lifetime of codependent training, performing the role of the daughter who endures. My father was simply continuing the performance of the man-who-takes.

And this time, it nearly destroyed me.

Destruction

He arrived already weaker than I'd imagined, frail but defiant, and immediately my apartment shifted from sanctuary to sick-room. I hadn't known colon cancer affected the body this way, loss of bowel control, violent illness, relentless fatigue. My father was quickly reduced to a shadow, angry and frustrated, and taking it out on me. Within days, my beautiful couch was stained, covered in feces, layers of it smeared onto the bathroom tiles, crusted around the toilet. I spent evenings after work scrubbing, gagging, quietly sobbing, feeling a mixture of pity, revulsion, and profound anger.

I cleaned it all, without complaint, without help. Secretly, though, resentment and exhaustion built quietly beneath my skin. It felt like punishment. And I accepted it, quietly, because that was my way of atoning for something I couldn't even name.

Since my dad moved into my apartment, I moved in with Arda. He tried so hard to show up for me during this time. He brought food, called gently to check in, held my hand quietly while I cried wordlessly in his car. But each day I grew further away from him emotionally. I was overwhelmed by guilt, shame, anger, emotions I didn't know how to share or articulate. I had no emotional capacity left for him. It was my failure, my inability to commit, that began unraveling us.

I was the bad guy. I pushed him away without meaning to, withdrew when he reached out, buried myself in a caregiving role that swallowed me whole. Arda deserved someone present, someone capable of partnership and love. I was none of those things anymore. I became the shadow, unable to hold space for love while I fought daily battles against the ruin unfolding in my apartment.

Delusion

I'd imagined, naively, that living in the same city during my father's final year might bring closure, peace, and understanding. Not some glossy Hollywood ending but maybe a tender dramedy about a daughter and father reconnecting in his final days. Dark enough for an Oscar nod. Redemptive enough to make the whole mess feel worth it. Instead, the days turned into endless cycles of tension and arguments. He was angry, bitter at his illness, and he took it out on the nearest person: me. His temper, previously tempered by distance, was now my daily companion.

And yet, because he was dying, I swallowed every retort. Every hurtful remark became something I convinced myself I had to endure. The guilt I felt for not loving him enough, for secretly resenting every breath he took inside my sacred space, tore at me daily.

There was one small flicker of common ground between us. Dead and Company.

Months after my dad moved in, John Mayer announced he was joining forces with Bob Weir. It felt like a mashup of worlds I never imagined colliding. My musical north star folding into the legacy of the Dead.

Of every musician in the world who could have stepped into that sacred space, it had to be mine. The one whose music had narrated my coming of age. The one whose lyrics I had studied like scripture. Suddenly, he was the one singing the songs that had shaped my father's life.

And now, somehow, they belonged to both of us.

It felt like the universe had pulled off a cosmic goodness inside joke that only the two of us would get. What were the chances? That the rock star would become the bridge. That two lives shaped by entirely different soundtracks could suddenly find themselves in harmony.

We still fell into the same old patterns. Still misfired, still missed each other in the ways we always had. But there were afternoons when we listened to the live shows in silence, bonding over something neither of us could have seen coming.

Eventually, I started going to the shows. I tapped into a world beyond just my dad's introduction to the Dead. Tie-dye, incense, strangers dancing like nobody was watching. And slowly, something shifted. I began to understand. I understood why my dad had been willing to uproot his entire life to follow the band around the country.

The Breakup

My relationship with Arda further frayed under this relentless pressure. He kept trying, gently, persistently showing up, but I had retreated too far inside myself to reach back out. He showed up again and again, steady and patient, holding space for me even when I had nothing to offer in return. He tried until he had nothing left to give.

The day he came over to end things, he wasn't angry. We had almost been together four years at that point. He seemed hollowed out by the weight of everything we couldn't fix. The kind of exhaustion that lives in the bones. He sat across from me and told me, gently but clearly, that he couldn't do it anymore. That the version of me he had fallen in love with felt further and further away, and no matter how hard he tried to hold on, it was slipping through his fingers.

I was stunned. Deep down, I knew our relationship had been unraveling, but I'd been too distracted to see just how far we had fallen. I had been so immersed in survival. Producing, caretaking, grief, that I had failed to notice him withdrawing. I had even forgotten to buy him a gift for his birthday. The date had slipped past me like everything else that year, buried under hospital visits and red-eye flights. I wasn't present. I wasn't available. I wasn't the partner he needed or deserved.

I had also become addicted to saying yes. I took every single assignment offered to me at *Good Morning America* and clung to them like lifeboats. They gave me purpose, control, and a reason to keep going. I traveled constantly, producing segments that required everything I had left. But between flights to cover mass shootings and national tragedies, I wasn't coming home to Arda anymore. I was rushing home to check on my dying father, navigating fights with a man who had never known how to love me in life and was even harder to love in death.

In trying to save my father, I sacrificed my relationship.

The grief that followed was immediate. It hit like a crash, loud and final. I was heartbroken. But this time, I was doing it alone. Arda's way of grieving was to erase the connection altogether. He didn't believe in slow goodbyes. No texts, no friendship, no residual warmth. Just finality.

And it killed me.

He had been my best friend for four years. My compass. My constant. I had built a life around him. One filled with Turkish tea and long car rides and inside jokes and quiet Sunday mornings. I had imagined a future even if I had refused to commit to it. I had never agreed to move to Turkey even when he asked. That had always been our impasse. I thought we had time to figure it out. But life has a way of ending things before you're ready.

When I told my father about the breakup, his response was dismissive. Flat. "Oh, that's too bad," he muttered, barely looking up from whatever he was watching on the hospital television. "He seemed like a great catch. I don't know if you'll meet someone like that again."

Rage flooded my body. Hot, fast, unforgiving.

"It was your fault," I wanted to scream. *I lost him because I was taking care of you. Because my life became about managing your decay. Because your mess bled into every corner of my world even the ones I tried to protect.*

And yet, a quieter voice inside me reminded me of something else too. That life is long. That if a relationship can't survive trauma and grief, maybe it wasn't meant to last a lifetime anyway. That sometimes love isn't enough when timing is wrong, and wounds are too deep.

But mostly, I just missed him. I missed the way he made me laugh. The way he always knew what I needed without me having to say it. I missed our rhythm, our closeness, our friendship.

About six months after the breakup, we met for brunch. My dad was still alive but rapidly deteriorating. It was the first time I had seen him since the night he left. We sat across from each other at a sunlit table, and almost immediately, the tears came on both our faces. Hot, wet, unfiltered. We didn't even try to hold them back. They streamed down both of our faces; grief and love tangled in the silence between us. There was still something there, but nothing had changed. And more importantly, I still wasn't willing to move to Turkey.

So, we hugged goodbye, and this time it felt final. Like the closing of a chapter neither of us expected to write let alone end.

In the months that followed, I surprised myself by turning to faith. With Marianne Williamson stepping away from her weekly lectures at the Saban Theatre to run for Congress, I found myself searching for another form of spiritual nourishment.

I started going to Churchome with Judah Smith on Wednesday nights. On Sundays, I sat quietly in the back rows of Mosaic, listening to Erwin McManus speak about transformation, redemption, and the hidden grace in suffering. And somewhere in those rows, beneath the colored lights and worship music and warm bodies around me, I began to heal. I leaned in. I got baptized. I joined a yearlong pastoral program. Not because I wanted to be a pastor but because I was starving for connection, for a safe place to put my grief, for a community that made room for the mess of becoming.

The grief over Arda never vanished completely. It softened, reshaped itself, and became quieter with time. But losing him cracked something open in me that only faith could reach. And even though I was the one who let the relationship crumble, even though I was the one who forgot his birthday and failed to show up in the ways that mattered most, he had left an imprint. One that reminded me what it felt like to be seen and cherished.

And even now, when I think of him, I feel both the ache and the gift of that.

Death

By then, my father had no choice but to relocate to an assisted living facility. I had reached my limit. I could no longer manage the colostomy bag, the endless parade of medications, the emotional whiplash of caretaking someone who had never truly cared for me.

The final straw came on a quiet afternoon when I stopped by to bring him groceries. I walked in, bags in hand, and called his name, but there was no response. When I turned the corner into the bedroom, I froze.

His pillow was drenched in blood. Fully soaked, deep crimson. It took me a few seconds to register what I was even looking at. My body screamed before my brain could. I dropped the bags and rushed to his side.

"What happened?" I cried out, frantic, my voice rising in panic.

He barely lifted his head. "I fell," he said flatly. "I hit my head."

There was a deep gash at the crown of his scalp, the skin split open in a jagged line. The sheets beneath him were stained. It looked like something out of a war zone.

To this day, I wonder if he would have just bled to death had I not shown up at that exact moment. I called an ambulance immediately. The EMTs arrived quickly, took one look, and rushed him to the ER.

After that, he finally agreed to move into an assisted living facility. The resistance, the arguments, the pride, all of it crumbled. He knew he could no longer be alone. I helped with the transition and then quietly moved back into my apartment, reclaiming the space that had once been my sanctuary.

Although we had been told he had about a year to live, the months kept passing. One year became eighteen months. Then, in the midst of my breakup, it crept towards the final twenty-four months. It stretched just long enough to distort everything I had mentally prepared for. Most daughters might have welcomed the extra time, might have viewed it as a gift, a chance to savor final memories, to say the unsaid. But for me, that second year didn't feel like borrowed time. It felt like a sentence. A slow, grinding unraveling.

I remember asking his oncologist for an update. He glanced at the chart, then looked up and said, almost cheerfully, that although it was still terminal, the chemo had been "remarkably effective at slowing the growth." I nodded, numb.

Inside, I wanted to scream.

I had committed to a year. I had braced myself for twelve months. I could survive anything for a year. But two?

Two felt like being buried alive.

It was the difference between endurance and depletion. Between holding my breath and forgetting how to breathe at all. That second year hollowed me out in a way that no one could see because from the outside, I looked capable. I looked committed. But inside, I was rapidly fading.

He grew weaker. Smaller. More fragile. More demanding.

Each day blurred into the next, a cycle of checking in, coordinating doctors, chemo, managing paperwork, answering late-night calls from nurses. I moved through it all like a machine, functioning, helpful, smiling when necessary, but something in me was shutting down. I couldn't access real emotion anymore. I couldn't cry. I couldn't feel anything. I wasn't living. I was numb.

People would say things like, "You'll be glad you were there for him," or "You'll never regret being the one who showed up." But those words rang hollow. I wasn't doing this out of love. I was doing it out of obligation and a distorted sense of duty. I was the daughter who stayed. But I no longer recognized the girl who had once longed for her father's approval.

Whatever time we gained in those final months came at a cost. And I paid it quietly. With my body. With my peace. With the part of myself that had tried, against all odds, to find redemption in a story that had never offered me one.

Finally, he slipped into a coma. His body was giving out, and he was transferred to Cedars-Sinai.

When hospice nurses finally came to Cedar in those last days, they explained to me carefully: the machines and medication bags were the only things sustaining his life now. "Do you want us to continue this, or would you prefer we allow him to go naturally?" they asked gently.

I remember feeling like an absolute monster when I quietly declined further intervention. It wasn't just for my sanity although by then I was threadbare. It was also mercy, both for him and for me. He wasn't living. I wasn't living. We were both suspended in a torturous limbo.

Three days later, I sat quietly in his hospital room at Cedars-Sinai as he flatlined. It was symbolic, profound, me being there as he took his last breath just as he had been there when I took my first. And yet, as the monitors went silent, I felt no sadness. Only relief. An almost-euphoric release from the heavy chains of caregiving and emotional labor.

I reached over his body and began to pray. My voice was trembling but steady.

Our Father, who art in heaven, I whispered, not sure if I was speaking to God, to him, or to the part of myself that still needed to believe this meant something.

Hallowed be thy name. The words felt ancient in my mouth, heavier than I remembered. I didn't know if I believed in any of it anymore, but I said them anyway, out loud, clear.

Thy kingdom come, I prayed, as machines clicked beside me. *Thy will be done,* I said, though I wasn't sure I truly surrendered to that. Not yet. *On earth as it is in heaven.*

His chest was still, his skin already beginning to cool beneath my hand.

Give us this day our daily bread, I said, my voice cracking now. I hadn't eaten. I didn't care. I wasn't asking for nourishment. I was asking for something I couldn't name.

And forgive us our trespasses, I said over him, the weight of those words almost unbearable, *as we forgive those who trespass against us.* That line held more than I could carry. It wasn't just scripture; it was our entire relationship. Everything I had forgiven. Everything I hadn't.

And lead us not into temptation, I breathed, barely audible now, *but deliver us from evil.*

I opened my eyes. The room was silent.

The monitor beeped. A flicker. A rhythm. A heartbeat. The line that had gone flat sparked back to life. Nurses looked at each other. The chaplain stepped closer. No one said anything, but we all saw it.

The flat line gave way to a flicker of rhythm. The monitor blinked. A heartbeat had returned.

It felt like electricity had passed through me. As if the prayer itself had been defibrillation. My words had reached somewhere unseen. He lived for only a few more minutes, but in that moment, the impossible happened.

When the flatline returned, I didn't speak again. I didn't beg. I didn't plead.

I just sat there.

And held his hand.

When it was over, I stood, kissed his cooling cheek softly, and left the room without a single tear. There were no tears flooding the hallway; nobody crumpled in grief. Just a strange stillness inside me like a switch had been flipped and all the noise had gone quiet.

I walked out of Cedars-Sinai and into the sunlight of a regular Los Angeles afternoon. The sky was clear. Traffic moved as usual. Nothing about the world reflected the enormity of what had just happened. It was all so ordinary.

As I stood at a crosswalk, waiting for the light to change, a car pulled up to the red light beside me. A friend from church leaned out the window with a big, easy smile.

"Cassidy! Hey! What are you up to?"

There was nothing casual in me. No small talk to offer back. I looked up at them and, disoriented, half-shouting across the distance, said, "My dad just died."

Their face fell, confused and startled, as if I had just spoken in another language. Before they could respond, the light turned green. They drove off. I watched the car disappear into traffic and stood there blinking, stunned by the awkwardness of it all. The absurdity. The impossible timing.

I got in my car and drove to Trader Joe's.

It wasn't planned. My body just moved. I knew I needed something, food maybe, or just to not go home alone yet. I pulled a cart from the stack and started walking the aisles, the cold air brushing my arms as I passed bins of organic produce and endcaps of seasonal snacks.

I picked up cereal. Pretzel bread. Fresh flowers. Almond milk. A bag of frozen mango.

I moved slowly, deliberately, placing each item in the cart with a strange, mechanical calm. My father had just died, yet here I was checking expiration dates and wondering if I had enough oat milk for my coffee. The dissonance was staggering. It felt almost performative—like I was playing the role of someone who had it together. But it wasn't a performance. It was instinct.

And then, Don McLean's *"American Pie"* poured through the speakers overhead.

It was almost too on the nose, too haunting to be real. I stood there holding a bag of cereal as the chorus drifted through the air.

The store felt frozen. I kept moving. Reaching for bananas. Grabbing a bouquet of roses for myself.

That single word—*die*—echoed in my head on a loop. Not dramatic, not heavy-handed. Just matter of fact. Eerily calm. As if the universe was narrating something I wasn't ready to admit.

I was alive. He wasn't.

And still, I moved through the aisles under fluorescent lights.

In the immediate hours after my father died, I ran errands.

I ran errands.

Not because I was in denial. Not because I didn't care. But because there was nothing left to do in that hospital room.

And so, I turned to the ordinary. To the familiar weight of a grocery basket. To prices and packaging and produce that didn't ask anything of me emotionally. I needed something to hold in my hands. Something that made sense. A receipt. A bag of almonds. A paper bouquet.

I didn't cry.

I felt only numb relief.

Because what died that day wasn't just my father. It was a chapter. A burden. A decades-long cycle of longing and disappointment, of caretaking and quiet emotional sacrifice. And in its place, for one brief, disorienting moment, there was silence.

Not peace.

But stillness. Empty and exacting. The kind that comes only after something heavy has finally been put down.

Grief, in the years that followed, didn't show up on the dates I have memorized. Not on his birthday or the anniversary of his death or Father's Day. It crept in through dreams instead, quiet and uninvited.

He simply appears, healthy, smiling, lighter than I ever knew him in life. In the dream, he explains that it was all a misunderstanding. That he never actually passed away, just quietly returned to China without telling anyone. No drama, no funeral, no goodbye. Just slipped away.

And somehow, despite how absurd it is, I believe him. Every time.

The dreams feel so real; his voice, his laugh, the easy way he brushes off the whole ordeal, as if death had been a clerical error. For a few fleeting moments, my body believes him. Believes he really did just vanish abroad without telling anyone.

But when I wake up, there's always a pause. Long, disorienting minutes where my brain tries to bridge the gap between dream and truth. I lie there, blinking at the ceiling, the weight of reality slowly seeping back in.

And then I remember.

He actually is still dead.

And strangely, that's when I grieve him most. Not in the hospital. Not at Trader Joe's. But in the quiet morning fog after those dreams when my mind has to relearn what my body never forgot.

Grief is complicated like that. It isn't neat or logical. It isn't even always about missing what you had. Sometimes it's about missing everything you never had, the possibility, the father he couldn't become.

And the truth is, Arda had deserved better too. He deserved a partner who could return love, reciprocate the kindness he offered so freely. I was not capable then, drowning as I was in the impossible weight of my past and the unbearable demands of my present.

I was the one who destroyed us, who broke our connection, who let the burden of caring for a dying, toxic father push away the one healthy relationship I'd had. I was the one who built a sanctuary only to watch it crumble. And now, I was left to pick up every broken piece alone, feeling relief mixed with regret, liberation alongside loneliness.

This is how that year went: brutal, exhausting, heartbreaking. And finally, over.

Signs

Years after my dad died, I pulled up to a stop sign, waiting for a small group of people to cross. Channel twenty-three, the Grateful Dead Channel, was playing on Sirius XM. I glanced up just in time to catch a bright shock of white hair passing in front of my windshield.

Bob Weir was standing right in front of me.

I burst into laughter. Not the kind that comes from humor, but the kind that escapes when something is too strange, too aligned, too much to explain. In that moment, I felt my dad's presence more vividly than I had in years. Not in some vague spiritual way but viscerally, like he had orchestrated the whole thing just to say, *"I'm here."*

I pulled over, stunned by the odds. Heart racing, I awkwardly called out, "My dad was a Deadhead!" His beautiful, goddess-like wife, Natascha, smiled and waved me over. I couldn't believe the timing. Couldn't believe the song playing. I filmed it, knowing I had to tell my mom later.

I shook his hand and told him I was named after the song he had carried through thousands of live performances.

I posted the exchange to TikTok because by then I was deep in my Deadhead renaissance, and there was no way I wasn't going to share this serendipitous moment.

A man in the comments joked, "What does Bob Weir smell like?"

I deadpanned, "A redwood tree."

Then the official Bob Weir TikTok account replied:

"Damn right I do."

It was all too funny. Too perfect. Too threaded with something larger than logic. And it left me feeling like maybe, just maybe,

Once in a while
You get shown the light
In the strangest of places
If you look at it right.

—Grateful Dead, "Scarlet Begonias"

21
Inheritance

"Poor planning on your part does not
necessitate an emergency on mine."
—Bob Carter

After my dad's death, I called my supervising producer and said the words flatly: I am single again. My dad is dead. Put me on every single assignment you have. To their credit, they did. No questions, no coddling. They flooded my schedule. And I let them.

The next several months were an emotional freefall disguised as professional productivity. The Vegas shooting happened in October 2017. I was one of the bookers covering the aftermath. I cold-called witnesses who had watched people drop next to them in a hail of gunfire. I asked them to recount it. To relive it. To come on national television and share the most horrific night of their lives. We combed through social media, mostly Twitter and Instagram, looking for blurry iPhone videos that captured the terror.

Then came the avalanche of the Me Too movement. I worked on the Harvey Weinstein coverage for *20/20*, booking survivors and advocates. I was the one coordinating greenrooms, prepping questions, talking softly to women in trauma all while the ground inside me kept cracking.

A few times, I had the privilege of producing Ronan Farrow. He was brilliant, steady, and carried the weight of his reporting like a soldier returning from battle. It felt like a privilege to be near it. But it also took something from me. The stories we were covering were not just news cycles. They were revelations of a systemic rot.

And I was single again. The world of dating felt like a minefield. Monsters in cufflinks. Secrets in conference rooms. Every time I looked at a man in a position of power, I flinched inwardly even if I didn't show it.

My loneliness took on new shapes. It didn't cry out. It hardened. It calcified. I was grieving my father. I was grieving Arda. I was grieving the version of myself that once believed I could have a family and also be a journalist. The version that thought I could compartmentalize. I couldn't.

Arda had shown up for me in ways no one else had. And I had failed him. I was unraveling, and I was too emotionally shut down to see it clearly. I wanted to believe I was still in control. I wasn't. I had inherited a mess.

It began, quite literally, at the senior facility where I had to collect the remains of my father's life. His belongings. His clothes. His scattered paperwork. The things no one tells you will fall to you. The loose ends. The emotional debris. I met Bing Yu for the first and only time the day he died. She hadn't shown up once during his long decline, but suddenly she was there in the final moments. Panicked. Hysterical. Overbearing.

Her presence felt like a gust of chaos in an already collapsing room. I remained polite. But I did not let her in.

My father had left nothing behind to guide us. No will. No power of attorney. No health directive. I called repeatedly to claim his ashes, but Los Angeles County informed me that "his wife" had already made arrangements. I assumed that meant Bing Yu. And honestly, I didn't want his ashes in my apartment. I had already absorbed enough of him.

When I picked up his death certificate, it read: "Scattering at sea, off the coast of Los Angeles County." A government employee had disposed of his ashes. Because no one claimed them. I stood there, holding that certificate in my hands, feeling the full weight of what happens when a person chooses denial over preparation. I tried to apply what I had learned from Marianne Williamson. I reminded myself that I had done what I could. That it was not mine to carry.

But the real firestorm hadn't even begun.

There was over a million dollars sitting in an inherited investment account. Money my father had received from his mother. And that money had a history. When my great-grandfather, Frederick H. Marcus, died in 1942 aboard the S.S. *Lexington*, a naval vessel that sank off the coast of Manhattan, my grandmother was devastated. She was just thirteen years old when she lost her father. The U.S. government, in one of its postwar settlements, gave his widow oil stock as compensation. That oil stock grew steadily, quietly, over the decades. By the time my father inherited it, the value had reached over three million dollars.

When he died, one-third of that remained in his name. And that portion should have gone, by every logical standard, to his wife and children.

My brother and I filed for probate. We followed the process. We tried to be fair. We didn't demand everything. We asked for what we were owed. One-third each, honoring the generational lineage of the inheritance. But Bing Yu did not agree. She tried to claim all of it. Every last cent. Despite California law stating that a surviving spouse is entitled only to community property and not inherited assets from prior generations, she fought for the full amount.

What followed was surreal. The judge eventually approved the sibling's proposed division. We submitted the necessary paperwork to the investment firm. And then came the call that changed everything.

The money had already been dispersed.

An investigation revealed that Bing Yu had hired a disbarred attorney, someone with a long criminal history, including multiple prison stints, to fabricate documents, forge a trust, and illegally transfer the inheritance. It was all fraud. The kind that takes months to unravel.

It felt biblical. Absurd. Like I was starring in a thriller I never auditioned for. And somewhere inside it, I was still the girl in hand-me-down clothes whose school counselor used to leave trash bags full of her own daughter's outgrown wardrobe on our front step.

This was never about money. Not really. It was about the principle. It was about justice. It was about not letting someone erase a lineage, a legacy, a story built on grief and survival and sacrifice.

We sued the investment firm. We went into arbitration. We won. But even then, 50 percent of the settlement went directly to the attorney who had represented us on contingency. The remainder was taxed, picked apart, reduced down to something small enough to hold in a single bank transfer. A single moment. After years of hearings, delays, continuances, red tape, and emotional labor.

We never heard from Bing Yu again. She vanished.

What stayed with me was not the money. It was the exhaustion. The way grief and injustice combined to make a second full-time job out of my trauma. The disillusionment. The lesson.

I thought of my seven-year-old self. I thought of how hard I had fought to build a life that didn't rely on any of this. How I had supported myself. Moved to cities on my own. Produced a national news show. Held the weight of trauma, both my own and others', without letting it crush me. Even after his death, I was still cleaning up the wreckage I had inherited.

But I also inherited something else.

The strength to tell the truth.

The strength to say no.

The strength to stop the cycle.

Because legacy is not just what we pass down. It's what we choose not to carry forward.

22

Wild Card

"Don't ever think I fell for you, or fell over
you. I didn't fall in love, I rose in it."
—Toni Morrison

When I emerged from that long, dark stretch of grief, I felt cracked open. But I was ready, open to something new. I had spent so long among media people that I'd begun to find the whole industry insufferable. Everyone was polished and sparkly. But it was performative. I could smell the spin. I wanted someone messy. Real. Someone who didn't perform charm but lived in their own skin.

That's when I met Miles.

He was younger than Arda and far more chaotic. A miniature Jewish Larry David meets Hugh Grant if you can imagine such a thing. He was wildly charming, neurotic, self-deprecating, and told stories with the erratic enthusiasm of someone who has never been edited. On our very first date, he laid it all out. His first marriage. The affair that ended it. The job he had been fired from. His crypto investments. His daily surfing routine. And the fact that he now sat on the board of directors for a high-profile company run by a white-collar criminal.

They had been college roommates bonded by history in a way that defied logic. Over time, he had become this man's confidante, pulled into the orbit of someone the rest of the world would eventually come to know through scandal. It was surreal to watch those headlines scroll across my professional news feed, stories I might have been assigned to cover, while knowing the truth behind the scenes. I saw things reported that didn't reflect reality. But I kept quiet. I turned down assignments that veered too close to the situation, unwilling to blur the lines between my work and my personal life.

It was a parade of red flags. And I ignored them all.

We went to Morocco for two weeks after knowing each other for only two months. I suppose that's better than going for two months after knowing someone for two weeks, but either way, it was impulsive. And that's exactly what I needed. After years of carefully curating every inch of my career, I craved recklessness. Thanks to a modest Bitcoin windfall, Miles didn't answer to a boss or a schedule. He was neurotic, often exhausting, and our dynamic sometimes felt like *Curb Your Enthusiasm* set in Marrakech. "Larry David Goes to the Atlas Mountains" was probably the best way to describe it. But I didn't care. I was just so relieved to be unreachable. No news cycle. No deadlines. For once, I was off call, and it felt like pure ecstasy.

There was something thrilling about booking a last-minute flight to Africa, switching my phone to airplane mode, and telling the newsroom I'd be out of the country for two weeks. I had never done that in my twenties. I had worked straight through them. He brought that into my life, a loosening of control I had white-knuckled for years.

He invited me to meet his mom right after that trip. She was radiant, silver-haired and effortlessly chic, the kind of woman who wore coordinated cashmere sets and threw dinner parties with perfect lighting. His family was a beautifully tangled web of half-siblings, remarriages, and longtime friends who felt more like relatives than guests. Holidays weren't about perfection. They were about belonging. They showed up for each other, messy and loud and loving. It felt like the thing I had wanted as a child but never had words for.

Growing up, it was just me and my mom. Some nights, dinner was nothing more than orange slices and a cut-up tomato. We had our own little mother-daughter rituals that were special in their way. Still, I often found myself wondering what it would feel like to sit at a long, crowded table.

I imagined the kind of home where people interrupted each other with affection, not annoyance. A dinner scene you might find in a Nancy Meyers movie only richer and more offbeat. A dad tucked into the Malibu hills. A mom in the Palisades. Both remarried. A swirl of siblings and step-siblings and exes who somehow still felt like kinship.

When I met him, that fantasy began to take on texture. Their family gatherings felt enchanted. Not glamorous but full of life. Eccentric and alive. His mother once told me she chose his name because when she was pregnant, her best friend at the time, Joni Mitchell, had suggested it. It felt like stepping into a time capsule of another world. One where stories were currency, little details you would never find in the news, but I tucked dozens of them away in my back pocket.

His family didn't impress me because of their legacy in Hollywood. I wasn't dazzled by the fame. I was fascinated by the layers. Curious in the way a journalist becomes when invited into a world worthy of a feature, one that feels both foreign and familiar all at once. But this time, I wasn't there to observe. I wasn't holding a notebook or framing the scene from the outside. I had stepped inside. I had fallen for the oldest son, and without realizing it, I had become part of the story.

His grandparents had been movie stars in the forties. The kind who had black-and-white headshots framed in silver, and yellowing clippings from the trades tucked into drawers. His grandmother had even won an Oscar. But no one in the family spoke of it with awe. It wasn't displayed like a relic or treated like a crown. It was just there, part of the landscape, tucked into a cluttered bookshelf in the living room. Familiar. Unremarkable. Almost easy to miss.

One night, Miles invited me to Passover with his family. The entire evening was etched with meaning. His mother guided me through the symbolism of each dish. I asked why there was so much parsley scattered across the table, and she explained that dipping it in salt water represented the tears of the Jewish slaves. I was breathless at the sacredness of it all.

His sister, Cleo, was a hippie vision to behold. Two wild little girls attached to her hip, nursing on demand, the poster child for holistic living. She radiated warmth and sunshine; she was someone I would have gravitated toward even if I had only seen her at the farmer's market.

Long prairie dresses by *Christy Dawn* draped over her frame, always falling just below the ankle. Always barefoot.

I liked her instantly.

And for people like me, who can get drunk on a daydream, it's hard not to think, "You are my dream sister-in-law."

Then, his five-year-old niece looked up and blurted, "So are you two going to have a baby or what?" The whole table erupted with laughter. His mom smiled at me and said, "One could only hope." My face flushed. My heart raced. I had wanted a family like this since I was old enough to understand that mine had gaps. At that moment, I thought maybe this was it. Maybe I had found the door in.

Miles was chaos to Arda's calm. Arda had offered me something stable. Steady. Real. But I wasn't ready. I had shut down. I didn't yet know how to receive love that was uncomplicated, love that stayed. So, I chased something else: love in its trick-mirror form. Shiny. Distorted. The kind that looked like depth until you tried to stand in it.

From the beginning, I knew Miles wasn't built for permanence. He told me as much on our very first night. A serial dater, self-aware enough to confess it but not enough to change it. And still, something between us sparked. It was messy, magnetic, strangely familiar. We were tangled up for two years with a six-month rupture in the middle when he panicked and pulled away. He said he wasn't ready.

I let him go.

I didn't wait around. That summer, I fell into a fast, fizzy romance with the founder of a cult-favorite ice cream brand at Whole Foods. It was all sweetness and no substance, but it felt good to be wanted by someone new. It gave me something to do with my heart.

By summer's end, Miles came back. Apologetic. But if I'm honest, he only ever seemed to want me when he sensed I had slipped away. I let him back in because we laughed more than I had in years. Being with him was like drinking something fizzy and cold on a hot day—light, intoxicating, addictive. For a while, it worked. Until it didn't.

Something in me had shifted. My biological time clock had started flashing like a warning light. I could feel time tightening. I didn't want to waste another year in limbo with someone who only offered half of himself. I wanted certainty. Solidity. A man who stood all the way in.

After one final wave of tension, another round of his indecision clashing against my growing clarity, I reached my threshold. One last conversation where he wavered again, vague and noncommittal. I had to summon every ounce of self-respect I had and block his number. I wouldn't have done it if there was anything left to fight for. But there wasn't. He just couldn't commit. I was done holding space for someone who couldn't name what he wanted. I needed to be chosen out loud. Not hypothetically. Not someday. Now.

And then something strange happened.

Two weeks after my thirtieth birthday, I woke up with Miles's father on my mind. There had been no recent conversations, no health scares, no reason. Just a persistent image of his face that wouldn't leave me alone. By late afternoon, I unblocked Miles's number.

My phone lit up. Missed calls. A long text.

His dad had died that morning. A sudden heart attack.

The grief in his voice felt familiar. I knew the way a death could knock the air out of you, how it made you feel like a child again. He needed someone who understood. I answered. Not as the woman he once dated. But as someone who had once stood in the same dark room.

I never stopped thinking about that morning. About how I somehow knew. How he floated into my consciousness without invitation. It defied logic. But I've stopped needing everything to make sense. Some truths live in the body, in the undercurrent.

Certain synchronicities feel like quiet evidence of something divine at work just beyond our comprehension. That reminds us how deeply connected we are even after we walk away.

This was one of them.

Years later, when the Los Angeles fires swept through the Pacific Palisades, I pulled up the evacuation maps out of morbid curiosity. Miles's family home sat inside the red perimeter. I hadn't seen them in years, but my heart raced. The next morning, I checked again. Their address was now marked in deep crimson. Burned. Gone. And I cried. Not for him. But for the memory. For the ghost of the life I once thought I might build there.

I kept running into him. At events. In passing. In strange intersections that made it clear: the world isn't random. Years later, I would discover that Miles and my future partner had known each other long before I met either of them. While I had been tangled in one man, I had already existed in the orbit of the one who would one day become my home.

That, to me, is the golden thread. The pattern in the noise. The divine choreography hiding inside all the mess.

One of the strangest moments happened in the bathroom at a concert. I was washing my hands when a girl came out of the stall, panicked because she had just started her period, and it had soaked through the back of her skirt. There wasn't a full-length mirror, so I helped guide her through how to wash it off and disguise the stain as best we could.

When we walked out of the bathroom, Miles was standing there waiting for his date. It was too absurd. I greeted him and quietly suggested he offer her his button-down shirt to tie around her waist.

He called me the next day and said, "That might have been one of the strangest coincidences that has ever happened."

I didn't disagree. Some moments don't need a moral or a reason. They just stick with you.

Only when I held my son did I understand what it had all been for. What I had survived. What I had been shaped by. When I met the man who would become my partner, there were no games. No panic. No performance. It was quiet. Steady. Clear. Like being handed a compass I had been looking for my whole life.

I didn't fall into that love. I rose in it.

Takeaways for Single Women:

- **Protect your center.** Never outsource your identity to someone else's expectations.
- **Red flags are not mysteries to solve.** They are exit signs.
- **Love should not make you smaller.** The right relationship lets you expand.
- **Time does not heal everything, but it will clarify everything.**
- **Divine timing is real.** It may not feel like it in the pit of grief, but trust that love can arrive in its right season.

These stories are for the women walking through heartbreak, for the ones redefining themselves after years of shrinking, for anyone rebuilding after everything cracked open. The fire is not the end. It is the forge. It is the beginning of the woman who rises from it.

23

ADHD is a Superpower

"People with ADHD often have a special feel for life, a way of seeing right into the heart of matters, while others have to reason their way methodically."
—Edward M. Hallowell, M.D., *Driven to Distraction: Recognizing and Coping with Attention Deficit Disorder from Childhood through Adulthood* (1994)

Ideas hover just out of reach. They circle overhead like birds deciding whether to land. I try to stay still, grounded, open. I wait for one to strike with force. But most of the time, they vanish before I can even hold them. They slip through my fingers before I can understand what they were trying to become.

I sit in silence as my thoughts spiral. So many options rush in at once that it makes me physically dizzy. I open tab after tab on my browser, convinced there must be a name for this restlessness. The fidgeting. The chaos. The way my brain won't hold still long enough for anything to form. I type my symptoms into Google and quietly diagnose myself with ADHD.

When I finally say the words out loud to my doctor, she doesn't flinch. She hands me a three-page checklist with instructions to fill it out honestly. I'm not sure whether what follows would be considered "passing" or "failing," but a week later, she confirms the diagnosis: Attention Deficit Hyperactivity Disorder. She writes me a prescription for Adderall.

I stare at the bottle for months before I ever take a pill. Just having it makes me feel better. Like maybe I have a parachute. Like maybe I won't fall apart if things get worse.

And then they do.

I hit a stretch of time where nothing feels possible. My thoughts get heavy. My body feels heavier. I am scared of everything and bored by everything at once. I feel like I'm disappearing into a version of myself I don't recognize.

My job is draining me. The news cycle never ends. There is always another tragedy. Another update. Another breaking headline that requires me to move fast and feel nothing. I am numb and overstimulated at the same time. I make good money. People return my emails. My job title opens doors. And still, I hate it. Every day I wake up and dread logging on. But I don't know what else to do or where else to land instead.

I was so young and bright when I first walked through the doors at *Good Morning America.* I was bright. Glossy. Grateful. I wore heels that clicked confidently across the floor, rehearsed my pitch lines in the mirror, stayed late to prove I was all in. That was seven years ago.

Now I wake up exhausted before the day even begins. The news cycle is endless. The adrenaline that once fueled me now feels corrosive. I sit in morning meetings with a tight smile and a caffeine headache, wondering quietly, *What is this all for?*

I picture an alternate version of my life. One where I'm not chasing stories or negotiating live hits before sunrise. In this other life, I'm a mom. I bake banana muffins in a soft-lit kitchen. I wear socks that match. I go to playgrounds and baby music classes. I push a stroller instead of a story. I make snack plates. I plan birthday parties. I am still exhausted, but the rhythm is different. It's quieter.

And then I wonder, *"Am I going to be thirty-five and still doing this?"* Still single? Still knocking on strangers' doors encouraging them to share their grief or joy or trauma on national television at 5:00 a.m.? Still booking experts for segments that will be forgotten before noon?

I look at my calendar and see four interviews scheduled back-to-back, and I feel the weight of my own ambition. I worked so hard to get here. I got the job. I got the title. I played the part. And yet, some days, it feels like the performance swallows the person underneath.

I'm not ungrateful. But I'm tired. Tired of selling urgency. Tired of pretending breaking news is always breaking me open in a good way. I crave softness. I want a life that doesn't feel like a constant negotiation between identity and exhaustion.

I skim *Extremely Loud & Incredibly Close*, holding tight to the familiarity of Jonathan Safran Foer. And there it is. The line that guts me every time:

"Sometimes I can hear my bones straining under the weight of all the lives I'm not living."

It feels less like a quote and more like a diagnosis.

Gut punch.

On one of those days, I do what I always do when I can't think straight: I clean. I pull every piece of clothing from my closet and dump it into a pile. I try to organize my external world, so I can make sense of my internal one. And then I see the bottle. Tucked into the sock drawer, waiting.

This time, I don't hesitate. I twist the cap open and take one.

Within the hour, I feel like I've returned to myself. Like I've been underwater for months and suddenly come up for air. I don't just feel better. I feel clear. Capable. Electric. My self-esteem, which had been scraping the floor, feels restored. I send a DM on Instagram to a reality television producer I barely know. Just a few lines: I'm ready to leave news. I want to work on the show you produce.

He replies within minutes. Then we're on an email chain. His assistant is looped in. Lunch is set for the following week.

I barely know him, but he's a senior producer on *The Bachelor*, the kind of job that once felt galaxies away from my world of breaking news and 5:00 a.m. live shots.

Now, somehow, it's just a calendar invite away.

When we meet, we click instantly. There's an ease between us, a shared language of production, even if the content we've covered couldn't be more different. He tells me there's a top-secret spin-off show in development. They're staffing cast producers and moving fast.

There's a moment of hesitation when he realizes I've never worked in reality TV. My background is hard news, not heartbreak montages or musical date cards. But something about our conversation makes him lean in instead of pull away. He tells me not to worry. He'll show me the ropes. He says I have the instincts, and the rest can be taught.

The show is called *The Bachelor Presents: Listen to Your Heart*. A hybrid of dating and music competition. Musicians falling in love while performing duets. It's not exactly my dream job, but I don't care. I'm just relieved. Relieved to take a break from trauma and disaster. Relieved to not be chasing body counts or booking survivors of mass shootings.

For once, I get to help people tell love stories instead of survival stories. It's a strange pivot. But it feels like oxygen.

It all happens fast. It feels like fate, but I know better. I was high when I got the guts to message him on Instagram of all places. And that bothers me. Not because I think I cheated. But because I'm scared that without it, I wouldn't have had the nerve to change anything at all.

On that four-month shoot, I discovered I am not alone. Most of the crew uses Adderall. It's how they survive the eighteen-hour days. It's how they stay sharp in the chaos. It's how they power through exhaustion. Everyone is tired. Everyone is trying to keep up. Everyone is medicated.

I signed an ironclad NDA to protect all the secrets of the show. But working on the show gave me a front-row seat to the architecture of reality television. I saw how storylines were shaped in real time, how characters were quietly framed and nudged into arcs that would keep audiences hooked. It was less chaotic than I expected and far more intentional. The emotion was real, but so was the strategy.

The season wrapped just as the world began to shutter. Our final episodes aired in the earliest days of the pandemic. Flights were grounded. Cities went silent. The usual noise of production faded overnight.

I had been slated to join *Bachelor in Paradise* that summer, finally stepping into a new rhythm after years of hard news. It felt like momentum was beginning to build. Then everything stopped. Right as I was dipping my toe in, the entire industry paused. The opportunity evaporated before it ever fully began. One moment, I was inside a new world. Next, I was quarantined.

I use the pills sparingly during that time. Never more than five times before throwing the rest of the bottle away. I had a pang of shame that if I took more, I wouldn't be any better than my own father's addiction. I don't want to lose myself to a chemical solution. I want to learn how to build that fire without gasoline.

So, I go inward. I start waking up early and sitting in silence. I read. I meditate. I walk instead of scroll. I put my phone in another room. I try to listen to the spaces between my thoughts.

Eventually, I start finding the same buzz I once got from the little blue pill—only now it comes from meditative stillness. From breath. From being alone with my own mind and not needing to run from it.

I begin rebuilding my ability to focus holistically. Not perfectly. But slowly. Day by day. Not because I'm disciplined. But because I've seen what it feels like to live completely scattered. And I don't want to live like that anymore.

I start going to the used bookstore every Sunday. The kind where nothing is alphabetized and everything smells like dust. I wander for hours, trusting that the right book will find me. That's how I met the words of Alan Watts. Ram Dass. Louise Hay. Joe Dispenza. Abraham Hicks. Glennon Doyle. Cheryl Strayed. Elizabeth Gilbert. I stack them on my nightstand like medicine.

I read until I begin to understand my own brain. The way it needs to move. The way it resists structure but still craves it. The way it holds a hundred possibilities at once and gets overwhelmed when forced to choose.

I stop seeing my mind as a problem to fix. I stop labeling myself broken. I begin to see it all—the chaos, the creativity, the sensitivity—as data. As information. As something I can learn to work with instead of against.

At my lowest, I thought the pill was my only way out. Now I know there are other tools. Other ways to access clarity. Other paths back to myself.

I think of the Lewis Carroll quote: "If you don't know where you're going, any road will get you there." There was a time when that made me feel lost. Now, it feels like permission. I don't need to know the whole map. I just need to keep walking. Keep listening. Keep choosing myself.

Again and again.

24

Rose

"Women's friendships are like a
renewable source of power."
—Jane Fonda

I didn't meet Rose until my final three years in Los Angeles, and maybe that timing wasn't a coincidence. Maybe I had to grow into the kind of woman who could recognize a friendship like hers when it arrived. The kind that didn't come wrapped in shared ambition or filtered through industry circles. It wasn't born in a writers' room or cemented on a press line. It was something quieter. Truer. A friendship not built on matching titles but on matching frequencies.

What I found with Rose was reciprocity. A true exchange of energy. Never one-sided. Never leaving either of us feeling depleted or used. There was no unspoken ledger, no social calculus behind the scenes. Just mutual care. That kind of balance was rare, especially in a city where so many friendships were transactional by design. Where the currency was potential connections, and the undercurrent was always competition. But with Rose there was no game to play. Nothing to prove. Only the quiet relief of being met where I stood.

I had gone through so many waves of community and then collapse. I had built friend groups that were extensions of the men I dated. And when the relationships ended, the friendships evaporated too. Like smoke after a fire. I'd find myself standing at the edge of the wreckage holding a few tattered connections, watching everyone else return to their camps while I walked back to mine. Alone. Feeling like the last kid left at summer camp.

In between those cycles, I spent a lot of time in solitude. I had what I came to call "seasons of friends." Some would arrive like a flash flood. Immediate and intense and then they would move away, find a new job, get married, have a baby, shift their priorities, and I'd find myself back at square one. Rebuilding. Starting over. Reaching out. Waiting for texts that sometimes never came. But through it all, it was mostly just me and my dog Hazel. We were a little team. She was my constant. My witness. My quiet, steadfast partner in a city that never slowed down.

The truth was, I still had a chaotically unpredictable schedule. At any moment, I could be assigned a breaking story. There were times I would wake up thinking I had a free day only to be packed for an airport and on a flight by noon. People didn't always understand that. I wasn't flaky. I hated canceling. But when there was a fire, sometimes literal and sometimes metaphorical, I was the one who had to cover it as a breaking news producer. I had chosen this life. I had signed up for the chaos. But that didn't mean it was easy.

Working for *Good Morning America* was a dream in so many ways, but it came with a cost. It made building any kind of consistent community nearly impossible. People grew frustrated with me. They thought I didn't care. But I did. I cared deeply. I just never knew when the next call would come. I lived inside a constant state of alert. It made it hard to make plans and harder still to keep them. I was always one text away from being needed somewhere else. And over time, that kind of disruption becomes isolating. It starts to feel like your life is happening to you instead of with you.

One time, I picked up a girlfriend to go to the beach. I packed it the way I always did. Sandwiches. Cold water bottles. Fruit. An umbrella for shade. Snacks for Hazel. I was prepared to stay until the sun dipped low, and the sky turned pink. That's how I did the beach. As a ritual. As restoration. But we hadn't been there ninety minutes before she turned to me and asked if we were heading back soon. It wasn't even noon! That was the moment I realized I preferred to go alone. From then on, if someone asked to join me, I had one rule: drive separately. Because I wasn't cutting a sacred six-hour day short.

Rose was the antithesis of all of that. She was game. She was easy. She was curious. She was down to frolic. I mean that literally. Frolicking was her baseline.

In a strange twist of fate, I have John Mayer to thank for meeting her. Yet another little guidepost from someone that has consistently popped up in my life in the most serendipitous of ways. I was in the *Bachelor* production office one day helping brainstorm segment ideas. One of our cast members was a superfan of John Mayer, and we were figuring out how to weave that into the show.

It reminded me of something. A memory from my time with Miles. He had brought me to a house party in the hills, and I had instantly recognized a tall man leaning in the kitchen. John Alagía. The record producer behind *Room for Squares*. I had devoured every behind-the-scenes video of that album in high school. So, when we crossed paths at the party, I couldn't help but mention *Room for Squares.*

To my surprise, he was kind and genuinely delighted that I recognized him. We ended up talking for a while and exchanged numbers not because it was flirty, but because how often do you meet the producer behind the soundtrack of your adolescence?

During that pitch meeting at work, I brought him up. Suggested that maybe we could get him involved for an episode. That was when I heard a bright voice chime in from a few desks away.

"I actually know John Mayer's manager. I know it's a long shot, but he's a fan of the show. Maybe we can try to get him on too?"

I looked up and saw Rose. Warm, stunning, disarming Rose. *"Wait, I know him too!"* I exclaimed.

We instantly did a debrief and realized we had both dated him. I had gone to Dead and Company shows with floor seats because of him. She had casually seen him too. We huddled over our Raya profiles and compared notes, laughing at the synchronicities. There is nothing like two women bonding over a shared man when it is lighthearted and fleeting and fully in the past.

That was our meet-cute. We leaned over the selfie camera, snapped a photo of the two of us grinning, and texted it to him at the same time: "Heard you have a type ;)" He "hearted" it instantly and sent back a laughing emoji. It was light, harmless, and easy. Exactly how new friendship should feel.

Flash forward a couple months later, and the world shut down. Pandemic lockdowns hit. And as it turned out, Rose lived less than a mile from me. We kept running into each other on power walks around Beverly Hills Flats. Those quiet, odd, beautiful pandemic walks where no one had anywhere to be, but everyone needed to move their bodies for their sanity.

We finally promised to hang out. And from that moment, everything changed.

At the same time, a friend group I had known for years began to quietly fall apart. These were my early-twenties "going out" friends, still playing dress-up in adulthood, collecting contacts instead of closeness, measuring their worth by who they knew and where they were seen. At one time, I had valued all the same things. When I was twenty-two. By now I was thirty and craving autonomy. We moved together like a school of fish, mistaking proximity for intimacy. I didn't want someone to split an Uber with after drinks. I wanted someone to walk through the wilderness with. Pursuing true sisterhood is noble in its aim but often messy in practice.

The truth was it started to feel like a performance. There was always someone missing from the table—and always someone being talked about in their absence. The compliments were edged with comparison. The laughter often masked something darker. And eventually, I began to notice how small I made myself to fit in. How quiet I became. I didn't trust them. I had this gut-deep knowing that whatever I shared would be passed around like gossip. That the same people laughing with me would dissect me the moment I left the room.

It shattered something inside me. It made me retreat. I started to keep more to myself not out of spite but out of instinct. I felt a deep calling to protect my peace, to shrink my circle to only those who felt like home. I didn't want to be surrounded by people who needed me to play a part in their own performance of connection. I wanted out of the charade.

By then, I was just tired. Tired of the low-level toxicity. Tired of the eyerolls, the cutting sarcasm, the nights that ended in hangovers and emptiness. Tired of friendships built on convenience, on codependency, and shared nightlife calendars. I didn't care about the events anymore. I didn't want to be the quiet audience to another man's monologue, nodding along as he mansplained something I couldn't care less about as I scanned the room for the delicate choreography of an easy exit.

I decided to disengage from the group chat, the one that used to light up my phone with invites, memes, gossip. I didn't pour any effort into explaining why. I just stopped responding. I couldn't articulate it clearly at the time, but the energy felt misaligned. I stopped saying yes to proposed gatherings that didn't light me up. I stopped overriding the tightness in my chest that always followed those nights out, the kind of ache that made me feel lonelier after, not more nourished. I didn't make an announcement. I didn't need to. I just quietly reclaimed my energy.

First came a quiet month of solitude. Rose was out of town producing a new season of *The Bachelorette*, so I had an abundance of free time in the withdrawal. With nowhere to be and no one to entertain, I hiked nearly every day, journaled each morning, and gave my apartment a minimalist reset. I poured myself into the small but sacred work of tending to my own life. Mind, body, and spirit. Like it was a temple. And then, as if on cue, because that is how the universe responds to conviction, two magnetic, vivacious souls entered my life.

It happened on the beach. Topanga, of course. Hazel had wandered over to a nearby blanket, her nose buried in someone's tote bag, and I followed to retrieve her already rehearsing my apology. But the women on the blanket smiled wide. They were radiant. Laughing about astrology, sipping matcha, talking about Mercury retrograde and joking about ex-boyfriends like it was all part of the same cosmic curriculum. Within ten minutes, we were talking like we had known each other in another life. Maybe we had. By the end of the hour, they had invited me to join their women's circle held in Topanga Canyon.

I showed up to that first gathering, not entirely sure what to expect but fully open. It was twilight in Topanga. We sat in a circle on the grass, hands clasped, eyes soft. Each of us brought a small offering—a candle, a stone, a note, something sacred—to place in the center. The woman leading the circle was of Native American origin. Her presence was grounded and clear like she had done this in many lifetimes before.

She asked us each to call in our ancestors and angel guides. She asked us to speak aloud one thing we were ready to release and one thing we were calling in. And then, one by one, the women began to share.

There was no posturing. No pretense. No filters or small talk. Just truth.

One woman asked for help in healing a broken heart. Another shared her deep desire to become a mother. A third admitted that she was struggling financially and needed a job. Their words came out raw and unguarded, and no one flinched. No one offered unsolicited advice or interrupted. We just held space. We witnessed. We blessed each offering with our presence.

I sat there in awe.

This, *this*, was what I had been craving without knowing how to name it. A gathering where masks weren't required. Where pain wasn't hidden. Where intentions were spoken like prayers, and the air felt holy with possibility.

I thought back to my journal just days earlier. I had written that I was ready to find a deeper group of friends. A new circle. One that didn't drain me. One that felt aligned with who I was becoming, not who I had been. And somehow, without effort or strategy, this invitation had fallen into my lap.

As if the universe had just been waiting for me to mean it.

I told Rose. She came with me to the next one. We started spending every free day in Topanga Canyon hiking to waterfalls, dancing at the farmers market, meeting wildly eccentric men who looked like they had wandered out of a Gabriel García Márquez novel. It was magic. It was exactly the chapter I didn't know I needed. We weren't going out to bars anymore. We were finding community. Spirit. Expansion.

We opened each other's worlds.

She showed me how vibrant life could be outside the traditional paths. She made me feel like my dreams were not only valid but inevitable. And I truly believe we crossed paths because the universe conspired to place us in that office on that day, connected by a guy we both dated.

Years later, we still laugh about it. What if I hadn't spoken up? What if she hadn't responded? What if that conversation about a *Bachelor* cast member and a rock star had never happened?

Women's friendships are not ancillary. They are not the side dish to the romance. They are the meals. They are the sustenance. Rose was my sustenance. She still is.

She was the first person who made me feel that a female friend could hold the same weight in my life as a life partner. Not a placeholder. Not a stopgap until I got the ring or the baby or the job. But a pillar. A permanent structure in my emotional architecture.

Rose taught me the phrase "woo-woo." As in: we want to be *woo-woo* but not *too* woo. Maybe just one woo, she would laugh. Someone who was equally excited about attending a full moon ceremony and going out to a fancy dinner at the Chateau. We could go from talking about manifestation and spirit guides to walking silently through a canyon trail, completely at ease in each other's company. That was the magic; there was room for it all.

Even now, we talk almost every single day. If a day slips past, and we haven't texted, she'll just send a simple message: "hi friend" with the little alien emoji. A transmission. A signal. A tether to something that has only grown stronger with time. She is the closest thing I have ever had to a sister, and I don't take it for granted. It lives in me like a landmark from the map of who I became.

And if you are a woman who is deeply yearning for that kind of soul-level connection with another woman, here are a few grounded, actionable ways to begin calling it in.

How to Call In a Soul-Friendship:

1. **Get specific in your journal.**

Write it down like you mean it. Not just "funny, nice, loyal." Get detailed. What do you want your conversations to feel like? Soft and nourishing, or electric and fast-paced? Do you want someone who texts you memes all day, or someone who lights candles with you under the full moon? Be as precise as you would be if you were manifesting a great love. Because this kind of friendship is a great love. Write about the energy you want in your orbit. Write about how you want to feel in their presence. And then get honest about how you want to show up too.

2. **Be visible to the women who already inspire you.**

If another woman's presence lights you up, tell her. Comment on her posts. Reply to her stories. DM her with kindness, not coolness. Don't overthink it. Friendship isn't about playing it safe. It's about resonance. Treat connection like you would if you were reaching out to someone you admire professionally. Let women know you see them. Sometimes the deepest friendships begin with, "I love what you said," or "You make me feel less alone."

3. **Say yes when it feels aligned. Say no when it drains you.**

If your body says no, listen. You don't owe anyone your energy. You'll know when it feels expansive, when someone's presence makes you sit up straighter, breathe deeper, feel more like yourself. That's your yes. And when something feels performative, obligatory, or like you're back in seventh grade pretending to be someone else just to be included, that's your no. You don't have to apologize for protecting your light.

4. **Go where the energy lives.**

The women you're looking for are already gathering somewhere. Women's circles. Retreats. Art classes. Book clubs. Full moon ceremonies. Dance classes. Breathwork. They're out there having meaningful conversations and making eye contact. Show up for something that calls to you even if you don't know a single soul in the room. Especially if you don't. That's the beginning of everything.

5. **Be willing to go first.**

Friendship requires a kind of bravery that doesn't get enough credit. Be the one who asks the deeper question. Who shares the real answer instead of the polished one. Who gives a compliment without expecting anything in return. Show up with your full attention. That is the magic. That is what makes someone feel safe enough to do the same. Soul-friendships aren't found. They're built, hand over hand, heart over heart.

6. **Honor the law of reciprocity.**

If you're always the one reaching out, always the one extending the invitation, always the one making the plan, pause. Friendship should be a rhythm, not a performance. There is a difference between being generous and being depleted. If your energy is not being met, matched, or returned, it's okay to pull back. Not in a bitter way. Not in a performative way. But in a self-respecting way. It doesn't make you unkind to protect your resources. Time, energy, and emotional labor are not infinite.

If you're constantly pouring into someone who never thinks to pour back, you are not in a friendship. You are in a transaction. And you deserve better than that. The right people will notice when you go quiet. The right people will text back. Show up. Invite you in return. Real friendship flows in both directions, like breath. If it always feels one-sided, let that be your signal. You're allowed to walk away from connections that only take. Choosing reciprocity is not about keeping score. It's about choosing mutuality over martyrdom.

25

Conscious Sobriety

"Recovery didn't open the gates of
heaven and let me in. Recovery opened
the gates of hell and let me out."
—Anonymous, Alcoholics Anonymous saying

The absolute best part of entering my thirties was that I had finally lived enough life to collect a personal belief system. I had walked through so many different seasons, Marianne Williamson, Christian church services that built a relationship with my version of Jesus, and a spiritual retreat in Malibu through SLAA that cracked something wide open in me. These guideposts, scattered across my twenties, taught me one thing: take what serves you and leave the rest.

After my breakup with Miles, I got really into Abraham Hicks. I listened to her teachings like sermons, organizing my closet while she talked about alignment and the vortex. She made me believe in the mechanics of energy. That what you attract has everything to do with how you feel. But that system started to feel convoluted every time alcohol entered the picture. I would go on a date and think a guy was magnetic, witty, charming, and mysterious, but the next day I would realize I had just added wine to a cardboard cutout. The alcohol had cast a spell that wasn't real.

So, I started to experiment. What if I didn't drink at all?

At first, I did it quietly. I just ordered sparkling water with lime or a mocktail. I loved watching men squirm when they asked what I was drinking, and I said, "Nothing." They would stammer or try to act unfazed, but their energy always shifted.

"You're not drinking?"

"No."

"Uhhh, okay.... Do you mind if I do?"

"Go right ahead."

But I could see it now. These were the kinds of men who needed alcohol to become interesting and needed me to be just drunk enough to believe they were. Sobriety gave me a new filter. I saw things more quickly. I lost interest faster. I no longer spent weeks or months convincing myself that someone was aligned when they clearly weren't.

It's worth noting that within the spiritual communities I found myself moving through in both Los Angeles and New York, there were unmistakable trends. A kind of zeitgeist around healing but one that had grown louder, more accessorized. Ketamine being administered like a multivitamin. Mushroom ceremonies hosted in chic rented spaces with crystal grids and sliding-scale donations. Breathwork paired with a side of toad venom hallucinogenic called 5-MeO-DMT. Ayahuasca circles held under the guise of medicine but administered more like experiential theater. MDMA-assisted therapy. Cacao ceremonies with sound baths and Reiki. A revolving door of tools, rituals, plant allies, and substances that all promised access to something deeper, truer, more divine.

I wasn't judging. Truly, I wasn't. Everyone is on their own journey. Everyone is looking for a way home to themselves. And maybe for some, this was the portal. Maybe a vision sparked in the middle of a psilocybin ceremony really did lead to a more conscious life. But I couldn't ignore the sense that for many, it wasn't about transformation. It was about relief. A fast track to transcendence. A beautifully lit shortcut. And something about that, something about the idea that these experiences were being bought, scheduled, and styled to look good on Instagram started to feel less like spiritual awakening and more like high-end drug use in expensive packaging.

I didn't know the answer. And maybe that was the point. But what I did know was that for me, the idea of altering my consciousness in any way, no matter how ceremonious, felt too risky. I needed my clarity more than I needed my curiosity. I needed to stay as far away from my father's legacy as I possibly could. His life was marked by escape. By intoxication. By using substances to avoid what was real. I knew my own edge. And I didn't want to get anywhere important by leaving myself to get there.

I had ADHD. A highly addictive personality. I'd been addicted to work, to earning, to the high of accomplishment. I'd been addicted to men who didn't see me, to relationships I could fix, to fantasy and future tripping, and the aching hope that something better was always just around the corner. I didn't need to alter my consciousness. I needed to be conscious.

I was afraid of ending up like my dad. Terrified, if I'm honest. I stopped drinking on January 16, 2022. I poured my craving into sobriety, into twelve-step meetings, into the literature of women who had walked before me and dared to tell the truth.

Not the Instagram-filtered version of truth, but the real, sticky, shame-tinged kind.

It was the height of the pandemic, and for the first time in years, I had nothing but time. No flights. No hotel rooms. No press junkets. I had space to slow down and listen. I wasn't in AA because I was addicted to alcohol. But I had what people in recovery call "the ISM." It lived in me. A restless, racing brain that didn't know how to settle. I had inherited it from my father, and over time it bled into so many other areas of my life via control, perfectionism, and codependency.

I didn't go to AA because I couldn't stop drinking. I wasn't waking up in parking lots. I wasn't losing jobs. But I still felt unwell. Restless. Untethered. Like something inside me kept short-circuiting any time I got too close to peace.

In the language of recovery, the ISM is what lingers even when the drinking stops. It's shorthand for what the substance numbs but doesn't resolve. In the world of Alcoholics Anonymous and Al-Anon, ISM means different things to different people:

I, Self, Me.

A compulsive inward orbit. The hyper-focus on how I am being perceived, received, misunderstood. The emotional narcissism that comes from untreated fear.

InSide Me.

The swirl of distorted thoughts, distorted longings, distorted needs. The chaos that lives not on the outside, but deep in the nervous system. Always buzzing.

I Sabotage Myself.

The quiet agreement to stay small. To pick the partner who cannot see me. To be everywhere but here. To chase exhaustion like a badge of honor then resent the world for not noticing the cost.

I inherited the ISM. My father had the addiction. I got the aftermath. He used alcohol. I used people. He escaped through the bottle. I escaped through fantasy. Through over-working. Through numbing. Through chasing.

Al-Anon taught me that even if I never touched a drop of alcohol, I could still be ruled by its shadow. That growing up with addiction doesn't just make you cautious; it makes you compulsive. It makes you learn to anticipate the moods of others before you've even figured out your own. You develop this sixth sense for danger and discomfort, and you build your personality around avoiding them.

I learned twelve sayings that were digestible, easy to remember, and always there when I needed a touchstone. When the noise in my head got too loud, I clung to the Al-Anon slogans like stepping stones. ***One day at a time*** became a lifeline when the future felt unbearable. I learned to ***let go and let God***, not because I wanted to surrender but because holding on was killing me. I reminded myself to ***keep it simple*** and ***easy does it***, especially when my instincts screamed to overcomplicate everything. I started to ***think*** before reacting and asked, "***how important is it?***" before spiraling. I practiced ***live and let live*** when I wanted to fix everyone around me. ***First things first*** grounded me. ***Keep an open mind*** softened the sharp edges of certainty. ***This too shall pass*** reminded me that nothing was permanent. I began to truly ***listen and learn***, especially from the women who had walked this road before me. ***Progress, not perfection*** stitched it all together, offering grace where shame used to live.

But it wasn't until **SLAA** (Sex and Love Addicts Anonymous) that I fully recognized my patterns.

In SLAA, I met women who weren't addicted to alcohol or drugs but were addicted to longing. To being wanted. To the storylines we'd been fed since childhood. We confused inconsistency with passion. We mistook adrenaline for love. We believed that suffering for someone was proof we loved them enough.

I was one of them. I had the fantasy addiction. I could take the smallest romantic gesture and build a cathedral of meaning around it. I lived in the potential of people, not their reality. I didn't just date; I cast people in roles. I didn't just listen; I narrated. I was addicted to the part of the story where the girl got chosen no matter how many red flags were screaming at her not to want it.

That is the ISM.

The part of me that kept chasing things I knew would hurt. The part that felt safest in chaos. The part that whispered, "You're only lovable if you earn it."

The part that confused validation with value.

When I got sober, not just from alcohol but from all the ways I used to abandon myself, I started to see it clearly. I wasn't going to match with a normie. I wasn't wired for casualness. I wasn't lighthearted when it came to love. I was someone with a history, a hunger, a spiritual curriculum. Emotional sobriety, I was learning, meant not letting my feelings dictate my behavior. It was the ability to stay steady without reaching for chaos, control, or someone else to carry what was mine to hold.

I needed tools. I needed structure. I needed a space where I could lay my compulsions out in the open and not be shamed for them.

Twelve-step work gave me that.

It gave me a way to map myself. To tell the truth without performance. To learn how to stay present even when the urge to escape came roaring in.

I stopped drinking not because I hit a traditional rock bottom but because I realized I was dulling my intuition. I was blocking my discernment. I was making boring men seem magnetic. Alcohol distorted my judgment and disconnected me from the signals my body was trying to send me. So, I stopped.

Sobriety became my filter.

It showed me what was real.

It reintroduced me to myself.

Now I understand that *conscious sobriety* isn't just about abstaining from alcohol. It's about living awake. It's about staying alert to your own needs. It's about resisting the cultural lie that you need to be looser, cooler, easier in order to be loved. Conscious sobriety says: your clarity is sacred. Your stillness is powerful. Your truth is enough.

And the most radical part?

I don't borrow light from a substance anymore. I generate it from within.

Unlike traditional abstinence rooted in rock-bottom narratives, conscious sobriety is rooted in *awareness*. You might not have a "problem" with alcohol in the clinical sense. But you start to notice what happens to your energy when you drink. You pay attention to how alcohol impacts your intuition, your nervous system, your decision-making, your mornings, your boundaries.

Conscious sobriety exists on a wide and inclusive spectrum. It isn't a one-size-fits-all identity. It's a practice. A lens. A lifestyle. And it's gaining momentum for reasons that reach far beyond any passing wellness trend. One of the most impactful things I ever heard in a room was this: *More will be revealed.*

Those words quieted my ISM in a way nothing else had. They gave me permission to pause, to stop trying to control every outcome with force or over-functioning. The only way I ever learned to surrender was by trusting that nothing I could do or say would tempt destiny more than simply letting people, places, and circumstances unfold in their own time.

My emotional reservoir was not limitless. And pouring into the same problems over and over left me depleted. *More will be revealed,* I would whisper to myself when I felt the ISM begin to soak up my precious energy. It was a sacred reminder that my job wasn't to manage the universe. My job was to stay grounded, to trust the process, and to let "Good Orderly Direction" guide the way.

Sober Truths

1. Energetic Clarity Is the New Currency

People are seeking alignment. More than ever, the ability to trust your gut, stay emotionally attuned, and move from inner truth instead of people-pleasing is seen as a superpower. Alcohol scrambles that frequency. Conscious sobriety preserves it.

There's a common saying in SLAA: *"Stop going to the hardware store looking for milk."* During my breakup with Miles, that single phrase guided me toward an epiphany. The vision I longed for was never going to be sourced through him.

If you are in the midst of a soul-shattering breakup, caught between the will-they-or-won't-they, know this: one day you will look back, and hindsight will arrive with pure gratitude that they weren't your person.

2. Healing Is Mainstream

Therapy, trauma work, nervous system regulation, somatic healing are part of the cultural conversation. As people explore inner work, they often reach a natural point of asking: what numbs me from the very things I'm trying to feel?

3. Sobriety Is Spiritual, Not Just Clinical

Conscious sobriety often coincides with spiritual awakening. You realize alcohol may not be ruining your life, but it's muting your magic. It's dulling your discernment. It's making the wrong things feel good, and the right things feel dull. So, you pause. You pay attention. And you reclaim the connection.

4. Women Are Choosing Power Over Performance

For many women, conscious sobriety is a feminist act. It's a refusal to self-edit for the comfort of others. It's saying, "I don't need to sip something to make you more tolerable." It's walking into a room fully in your body, not slightly outside of it.

5. One Day at a Time

This isn't prohibition. It's permission. Conscious sobriety says: you can choose clarity whenever you want. For a season. For a lifetime. There's no medal, no label, no rules. Just presence. Just you

PART IV

Montana

26

Paradise Valley

"The mountains are calling and I must go."
—John Muir

When the world shut down in March 2020, I was living alone in my studio apartment. It felt nothing like it had when I moved in at twenty-one, buzzing with optimism and possibility. Back then, it felt like freedom. Now the air was stale, the walls felt closer, and the energy had gone flat. Four months earlier, I had turned thirty. I found myself quietly doing math in my head, those silent calculations women do to figure out if they're behind or still on track. The fear of being the last kid left at summer camp had crept in again. It felt like everyone had paired off, and I was still standing alone, holding my sleeping bag with nowhere to go.

I wanted a partner. Deeply. But after years of working nonstop, when I finally had the space to date, the world closed its doors. A global pandemic. It felt like a joke from the universe, the punchline being: not yet, not for you, not now.

At the same time, there was a district-wide rule across the newsroom. All nonessential travel was grounded. I remember feeling relief. Finally, I could breathe knowing I wouldn't get a call asking me to jump on a plane with only hours' notice. Each time the news desk called, my body revolted. A wave of nausea. The quiet voice in my head reminding me not to mess this up. There were a hundred people ready to take my place. I was burned out. I had been running at full speed for so long, I hadn't even noticed I was bleeding. For the first time since I was fifteen, I didn't have a job. The news cycle, which had ruled my life for years, went quiet.

Then, one week after the new no-travel rule was implemented, they asked me to fly to Seattle to cover the first ground-zero case of COVID in the United States. My stomach dropped. Were they providing hazmat suits for the crew? Did they understand how unpredictable this disease was? We didn't know the long-term effects.

This time, I didn't flinch. I had tools in my belt now. I simply emailed the news director back, "I am unavailable to travel for this assignment."

My cell phone rang within seconds. I didn't pick up. I had already said no. It rang again. And again. Finally, I just silenced it.

They sent someone else to replace me. By the end of that trip, the correspondent, the producer, and the camera operator all had COVID and were quarantined.

I was proud of myself for setting a boundary, but that moment created cracks with my supervising producers that were hard to ignore. I knew they were agitated I had blown it off, but I didn't care. The New York bureau called me directly to give me a new assignment, a much better one than going on the scene to COVID sites, which I had already made clear I wasn't going to do.

This one was a fully remote story for Diane Sawyer. Nursing homes across the country were in lockdown. Patients and families were being separated. Final goodbyes were happening over FaceTime.

I booked half a dozen nurses and began overseeing their daily video diaries. It became a powerful series for Diane's primetime special on the pandemic. Our team operated entirely on Zoom, and for the first time, it felt like we were proving something new was possible. We were producing meaningful stories from our homes. It felt revolutionary.

My days began early, combing through hours of footage, organizing clips, doing rough edits, and building the emotional narrative from what was happening on the ground. Around lunchtime, I would take long walks with my phone, waiting for calls about editorial feedback. In the afternoons, we'd have our team meetings, sometimes with Diane herself.

She was a class act. Working with someone so iconic but connecting with her as a fellow storyteller felt deeply impactful. I admired how clear she was in her vision. Always direct. Always respectful. One day, she left me a voicemail thanking me for my work on the project. I emailed the audio file to myself. I knew I would want to keep that forever.

Two months into lockdown, the walls started closing in again. Without the newsroom, without the chaos, I cracked.

And then, a thought drifted in like a whisper, *"What if I just road-tripped to Montana?"*

I had never been. I didn't know a single soul there. But when I feel trapped, I tend to reach for the voices that once saved me. In 2014, John Mayer released an album called *Paradise Valley* and spoke openly about leaving behind the noise for a quieter life in Montana. Something about that lodged in my psyche. Montana took on a mythic shape, less a place and more a symbol. It felt like a kind of frontier for the soul. I had once scribbled *"Paradise Valley, Montana"* into my journal, a place I dreamed of seeing someday. Why not now?

At the same time, there was a quiet exodus happening. Millennials were fleeing the cities in droves, trading cramped apartments and restless ambition for open skies and space to think. Between March and May of 2020 alone, over 250,000 people left New York City, according to data from the *New York Times*. Los Angeles saw more than 40,000 residents move out. In total, nearly sixteen million Americans relocated between February and July, based on U.S. Postal Service change-of-address requests analyzed by Pew Research Center. It wasn't just me. A collective migration was already underway.

This was one of those rare moments when your instinct speaks so loudly that ignoring it feels like betrayal. I believe those moments are led by something higher. You don't always get the full map. Just a single, luminous step. And that step was, "Go. *Go now.*"

On the morning of June 1, 2020, I woke before dawn, loaded up my little SUV, and hit the road with my dog Hazel riding shotgun. I wore oversized, white cat-eye sunglasses, tied a bandana in my hair, and blasted Springsteen like I was the heroine in the opening credits of my own film. With every passing mile, something inside me loosened. The tight coil of anxiety I had been living with for months began to unwind.

I landed in Livingston, Montana, and it felt like I had stepped into a Hallmark movie with a cliché plot line, "Disillusioned City Girl Escapes to the Mountains to Find Herself." I wandered the aisles of the local Albertson's, piling my cart high with fresh fruit, vegetables, and just enough groceries to stock the tiny fridge in my motel room just off the freeway. I had no idea how long I would stay.

The first two days, I took myself on long hikes with bear spray clipped to my hip and floated solo down the Yellowstone River in a borrowed tube leaning back and letting the water guide me wherever it wanted. Then, on the third day, out of the blue when I was getting out of the shower, a thought came to me.

"I wonder what the real estate market is like here...."

It made no sense. But something inside me stirred. I had spent so long worrying about being single in my thirties, about not having a traditional family structure, about doing things out of order. But at that moment, I felt none of that. Just clarity. I didn't need to ask anyone's permission. I had nothing tying me down. The project for Diane was wrapping. And while some people feel restless in chaos, I get uneasy in too much stillness. I needed something to sink my teeth into.

I sprawled across the bed and pulled up Zillow, eager to see what was possible. I scrolled endlessly, eyes skimming over sprawling ranches and glossy, oversized homes well beyond my budget. Nothing felt right. Nothing felt like mine. Until I saw it, buried at the bottom of the listings.

A tiny, 700-square-foot cabin on six acres. Just one bedroom with a lofted living room and windows that seemed to drink in the light. It felt strangely familiar, which made no sense. I had never seen it before, but something in me recognized it. The listing noted it was a thriving vacation rental with a fully booked calendar through the rest of the year.

That was the part that caught me. It wasn't just a real estate listing. It was a business. A functioning, income-generating property. I had just listened to a podcast about the importance of creating multiple revenue streams, and here it was, an opportunity waiting quietly at the edge of the screen.

I called the realtor. He said he could meet me in fifteen minutes.

When I stepped inside, I knew.

This wasn't just a house. It was a landing place. A container for the energy I had spent years giving away to deadlines, to headlines, to everyone else's urgency but my own. Here, I could rebuild a version of myself that felt nourishing instead of draining. Shape the space with my own hands. Press my feet into the earth and create something that was finally, unquestionably mine.

The previous owners were moving to Ocala, Florida, the very town where I had spent the first seventeen years of my life before moving to New York City. Of all the places they could have gone, they were headed to the place where I had grown up. It felt less like coincidence and more like divine choreography. A quiet wink from the universe. I made an offer. It was accepted. Just like that, I was a homeowner in Montana.

Every good property in Montana needs a name, and I chose *Cosmic Goodness* for mine. It wasn't just a title. It was a mantra. A quiet prayer. It also happened to match my initials *C* and *G*, but more than that, it captured what I was clinging to at the time. A reminder to keep reaching for even the smallest shimmer of grace. To try, every single day, to find some layer of cosmic goodness I could hold in my hands. Something to anchor me. Something to name this new beginning.

How do I hold both truths at once? That this moment in time cracked something open in me and led me toward a life I never would have chosen otherwise while also knowing that for so many, it was a season of unimaginable loss? I didn't lose a loved one. I didn't lose my home. I know how rare that is. My mom, in that very same month, told me her breast cancer had returned. And even if I flew to Florida, I wouldn't be allowed inside the hospital for her surgeries or treatments. The world was locking down just as my worst fears were unlocking. Every day, I worried that she would catch COVID during recovery. That I would lose another parent to cancer. That I would lose her alone.

There's a particular kind of grief in being helpless. In carrying the weight of fear with no one to share it. That's the truth of being an only child. There was no sibling to split the worry. No one to call when my thoughts spiraled at 2:00 a.m. Just me, hoping daily check-ins were enough. Hoping silence on the other end of the phone didn't mean the worst.

I carry that awareness with care. I don't take for granted that while I was discovering a doorway into a new version of myself, others were walking through endings they never imagined. I can't reconcile the contrast. But I can honor it. Because the stillness of that year gave me something I didn't know I was missing. A quiet, unexpected sliding door. And I chose to walk through it.

I didn't know exactly what I was building. I just knew I was done shrinking to fit someone else's story. I stopped chasing titles and started chasing quality of life. I stopped asking what I should accomplish next and started asking how I wanted to feel.

That first summer, 2020 was one of the most transformative times of my life. I dug up hundreds of noxious weeds with a shovel, refusing to use poison, and burned them one by one in a fire pit far from the cabin. My legs grew strong and my arms defined not from overpriced Pilates classes but from hauling brush and swinging a shovel. The land had been wildly overgrown, and each day I carved it back into open prairie. I planted and landscaped the area around the cabin, shaping it into something that reflected care and intention. I even hired a crew to help move an old hunting cabin I had found at the local dump. Once it was on my property, I gutted and rebuilt it by hand, transforming it into something entirely new. I became obsessed with the before-and-after. There was something deeply satisfying about watching a forgotten structure come back to life under my care.

The main cabin was fully booked for the season, and I didn't want to cancel dozens of reservations. I bought a $2,500 RV and moved it onto the land, parking it in the middle of the field. At night, the RV would get cold, and I would fall asleep to the sound of animals calling across the hills. Every evening around 8:00 p.m., I drove to Pine Creek Lodge to take a hot shower after working outside all day, my feet caked in black dirt before I started again the next morning.

I used to dream of New York and Los Angeles, of being in the center of the action. But now, I craved something rooted. Something holy. I wanted to cocoon. Montana gave me my sanity back. It gave me permission to leave the familiar. And when you do that, when you step away from what you've always known, you begin to change. From the inside out. And I was no exception.

27

I'm Not Easy and Breezy, I'm Windy and Complicated

"I wanted so badly to lie down next to her on the couch, to wrap my arms around her and sleep. Not fuck, like in those movies. Not even have sex. Just sleep together, in the most innocent sense of the phrase. But I lacked the courage and she had a boyfriend and I was gawky and she was gorgeous and I was hopelessly boring and she was endlessly fascinating. So I walked back to my room and collapsed on the bottom bunk, thinking that if people were rain, I was drizzle and she was a hurricane."
—John Green, *Looking for Alaska*

I am the hurricane.

If you're not sure whether you are one, then you probably aren't. Hurricane Women know. We don't try to be this way. We were born into it. Emotional weather systems with tempers, intuition, sensitivity, and something wild in our blood.

Once we were little baby thunderstorms. Emotional outbursts. Quick to cry and just as fast to collapse into laughter. We were told to "calm down," to "take it easy," to "stop being so sensitive." And we tried. God, we tried. I used to apologize for it. Tried to quiet it. I was told, more than once by a man I was dating, to "just be easy and breezy." Certain women were born to be easy and breezy, and it comes naturally to them. I think for a long time I tried to water down the parts of myself to be more like that, but it made my chest feel hot and claustrophobic.

I've been called intense. Dramatic. In Montana, I started to see it in the context that I am a cowboy at heart. I'm a force. And eventually I stopped trying to shrink myself into a palatable draft. That last time a drizzle man told me to be easy and breezy, I looked him dead in the eyes and said, "I'm windy and complicated." And I meant it.

Montana cracked something open in me. It was the land that first pulled me in. The big sky. The horses. The sacred silence. But it was also the resistance. The tension. The pushback from locals who didn't want outsiders like me arriving with license plates from California. It was subtle at first, then not. Cars keyed. Passive aggressive signs. Glares at the gas station.

A neighbor gave me grief about the land I bought. He didn't know me, didn't know my name, my job, or how long I'd been working to build a life I could call my own. All he knew was that I was from California, and that was enough to rile him up. A local realtor had given him the scoop. A single lady. From out of town. Buying up land.

He came at me with that puffed-up small-town entitlement some men wear like armor. But one thing about being an investigative reporter, you can't fuck with me. I've sat across from accused murderers, made cold calls to grieving families, held my own in rooms that most people would tiptoe out of. I'm not going to shrink just because someone calls himself a local.

I asked him plainly, "Were you born here?"

He hesitated.

"Nah," he said finally. "I'm from Maryland. Moved here in the eighties."

I nodded. "And how old were you when you moved?"

"Thirty."

"Well, I'm thirty. So, it looks like we came at the same time, just in different decades."

Silence.

I didn't say it to be clever. I said it because I was tired of the mythology. As if being born a few zip codes over gave you more of a right to belong. As if this place, this piece of land, this open sky, belonged more to him than it did to me.

I wasn't going to be sweet about it. I had found a piece of heaven, and I was going to fight like hell to protect it.

After my car got keyed, I installed cameras. I felt exposed, like I was trespassing, even though my name was on the deed. I had every legal right to be there, but I could still feel the suspicion in the air. I had been one of the first to relocate to the valley during COVID, and the locals didn't hide their stares. Their silence wasn't quiet. It was loaded.

They had guns. I had cameras.

I'm a news reporter. Surveillance is my armor. It's how I protect myself. The entire property is under twenty-four-hour watch. I do not flinch when someone tries to intimidate me. I have footage. I have timestamps. I have evidence.

The land was vast, open, wild, and I loved it. I did feel uneasy at times, alone in that cabin at night, the wind howling like a warning. I wasn't going to let that fear shrink me. I had claimed that patch of earth with every fiber of my being. And I would defend it with everything I had.

I understand the frustration about Airbnbs in small towns. But that business saved my life. It gave me the freedom to stop accepting newsroom assignments that drained me. It gave me a real shot at sovereignty. And I guard it fiercely. It was real estate investing that allowed me to stop chasing hustle and start living with intention.

It taught me something I never would've learned if I had waited for a man to handle it. The repairmen tried to take advantage. The contractors talked down to me. Men underestimated me until they didn't. I learned to hold my ground, to negotiate with clarity and calm authority. I walked the property like I owned it because I did.

I had been too scrappy for too long, too careful with every dollar, to get taken for a ride. I wasn't going to throw thousands of dollars at a repair I knew should cost $300.

And still, Montana tested me. The undercurrent here is unmistakable. Misogyny runs deep, quiet, local, and sharp as barbed wire. It isn't just women in power they resent. Out here, a woman claiming space is a quiet rebellion. And I was done shrinking to soothe someone else's discomfort.

I am windy and complicated.

And I have Montana to thank for giving me permission to lean all the way in, without apology, without softening the edges, without asking for permission.

It made me feel like I belonged to the land as much as it belonged to me. When I named the property *Cosmic Goodness*, and the neighbor scoffed, "What the hell is that?" I just smiled. He'd never get it. I'm a hurricane. He's a drizzle man. Of course he wouldn't understand. This wasn't a place you named after something practical. It was a place you named after something sacred and ineffable; the kind of thing you feel in your bones but don't waste time explaining to men who demand definitions.

28

Spirit Babies

"Dreams are illustrations from the book
your soul is writing about you."
—Marsha Norman

When I was thirty-one, the longing to meet someone and have a baby began to pulse louder than any career goal I had ever chased. I was deep into my manifestation practice, a true student of vision. I had journals full of scripted pages where I wrote in the present tense about the life I was building. I didn't just imagine it. I lived inside of it before it arrived.

One night, after an especially powerful full moon circle with my women's group, I came home charged with insight yet completely spent. The kind of gathering that cracks something open. Illuminating, yes, but also consuming. I had taken in so much, stories, grief, breakthroughs, energy. My body buzzed with it, even as it begged for rest.

I collapsed into bed with a kind of fatigue that settles into your bones. The kind that doesn't just ask for rest. It demands surrender. Hours later, deep in REM, I slipped into a dream.

In the dream, I was standing on the grounds of an outdoor school. The air was crisp. The trees were tall and quiet. There were children everywhere, laughing and weaving around me like sunlight. To my left, two blonde heads bobbed in and out of view. One taller than the other. Maybe two and four years old.

I remember thinking clearly, *this is what it will be like.*

It felt more like a memory than a dream. As if I had time-traveled forward and stepped into the future that was already waiting for me. I could feel the texture of the moment. I could smell the air. I could feel what it was like to be their mother. Not just the image of it. The cellular experience of it.

When I woke up, I felt an immediate, quiet knowing. I didn't have to worry anymore. I hadn't missed my chance. It was already on its way to me.

There have been a handful of dreams in my life that didn't feel like dreams at all. They felt like doors. They felt like messages. This was one of them.

Years later, when I became pregnant with my son, his name came to me the same way. In a dream. Clear as anything: *Golden.*

It was not a name I had ever considered. But when I heard it, I knew. It felt like sunshine on your skin after weeks of rain. Like a promise that no matter how dark it gets, the light will always find its way back in.

Even now, when I say his name, it stirs something in me. A softness. A reminder. That he chose me long before I knew how to choose myself.

When he was old enough to talk, I would sometimes ask him questions about when he was a baby. He would answer with a kind of certainty that made me pause. We joked about it, but deep down, I believed him. I still do.

There is a bond with him that feels older than this lifetime. When I see him now, his little blonde head racing ahead of me on the sidewalk, I remember that dream. I see it playing out in real time.

And I know with every fiber of my being, it was him.

I think a lot about the invisible tug-of-war many women face. The pull between building something in the world and building a family. It is our bodies that transform, our hormones that surge, our sleep that disappears. We are the ones who become portals. And while that process is sacred, it also slows everything else down. Slows our ambition. Slows our ability to produce. Slows the momentum we worked so hard to build.

What no one tells you is that for some of us, the moment we cross that threshold into motherhood, the hunger to chase the external fades. The sharp edge of our striving softens. Careers we once clung to with white knuckles begin to lose their appeal. I used to fear missing the moments, the first words, the sleepy cuddles, the everyday miracles that vanish if you're not paying attention. And I was right to fear it. Because I would have missed them. And I would never get them back.

I know every season brings its own lessons. But sometimes I still wonder what all those years were for. I spent so much time chasing status and security in a high-value career. I made good money. But my nervous system was fried. My joy evaporated. My health deteriorated. What was the real cost of that?

As I got older, and the longing for a family grew louder, I threw myself into preparing for conception like it was a job. I tracked my cycle religiously. I read everything I could find about egg quality and fertility. Rebecca Fett's *It Starts with the Egg* became my holy grail. It felt like the only thing I could control. A way to participate in a process that otherwise felt slippery and unknowable.

There's something deeply absurd and almost laughable about trying to schedule a baby the way you'd plan a vacation. I remember Googling things like "best month to get pregnant for a spring baby" while holding back tears because I didn't even have a partner yet. That's the part no one prepares you for: the limbo. The not knowing when or how or with whom. Just a deep cellular hope that someday, somehow, the right soul would choose you.

A Practice: Becoming the Portal

If you're here feeling a deep call to become a mother, then you may already feel the presence of a child who hasn't arrived yet. A child you've dreamed about. A child whose soul might already be circling you.

This practice is not about ovulation charts or hormone levels. This is about opening the door. Not just to pregnancy, but to possibility.

Step One: Create Space to Listen

Find a moment where you can be completely alone. No phone. No distractions. Just you and a notebook. Light a candle if it feels right. Breathe. Place one hand on your heart, the other on your belly. Imagine you're making contact with the part of you that already knows how to hold life. You don't have to try. You just have to listen.

Step Two: Ask the Questions

Use these prompts to open a dialogue between you and the soul who may be choosing you.

- What are you here to teach me?
- What do I still need to heal before I meet you?
- What are you waiting for me to remember?

Let the answers come in fragments, feelings, metaphors. Don't try to interpret everything. Just write.

Step Three: Name the Altar

You don't need crystals or incense to build an altar. Sometimes an altar is a single object that carries meaning. A tiny pair of shoes. A feather. A photograph. Create a physical space in your home where you can return to this intention. Somewhere you can place your longing without it overwhelming you. Somewhere that says: I'm open.

Step Four: A Letter to the Spirit Baby

Close the practice by writing a letter. Even if it feels strange, write it anyway. Begin with: *To the soul who may choose me…*and let it flow. Tell them what kind of world you hope to create for them. Tell them who you are. And tell them they are already loved.

This is how you begin to prepare not just your body but your spirit. Not just your calendar but your capacity. And when the time comes, whether it's this year or in ten, you will already be in a relationship with the life that is waiting to meet you.

PART V

2/22/22

29

Love Letter to the East End

"I don't look at the view, I watch it. The land
is alive, tells you things when you let it."
—Jackson Pollock on the Pollock-Krasner House
and Study Center in Springs, East Hampton

Exactly three months to the day before I met Squirrel, I made a bold, impulsive decision to become bicoastal. I had outgrown the seams of my West Hollywood studio. Moving to New York City felt like more of the same. In a twist of fate, I was connected with a Deadhead from Montauk and booked a spontaneous flight for a weeklong escape. It started as a visit. A week to clear my head. But the air out here rewired something in me.

Montauk reminded me of Malibu in some ways. Ditch Plains had grand sweeping cliffs, but the air felt more expansive than Malibu's, which was still suffocated by the sprawl and haze of Los Angeles pressing in from just beyond the shoreline. They call it the end of the world for a reason. Everyone in the Hamptons is escaping something. Most are escaping New York City, one of the greatest cities in the world, just two and a half hours away.

I went in June and then again in July. By August, I was finding every excuse to return. The East End pulled at me with a quiet force. The landscape. The ocean. A kind of mystical intrigue in the characters who had chosen to build their sanctuaries there. Renting even a modest guesthouse for a weekend was astronomical. I couldn't justify spending $4,000 for three nights. My frugal, scrappy side refused. So, I floated between a yurt tucked in the backyard of a friend-of-a-friend, and, when it was taken, I borrowed an SUV from Brooklyn and car camped with Hazel curled beside me, parking deep in the woods of Springs.

At thirty-one, I felt a little too old to be car camping in the Hamptons to save money, but I also found it to be a quiet rebellion. A return to something I thought I had outgrown. It reminded me of my late teens when I could fall asleep on a futon in someone's kitchen without a second thought. But my ability to stay flexible, to say yes to less-than-perfect conditions has always served me. It has kept me from growing too rigid to follow wonder when it knocks. I'd wake with the sun and shower at the beach in the comfort stations. A full day ahead with no plan at all. There was a sense of wild spontaneity in it. A last breath of complete detachment, not knowing that by the next summer, I would have met Squirrel.

At the time, I was one of the lead bookers on a two-hour *20/20* special detailing the tribulations of Robert Durst. I would usually grab my laptop and set up at a coffee station while working through booking efforts. That often meant staying in close contact with the family of his first wife, Kathy Durst, who had gone missing decades earlier. Infamously, Ryan Gosling played Durst in a film with Kirsten Dunst portraying Kathy.

While my colleagues were perched in their home offices, I carried a silent joke with myself knowing I had car camped the night before. The contrast felt surreal.

The trial kept getting paused for various reasons; one of the defense attorneys caught COVID, then Durst himself tested positive. I was essentially being kept on to maintain the relationships, to keep family members and close contacts warm until we were ready to film.

I felt I had earned the right to be on location in Montauk after years of crisscrossing the country, sacrificing everything to help tell these stories. In an unpredictable way, the pandemic unshackled us. Those of us in production could suddenly work remotely. Return-to-office rumors were swirling, but the real pressure wouldn't come for another two years.

Everything inside me whispered: root, root, root. It made no practical sense. I was single, untethered, not exactly in a position to buy a family home. It was that strange sliver of time when everyone was talking about low interest rates, and it felt like a "strike-while-the-iron-is-hot" kind of window. I didn't want to be one of those people, decades later, muttering, *"I should have bought there when I had the chance in 1970."* Only for me, it was 2021, a year into the pandemic. I opened Zillow, adjusted the listings from least to most expensive, and one jumped out at me. I felt the same pull in my chest that I had when I found the place in Montana.

I had met plenty of people who rented their homes during peak season, June–August, and covered their entire mortgage for the year. May was when it started to wake up. September was when it began to settle before the exodus after Labor Day. The locals called it "Tumbleweed Tuesday," a nickname that stuck.

As someone with an entrepreneurial spirit and a deep love of real estate, it actually seemed possible. If I could rent it in the summers, I wouldn't carry the burden of a year-round mortgage. That was the way in. The only way that buying a home in the Hamptons felt remotely within reach.

In full transparency, none of this would have been possible without my mother. Her help with the down payment turned a pipe dream into something real. It feels important to say that out loud. Homeownership in this market can feel like a locked door. I did not do it entirely on my own, and I will not pretend that I did. It was a full circle moment from the universe that my mom could give my adulthood something we never had together in my childhood, a beautiful home. She has shown up for me as an adult in so many ways we did not have the resources to manage earlier. I am grateful for the ways she has shown me a generosity we could not afford when I was a child.

I understand the kind of privilege that comes with having a parent who can help financially. I know it can be infuriating from the outside. But we had struggled through so many years of my childhood. Shame over our poverty had become second nature to me. It wasn't until deep into my adulthood, after her parents passed, that she was finally able to stop struggling. And when she had the chance to make different choices, she did.

Her generosity repaired something in me. She gave me the gift of stability when she finally had the resources to do so. We didn't have that when I was growing up. To know she was willing to invest in my future after all the instability of our past meant more than words could ever say.

Within two months, the deal had closed, and I had the keys in my hand. I flew my mom up from Florida, so we could work on the project together. In every brushstroke and small repair, we tended to something we had never been able to fix in the rented home I grew up in. What had once been out of reach for her, we were finally doing side by side.

The Hamptons home became my sanctuary. A nest to repair in, to root into. It needed work, and I threw myself into every detail. I had done all of those things in Montana too, but over time, that property became a thriving business. It got to the point where staying there meant giving up valuable income, and living elsewhere full-time made more sense.

I couldn't picture myself in Montana full time. I had to stay sharp there. In the Hamptons, I could soften. Something in the light, the salt air, the rhythm of the days invited a different version of me forward. Not the fast-paced TV producer chasing commitments on a deadline. This version had recalibrated her nervous system and was determined to protect that peace. She wasn't going to be rushed for anyone's convenience.

My only hesitation about the Hamptons was the small-town visibility. You run into someone every day everywhere you go. It can be hard to disappear, to go inward, the way you sometimes can in the anonymity of a big city. But when I pulled back from the events, the dinners, the social scene, I found something else. A quiet, rooted undercurrent of locals. Families that had fished these waters for generations. Farmers who knew the land and lived holistically as close to the earth as possible. The groundedness is embedded into the lifestyle here if you know where to look for it.

It exists in the soil. In the people. In the way children run barefoot through the dunes with salt still drying in their hair. After the pandemic, there was a shift. Families who once came for weekends began to stay longer. What had once been a seasonal destination quietly transformed into a year-round ecosystem of young families growing gardens, forming school pods, starting farm stands, and embedding themselves into the community here. I became an active and committed member of that ecosystem, and it felt pure.

I never imagined owning a home here. But the quiet parts of me, the ones that had long gone unheard, felt seen here. Something anchored. The land was a nest that carried me through pregnancy, into birth.

30

Joshua Tree

"The words we speak become
the house we live in"
—Hafiz

In the summer of 2021, a viral video crossed my TikTok feed. It was a conscious event in Los Angeles. Events like sound baths, breathwork, and musicians wired to plants, playing duets with their vibrational field as if translating the secret language of the natural world into music. At the time, I was spending more and more time in New York, but something about the video made me pause. I followed the account. I joined the text list. I wasn't free to attend any of the events, but I stayed connected. I knew, on some intuitive level, that I was planting a seed.

A few days before February 22, 2022, I received a text alert about an event happening in Joshua Tree. Leading the ceremony was Pauli Lovejoy, best known as Harry Styles's percussionist and musical director during the Love on Tour shows. An unexpected detail that somehow made the entire experience feel both cosmic and culturally grounded.

The event was timed to align with the rare numerological portal of 2/22/22, a once-in-a-lifetime vortex day. In numerology, the number two is associated with balance, intuition, divine timing, and partnership. When repeated, its power amplifies. A sequence like 2/22/22 is considered a master alignment, a rare window where the veil between intention and manifestation is thinner. It represents a moment of energetic clarity, inviting you to align with your higher purpose, call in meaningful connections, and trust that what's meant for you is already making its way. Quiet openings where life shifts course and something new begins. The next time this alignment will occur is not until 2/22/2222, two centuries from now.

I called Rose immediately and told her, "We have to go." She didn't hesitate. That's the kind of friend she is. Within the hour, she had sent me a yurt listing and said, "Here. This one." We booked it without a second thought. We didn't even notice the fine print about how it was unheated and required us to bring our own firewood. It didn't matter. When I'm with Rose, everything feels like an adventure.

The day before we left, I ended a short but emotionally draining fling with a man the algorithm had assigned me on Hinge. He looked good on paper. Founder. Forty-five-million-dollar exit. Impeccable taste in watches and architecture. But he didn't feel like home. He felt like a cold, modern hotel lobby. Sleek. Well-curated. But ultimately empty. I tried to talk myself into being more curious. I told myself I could learn from his entrepreneurial mind. But the truth was I was uncomfortable every time we were together. My body never fully relaxed in his presence. It was a push-pull that left me depleted.

When I left for Joshua Tree, I was raw but clear. I had done the thing so many of us are terrified to do. I let go of something that wasn't right, even though it looked right on paper. I released the safety net. The glossy version of love. The curated compatibility. I wanted to show up to 2/22/22 unbound. No emotional debris. No lingering what-ifs. Just me, standing open to possibility. Even if I didn't know what would come next, I knew I had to be clean for it. Empty enough to receive.

As Rose and I drove through the desert, a rainbow arched across the highway. It was one of those cinematic moments that takes your breath away. We both went silent. It felt like a blessing. Like a confirmation. Like something sacred had already started unfolding.

We pulled over and ran through a field beneath the rainbow, and I whispered a prayer to my angel guides. It was exactly 2:22 p.m. because of course it was. With Rose, moments synchronized like magic. The time, the energy, the unfolding. It was as if the universe adjusted its tempo whenever we were in the same place.

I didn't ask for a boyfriend. I asked for a life partner. I asked to be found by the man who would one day help me build a home. I asked to be met by someone whose spirit recognized mine. Someone who would want the same things I did. A family, a home, a shared language. I had no idea that prayer would be answered that very night.

Dating in your thirties is strangely similar to house hunting. Both require vision. Both demand discernment. Both become easier when you learn to trust your body. My breath has always been my compass. When I bought my home, I felt it in my chest before I even saw the listings. A quickening. A knowing. When I searched Zillow, I always ticked the box for "No HOA." I wanted autonomy. I didn't want to answer to anyone else's rules.

Freedom is one of my non-negotiables. I have learned to listen for what feels like mine.

I approached dating the same way. Hinge would send me their earnest suggestions. Ten men they thought I might love. Just like Zillow. Ten homes they thought I might want to live in. The algorithm meant well, like an overly involved aunt who tries to set you up with someone she met at the grocery store. But there are some things an algorithm will never understand. Chemistry. Safety. Breath.

We arrived at the event just before sunset. We walked through the open-air venue, a mixture of candlelight and distant music, and that's when I saw him. He was standing in the hallway, still and quiet.

He turned, looked at me, and simply said, "Hello." That was it. One word. But my breath caught in my throat. There was an electric awareness between us. I knew. And I could tell he knew, too.

We didn't talk again that night. But I kept sneaking glances. Watching the way he held space. The way he moved through the room. His presence was calm. Self-assured. His brown ringlets brushed the top of his glasses. His beard was thick and soft-looking. He looked like someone who had done the work. Someone who had come through something and found himself on the other side.

Later, when we finally got to know each other, I would learn that he had been sober for six years. That detail mattered. I had taken my final drink on January 16, 2022, a Bloody Mary on a too-intense day with the tech founder. I wasn't drinking every day. But I had started to question my relationship with substances. I didn't like who I became when I drank. More than that, I didn't like who I tolerated. Alcohol dulled my intuition. It made mediocre connections feel magical. It blurred the red flags I was learning to see clearly.

I had journaled about the kind of partner I wanted. I had written it down with the same precision I used when listing out my real estate goals. I even remember sitting on Rose's floor the night before and reading her my list.

"Brown curly hair. Beard. Entrepreneur. Sober. Family-oriented."

He matched the list I had written down almost word for word. At first glance, it was his aesthetic that caught my eye. But it was the stillness in him, the grounded presence, that kept pulling me in. I would later find out he was the founder of the event we were attending. Something he never mentioned. There was no personal social media to scroll through, no curated digital footprint. Just him. Present. Rooted. I found out from him directly, not through a Hinge profile, that he had studied drumming at the Berklee College of Music but ended up working in the music industry on the business side. I blurted out, "John Mayer went there too!"

He laughed. "Trust me, I know. They mention it every chance they get."

He didn't feel algorithmically placed. He felt orchestrated. Like someone sent by something larger than logic. A resonance not just with my preferences but with my values. A match to my nervous system. To the most sacred parts of me I didn't even know were still hoping to be met.

Our first date came a week later. We went to a tea house on Sunset Boulevard. At one point, he turned to me and asked, "Do you want kids?"

Not someday. Not maybe. Just a calm, clear question. And I felt something unspool in my chest. Relief. Recognition. This wasn't someone I needed to explain myself to. This was someone who wanted what I wanted.

We often talk about that night in Joshua Tree. About how so many things had to align for us to meet. The location. The timing. The decision to show up at all. It feels divine but also human. Like all the angel guides in our orbit had pulled a few strings and then whispered, "Okay. You two take it from here." And so we did.

31

Foundation

"Babies are bits of stardust, blown from the
hand of God. Lucky the woman who knows
the pangs of birth, for she has held a star."
—Larry Barretto

The next six months were sacred. We honored everything we had each learned in twelve-step recovery and built something that felt less like a conventional relationship and more like a spiritual container. It wasn't about romance for the sake of distraction. It was about presence. Discipline. Intention. He had been devoted to Alcoholics Anonymous and protected his sobriety for nearly six. There was a sacredness in how he treated it, like a vow he had made to himself, quietly, and kept. I was brand new, only thirty-seven days into my declaration of conscious sobriety though I had been attending SLAA, Al-Anon, and AA for nearly two years, excavating patterns that had ruled me for a lifetime. He was adamant that our palpable chemistry not become a stand-in for our old addictions. We both knew how easily obsession could masquerade as intimacy. So, we made something different.

We set boundaries—real ones. We declared friendship and used a composition notebook to draft our rules. No hanging out past 9:00 p.m. No physical intimacy beyond hugging. No texting or calling more than twice a day. These weren't restrictions. They were a form of respect for the healing we were both doing and for the intensity between us. They were a way to keep the spark from consuming us before we had built something steady underneath it. When people like us collide, it can be cosmic, yes, but also combustible. We slowed everything down. We treated what we were building with intention. We didn't want to accidentally burn it before it had a chance to grow just like a sapling in the woods.

For four months, we kept the heat low, trying to contain what was clearly simmering between us. But desire has a way of building pressure. One night, it reached a boil. We kissed for the first time. That kiss carried the weight of every moment we had held back. It surged through me like a live wire, igniting something that had been waiting to be unleashed. To this day, it remains the most electric kiss of my life. After that, we tumbled. Summer 2022 played out in fast-forward. There was no going back. The chemistry had been rising for months, and once it spilled over, there was no putting the lid back on.

We took road trips. We met each other's families. Went to Lollapalooza where we saw his old buds in the Manchester Orchestra play a private, secret show. We played The New Basement Tapes on repeat. One song in particular, "When I Get My Hands on You," became our anthem. It was built around forgotten Bob Dylan lyrics and carried a haunting sweetness. It was the most romantic song I ever heard in my whole life.

Just seven months in, we made the quiet decision to stop preventing pregnancy. We didn't make a big announcement to ourselves or each other. There was no calendar, no ovulation tracking, no checklist of signs to decode. It was more instinctual than strategic. We looked at each other one night and said, "Let's just see what happens."

It wasn't a plan so much as a permission slip. To let life in. To allow something bigger than us to enter the conversation.

And then, it did.

We were in East Hampton. September had just begun. The air had thinned out in that particular way it does after Labor Day when the town finally exhales. My period was late. By the fifth day, he turned to me and said, "We need to get a test. I'm dying to know."

We drove to CVS and picked up a box. But I didn't want to go back to the house. I needed the ocean. I needed to be near something vast. Something familiar. Indian Wells had always been my place during seasons of change. When I used to car camp, I would shower in the comfort station just off the beach. This time, I was there for a different reason.

I took the test in that same little bathroom and tucked it under my palm, so I wouldn't accidentally see the results too soon.

We found a quiet patch of sand above the dunes. Just the two of us, suspended in possibility. I held the test like it was sacred. We counted to three and turned it over together.

Two lines.

We squealed with joy. We laughed. We cried. We held each other like we knew everything was about to change. Because it was. Because it already had.

We were going to have a baby.

Something shifted in Squirrel overnight. He became instinctively protective, almost primal in his attentiveness. Watching how much I was lifting. Nudging me to swap the sweets for more protein. Quietly checking labels and gently rerouting anything that didn't feel right for the baby. It wasn't controlling. It was tender. Subtle. A thousand small gestures that said, *I'm all in.*

It was the beginning of family. Before diapers, before ultrasounds, before we had even told most people. We were already changing the way we moved through the world. Our choices were no longer just about us. They were about this new little life we had invited in. Something bigger than both of us had entered the conversation. And we were learning, slowly, how to listen.

Two months later, we found out it was a boy. It stirred a quiet fear in me; one I didn't expect. Girls I understood. I had been one. I knew the terrain. But a son? That felt like stepping into unfamiliar territory. I imagined dirt and sweat, broken toys and wild energy, sports I didn't watch and trucks I didn't know anything about. I was scared I wouldn't be enough for a boy. I was scared I wouldn't know how to connect with him.

I was never chasing a certain gender. I was grateful, deeply, for a healthy pregnancy. But beneath the surface of that gratitude was the truth: I feared the unknown. I feared being out of my depth.

What I didn't know yet was that parenting isn't about matching energy. It's about meeting it. I didn't need to become the kind of woman who thrills at the sound of a garbage truck. I just needed to watch his face light up at one and stand beside him in his wonder. His joy would become mine. That's what love does: it gives you access to someone else's world. Not because you understand it but because you care enough to witness it.

As my belly grew, our lives shifted. Quietly, steadily, we began disentangling from Los Angeles. There wasn't a single moment of decision. Just a growing sense between us that this wasn't where we wanted to raise our child. The city had shaped us, but it no longer matched who we were becoming. We didn't need billboards and traffic. We needed space. Room to breathe.

At the time, I had just completed my final long-form feature for *20/20.* A two-hour special on the Robert Durst trial. I didn't know then it would be my last assignment. There was no tearful goodbye. Just a soft, steady knowing in my chest. A quiet voice said, *"You are done here."* And I listened. I didn't mourn that chapter. I had lived it fully. I was ready to write something new.

We began to move intentionally. Slowly. I taught him about "the bubble." My name for the sacred membrane around home and family. If something depleted our energy, it didn't belong. If a commitment pulled us further from each other instead of closer, we passed. It wasn't rigidity. It was clarity. The kind of commitment that only arrives after years of distractions.

There were still echoes of my old self. I didn't want to become legally bound to anyone; it made me feel panicky inside. I didn't need the paper or the ring. I had always said I'd be a Goldie Hawn to his Kurt Russell. They raised a child together, stayed in love, stayed sovereign, and made it last without ever walking down an aisle. I respected marriage, but I never longed for it. Not in the traditional sense. Every time I imagined being legally required to show up, something in my chest tensed. It wasn't about him. It was about me. I am windy and complicated. I always have been.

Even living together was new. I had never cohabitated with a man longer than a couple of months. Certainly not one with a six-inch beard who shed like a golden retriever. I vacuumed constantly. His hair was everywhere. In the bathroom, the kitchen, the laundry basket. I fantasized about having two guest houses on the same property. Separate homes. Parallel paths.

In the mornings, he was always ready to talk. My brain, still foggy and wordless, was not. He'd ask, "What's wrong?" and I'd reply, "It's 7:00 a.m. It's quiet time." It became a running joke. We learned to adjust to each other's rhythms. These were the micro-negotiations we practiced long before parenthood arrived.

In my dream world, we would share breakfast and then part ways for the day. Not out of avoidance but to carve space for anticipation of reuniting. How could I have that if we saw each other all day long, both working from home? A woman in her own space, unobserved and uninterrupted, is not retreating. She is returning to herself.

As Esther Perel says, *"Fire needs air. Desire needs space. We need separateness to be able to come together."*

It wasn't commitment that scared me. It was the quiet blending of the woman I had worked so hard to become. To Squirrel's credit, he never asked me to shrink. He celebrated my complexity, never flinched at my wildness, never tried to tame what made me vivid. But I protected my alone time fiercely from the start. Not to pull away but as a way to stay intact. Because some women don't just want space. They need it. Not to escape love but to remain whole inside it.

This is my birth story. Not just the story of one day in a delivery room. But the slow, sacred reorientation of my entire life. Becoming a mother is not one moment. It is a thousand small choices to step toward something bigger than yourself.

My pregnancy asked me to soften. To trust. To stop bracing for the worst. It invited me to see the world not as something to conquer but as something to behold. The same way I would soon behold him.

Motherhood doesn't just change your schedule. It rearranges your soul. It expands your heart in directions you didn't know existed. It humbles you. It asks you to listen not just with your ears but with your whole being. It teaches you to show up when you're exhausted. To try again after you've failed. To stand in awe of the ordinary.

There is no checklist for that kind of becoming. No blueprint. Just a deep, cellular transformation that begins long before labor and continues long after birth.

And I was in it. All of it. The stillness. The nausea. The nesting. The letting go. The falling deeper into the unknown. I was being rewritten from the inside out.

I didn't become a mother the day he was born.

I had been becoming her all along.

PART VI

Out East

32

Becoming Mother

"When the winds of change blow, some people
build walls and others build windmills."
—Chinese Proverb

I remember the months leading up to his arrival as a blur of disorientation and mounting anxiety, unsure how to brace for the upheaval quietly taking shape inside and around me. Everyone had warned me how hard it would be. But the word "hard" is too blunt, too flat. It didn't account for the nuance. The kind that rearranges your sense of purpose even as it strips you raw.

I was anxious, hormonal, and unmoored. I couldn't find my footing, physically or emotionally. My body felt foreign to me. It was like I was carrying two bowling balls fused together, blocking the sight of my own feet. I bumped into furniture. I dropped things. I cried with both fear about the impending birth and also joy for how close my dream was to reality.

One afternoon, I was rushing out the door when I accidentally caught the tip of my dog Hazel's tail in it. She howled with a pain I had never heard from her before. I dropped everything. Plans, errands, time itself, all suspended for an emergency vet visit. In twelve years of loving her, I had never heard her make that sound. Her tail was bent, and they suspected a fracture. During the exam they also found decaying teeth that needed to be pulled. The rest of my pregnancy was spent coordinating surgeries, managing medication, and trying to calm a dog who already knew that everything was about to change. The more anxious she became, the more my own nerves tangled.

We were still in my tiny West Hollywood apartment. It was the place I had moved into in my early twenties when I was still just a girl trying to become someone. It had become too cramped, too chaotic, and not at all suited for a baby. But I couldn't bring myself to leave. The alley behind our building had turned into a fragile ecosystem of tents and suffering. Unhoused strangers with glassy eyes and fractured minds paced outside the back door. Some were quiet. Others screamed through the night, their voices echoing into my third-floor window. It had never been that bad before, but post-COVID, the housing crisis had mounted, and it only got worse each month.

I lay in bed most mornings staring at the ceiling, not just tired but quietly undone by the weight of what was coming. It wasn't fear exactly. It was the realization that everything familiar, everything that once felt manageable, was about to be dismantled and rebuilt in a new shape I couldn't yet see. I knew I wouldn't be able to leave the house without thinking ahead. No more spontaneous errands, no quick walks to clear my head. Every movement would require intention. Every hour would belong to someone else first. Even the smallest freedoms were slipping through my fingers before I had the chance to properly grieve them.

Motherhood was still a few months away, but it had already begun the slow and sacred work of changing me. Not in one sweeping gesture but in the subtle ways I was being softened and sharpened at the same time. My thoughts were heavier. My body was unfamiliar. I could feel my identity stretching to make space for something that was both entirely new and deeply ancient. This wasn't just a shift in lifestyle. It was a quiet, profound rearranging of who I had always been.

After all the wishing and waiting, the years of writing him into existence with hope-soaked prayers and future scripts, I continued to feel his spirit nearby. It felt quiet and steady. Not dramatic. Just present. Like he was sitting beside me in the waiting room of my own life, letting me know he would arrive when I was ready.

At thirty-two weeks, I boarded a flight to the East Coast to prepare our home for the summer rental season. I hadn't taken on any new assignments in the newsroom, and while I wasn't drawing a steady paycheck, I had the unexpected cushion of income from the Montana property. It allowed me to step back for a moment. I know that kind of pause is a luxury, and I hold that awareness with humility. For a short window of time, I had the space to breathe without a deadline looming overhead.

When I arrived at the eastern tip of Long Island, something inside me exhaled. The salt air, the farmland running parallel to the Atlantic Ocean. Everything slowed. It was the same place I had fallen in love with two years earlier when I was still single and scripting nightly. A town that still felt like a secret when the tourists were gone. In the off-season, it hummed at its own pace.

I had never imagined living somewhere long enough to be considered a local, the kind of person who knew which bakery closed early on Wednesdays or which farm stand sold the best eggs before noon. But somehow, here I was, growing quietly territorial over a place I had once only visited. In April, before the high season kicked in, the town still felt like a secret. The sidewalks were quiet, the beaches mostly empty except for a few year-rounders walking their dogs in old sweaters and beat-up sneakers. The small businesses like family-run fish markets, hardware stores with handwritten signs, cafés with mismatched mugs relied on our off-season loyalty. And I found myself becoming protective of them, hoping they would still be here when the summer crowd cleared out again.

Come Memorial Day, it would all change. The Teslas would start rolling in, polished and humming, driven by couples with matching sunglasses and toddlers in designer sneakers. Every restaurant would be booked three weeks in advance by someone wearing linen and talking loudly about hedge funds. The quiet rhythm of the town would shift to accommodate the temporary pulse of new money. The local wine shop would be cleaned out of anything rosé. The once-empty beach paths would be filled with people who saw the ocean as a photo backdrop, not a place to wade in and listen.

But in April, just before all that began, it still felt untouched. It still felt like mine.

When I packed my suitcase, I had no plans to stay longer than a week. The thrifted baby clothes I had collected and washed with care were still folded in drawers back in Los Angeles. That was home. That was where the nursery was meant to be. But within forty-eight hours of landing, everything started to shift.

Hazel, loyal as ever, was finally starting to recover from her surgeries. I watched her stretch out in the sun each morning, settling into the warmth of the backyard like it was her birthright. For twelve years, she had only known apartment floors and leash walks. Now, with her own half an acre to roam, she looked like she was also opening up to a new possibility. That alone felt like a sign. Maybe this place could hold us. Maybe I could stop searching and start staying. Moving from our cramped studio to a house with three actual bedrooms felt like a mansion. We even had separate bathrooms. On the second night, Squirrel looked at me across the kitchen and cautiously inquired, "Should we just not go back?"

I had been holding the same thought, but I was afraid to speak it. I had lived in Los Angeles for over a decade. I had built my entire adult identity there. Every version of me from age twenty-one onward was formed in that city. It was a place of ambition, distraction, hustle, and reinvention. I was proud of the life I built there. But now, I could not shake the sense that I no longer fit inside it. My body was expanding with new life, and my mind had begun rearranging itself in preparation. The thought of returning to my tiny apartment made my chest tighten.

Without fully realizing it, I had crossed into a new season of my life. I was no longer a woman imagining motherhood. I was a woman standing inside it, letting it rearrange her from the inside out. I wanted to meet my baby here, in this sanctuary of slow mornings and salt air. I didn't need to go back. The future had already begun.

I didn't know it at the time, but I had already spent my last night in the apartment that had been my nest for over a decade. There was no farewell, no final look around the room to let it all sink in. Just a quiet departure. A week later, Squirrel flew back alone to pack up the stroller, the tiny, folded clothes, and the sentimental pieces I had collected over the years for a baby I had long imagined.

What stayed with me most wasn't the stuff left behind. It was the pang of guilt that I hadn't gotten to tell the apartment what she had meant to me. I always thought of her as a living, breathing thing, an old, creaky, temperamental organism built in the 1920s that had somehow held me through every version of my twenties and early thirties. She had absorbed so much of my life. Late-night breakdowns. Early morning coffee rituals. First love. First heartbreak. Career wins. Career collapses. She had been more than just walls and floorboards. She had been my witness. My container.

And I never got to thank her. Not properly. Not with the reverence she deserved. If I had known I was walking out for the last time, I think I would have placed my hand on the doorframe and whispered something to her.

33
Threshold

"When a child is born, so is a mother."
—Osho

After Squirrel and I finally agreed to rest ourselves out east, we felt an unfamiliar calm settle over us. It was quiet in a way we hadn't known before. We didn't know a single soul there. No friends. I had no women to meet for tea, no one to go on a walk with or sit beside and confide how scared I was of the unknown newborn bubble I was about to enter.

That might sound small, but in Los Angeles, specifically in Topanga Canyon, I had been part of a women's circle so alive it pulsed with purpose. We met under the new moon. We sang and cried and spoke in phrases that would have made easy punchlines for an internet meme on, "Shit you hear Angelenos say." And yet there was nothing ridiculous about it. That space held me. It gave me room to be a woman becoming something more.

I went from that richness to nothing. No touchstones. Just me and Squirrel, orbiting each other in this new town, trying to stay grounded as the days ticked down toward everything changing. We were in a bubble, yes, but it was an isolating one of just the two of us.

We had been social people in Los Angeles. Our lives had been full. So, the silence wasn't gentle. There were still eight weeks to go. Eight weeks until I would meet the child who would rearrange the architecture of my body, my life, my name.

Nesting is real. It's instinctual, primal, and impossible to ignore. Just like birds gather twigs and string to build a place to lay their young, I found myself gathering, preparing, arranging. I became singularly focused on making space not just physically but emotionally for someone I hadn't met yet. A tiny being who was about to rearrange everything.

I scoured Facebook Marketplace for baby items that sparked joy, small pieces that helped me channel all the anticipation into building a nest. The one that melted me was a Restoration Hardware wicker bassinet in the most perfect shade of olive green. It was whimsical and slightly absurd and completely spectacular. When I brought it home, I placed it by the front window. Every time sunlight filtered through and lit it up in shadowed patterns, I pictured our baby boy curled inside it. That small image of him finally here was enough to calm my nerves.

I hadn't had a yard since I was a child in Florida. Suddenly, I had half an acre. The grass grew fast and wild like it had been waiting for someone to care about it. It became my obsession. I threw myself into the garden like it was a second pregnancy. When people asked what I was doing to prepare, I'd laugh and say, "Mowing the lawn…a lot." I wasn't exaggerating. I was out there every other day pushing the mower with my swollen belly in front of me. I bought bags of black mulch and spread them with my bare hands. I trimmed the hedges and mapped out flower beds, feeling a quiet satisfaction each time I stepped back and saw the yard coming together.

I didn't take on any big projects. I didn't do any consulting. I didn't work with any brands. I just worked in the yard. I walked long loops through our neighborhood. I wrote letters to Golden in my baby journal, one after another. I was planting, preparing, and clearing space. Not just in the garden. In me.

Waiting. Waiting. Waiting.

My mom flew in just before my due date. She had just finished treatment for breast cancer. Her third time getting it in twenty years. Watching her face another health scare had softened me. Not all the way, but enough. Her being there gave us something to do with our attention. Preparing for his arrival gave us something bigger to focus on. We didn't talk much about the past. We didn't try to fix anything. We just moved around each other organizing tiny onesies.

My due date was June 4. That morning, I had it in my head that if I went on a marathon beach walk, maybe I could get my water to break. I dressed in my workout clothes, laced up my sneakers, and asked my mom to come with me. I didn't want to sit still anymore. I didn't want to wait.

We drove to the beach. And instead of pulling into the parking lot like I normally would, I turned and drove straight onto the sand. I wasn't thinking clearly. I had the beach sticker on my windshield, and I figured that was enough. I also had a Jeep Commander. I figured that would be enough. The commercials always showed people gliding over sand like it was effortless. Turns out, it wasn't.

I kept driving until I felt the wheels start to spin, this slow, sinking resistance that told me I had made a mistake. The car stopped moving forward. The sand kicked up behind us, dry and wild. I felt the dread immediately. I stepped out of the car and saw what I already knew. We were stuck. The tires were half-buried, sunken into the dune like someone had pressed pause on a bad idea.

My mom and I started digging with our hands. We tried placing the car floor mats under the wheels. Nothing. The more we tried, the deeper we sank. Finally, I called the police. They transferred me to Marine Patrol. I told them it was my due date hoping that would speed up their rescue.

An hour later, the truck arrived. I have never felt so relieved to see a stranger in my life. He didn't ask questions. He pulled up, attached a chain, and started the engine. I stood back and watched as our Jeep lifted and slowly, finally, rolled across the sand to solid ground.

I went home covered in sweat and sand. No contractions. No water breaking. Just a lesson I wouldn't fully absorb until later that planned control is the last thing you get to hold onto at the edge of motherhood.

When I got home, I collapsed on the bed, completely deflated. My due date had come and gone without a single sign of labor. It felt like a deadline had passed, and I had failed to meet it. I started frantically googling every holistic method possible to break my own water. I watched YouTube videos of women stepping up and down on stairs. I bounced on my yoga ball. I danced in the living room hoping to jostle him out.

By the next evening, he had dropped lower in my pelvis. The contractions started slowly, almost politely, and then began to settle into something steady. The kind of rhythm that tells you this isn't a drill.

Every woman I had ever encountered in pregnancy had the same advice: labor at home as long as you can. They sang it like a mantra. Don't let them admit you too early. Don't let them put you on the clock. Don't let them intervene. That word, *intervene*, had taken on a dread for me. I had devoured the documentary *The Business of Being Born* made by Ricki Lake and Abby Epstein.

I knew the hospital was a machine, and if I entered too soon, I might be swallowed by it. Pitocin was the villain. I had heard enough stories to know it could cascade me into a kind of pain I wouldn't be able to manage. And I wanted to manage this. I needed to.

I had a hypnobirthing app on my phone and wooden combs pressed into the palms of my hands to act as acupressure. Supposedly the ridges could redirect pain through the nerves, giving your brain something else to process. I don't know if it worked, but I held them tight. I kept bouncing on the yoga ball. I focused on my breath. I tried to surrender.

There is something animal about labor. I read once that mammals go into hiding before birth, so they can focus without threat. I understood that. I didn't want to be looked at or spoken to. I didn't want to be asked how I was feeling or if I needed anything. I didn't want comfort. I wanted solitude. I needed the full force of my attention on what was happening inside my body. I wanted to stay in that cocoon of awareness for as long as I could. It was instinctual, primal, and deeply private.

I labored through the night with only Hazel by my side. At no point did it occur to me to go to the hospital. Not because I was brave, but because I was determined. Because I had prepared for this. Because I was afraid that if I left too soon, I'd lose control of the experience. That I'd be rushed into an emergency C-section or pressured into interventions I didn't want. I had a birth plan, and I wanted to give it every chance to unfold on my terms.

Around five in the morning, Squirrel walked into the room. His voice was calm, but I could hear the concern underneath it. He asked how far apart my contractions were. I told him I didn't know. I had been using an app to track them but gave up an hour ago because they were so close together it stopped feeling useful.

He looked at me and said quietly, "I think we should probably go."

I have never believed there's one right way to bring a baby into the world. I know women who grow their own vegetables and deliver their babies via scheduled C-section. I know women who meditate daily and choose an epidural at two centimeters. None of it matters. Not really. The only thing I know for sure is that the mother always knows. Her gut will guide her if she lets it. She will know what her baby needs.

There's this strange righteousness that hovers around the idea of an "all natural" birth. It's subtle, but it's there. This unspoken suggestion that if you can breathe through it without intervention, you're somehow stronger. Better. Wiser. I don't believe in that. Pain is not proof of devotion. Birth, in any form, is a transformation. What counts is that you make it through and meet your child on the other side.

I had a deep conviction that I wanted to feel my body. Every inch of it. I was scared of being numbed. I didn't want to be confined to a bed or have a catheter threaded into me. I didn't want a longer recovery. I wanted to move.

My water hadn't broken yet, so I figured we still had lots of time. He was still sealed in the amniotic sac, floating in his little universe. I assumed delivery was hours away. We were heading to the car, my mom and Squirrel walking ahead, and I was waddling behind them with my bag in hand when it happened. A sharp, undeniable *pop*. Then the rush.

Blood. Fluid. Heat. Everything released at once all over our wooden deck.

I had imagined it would be clear. Maybe a soft trickle. I wasn't prepared for the color, the sheer volume. It soaked the wood of the deck beneath me. I stood there, stunned. It wasn't fear exactly. It was something closer to awe. The moment you realize your body has made a decision, and there's no turning back.

I hadn't researched much about what to expect. I didn't want to fill my head with other people's stories. I didn't want someone else's fear to become my own. I had wanted to stay close to my own instincts, to let my body guide me without interference.

The drive to Southampton was unbearable. Walking had been manageable. But sitting in the car, strapped in with the pressure against my pelvis, I thought I might come apart. By the time we reached the ER, I could barely walk, but I refused a wheelchair. I didn't want to have to sit back down. So I knelt in it backwards, hands gripping the handles, swaying with each contraction as they rolled me to Labor and Delivery.

We arrived at exactly 6:00 a.m. The nurse met me with practiced calm. They led me into the room and moved quickly. An IV was inserted into my arm. Squirrel was still downstairs parking the car. I lifted my head and said, clearly and without apology, "I have a birth plan. Please don't give me anything in the IV."

Then I heard it, one nurse calling out: "Eight centimeters!"

Eight.

Everything snapped into focus. I wasn't early. I was nearly there.

How am I at eight? The baby comes at ten. That's only two centimeters away.

The doctor hadn't even arrived yet. Nurses filled the room, checking monitors, preparing trays. Then suddenly, this absolute badass came rushing in wearing a burgundy Adidas tracksuit. I had never met her before, but the moment she walked in, I felt something loosen inside me. Her energy was grounded. She met the chaos with calm, and I trusted her instantly.

Labor blurred and crystallized in strange ways. Some moments are still lost to haze. Others remain vivid, seared in memory. I remember the wooden combs pressed deep into my palms, the pressure anchoring me. I remember the ice, circular, crunchy hospital ice. I couldn't get enough of it. I was gulping it down, cup after cup.

Enya's "Orinoco Flow" played in the background on repeat. It had been part of my labor playlist. Somehow it ended up on a loop, and no one changed it. It became the sound of transition.

I had one clear instruction for Squirrel before we left for the hospital: *"You have to get the moment. The moment he comes out. The moment he's placed on my chest. I know I'll want to relive it again and again. Just get it."*

With one final push, Golden came into the world. Seventeen minutes after I entered the room. 6:17 a.m.

Exactly sixteen years earlier, on June 7th, 2007, I had sat in the front row of a Greyhound bus watching the sky light up with sunrise as it carried me into New York City. That date had always carried weight. It marked my first coming-of-age, the day I left behind the familiar and stepped into a dreamland that had always enchanted me.

This time, it marked a different kind of beginning. My birth into motherhood.

They wrote "precipitous delivery" on my birth chart. We arrived at the hospital at 5:43 a.m. I was fully dilated by 6:00, and by 6:17, he was in my arms.

For years, I had felt an energetic pull away from my career, an urgency I couldn't always name. A quiet fear that if I didn't restructure my life, I might miss the chance to become a mother. So when he arrived on that very same date, it felt like a gentle nod from the universe. A winking kind of confirmation. Like it had all been timed with quiet precision.

I remember being alone in hotel rooms on assignment, waiting for my three alarms to go off before dawn, and thinking, *God, I wish there was a baby on my chest right now.*

And then, on 6/7/23, there was.

The video Squirrel captured is primal. There's no softness, no slow fade-in. It's the head, the exit, the swift placement on my chest. It's shaking and crying and my whole body convulsing from adrenaline. I had no idea how intense that moment would be. I couldn't stop shaking. Not just a shiver. My body was violently trembling, like it had just survived something massive and hadn't caught up yet. I was in shock. I was in disbelief. I was not okay, and I didn't expect that.

As soon as he was out, the doctor told me I had torn. Badly. There was blood everywhere.

I had forgotten my labor wasn't over. I still had to birth the placenta. But it wasn't coming. So, they began pressing down on my stomach, using the full weight of their bodies to coax it out. It felt like being wrung out from the inside. There was nothing gentle about it—just firm, unrelenting pressure and the growing urgency in the room.

Squirrel stood beside me, grounded and calm. He stroked my head as they worked on me. He cut the cord. I had listened to a hypnobirthing app throughout pregnancy, and one line had embedded itself in my mind so deeply it haunted me during labor. One track said, in essence:

> You are in the ocean with your baby. The waves are crashing all around you. And he is counting on you, only you, to keep him safe. The more frantic you are, the more danger he feels. You must stay still, you must stay calm. If you scream, if you cry, if you lose control, your baby will feel that chaos in his body. You are the only thing keeping him above water. If you flail, he will sink. This is his first impression of you. Be a harbor. Be serenity. Do not alarm him. Do not show fear. Show him only peace.

I must have heard that passage a hundred times. I had internalized it like gospel. And somewhere along the way, I started to believe that my baby's first impression of me, his first moment outside the womb, depended on how composed I was. That if I screamed too loud or lost control or asked for help too frantically, it would leave a mark on him. That my distress would be imprinted as his welcome into the world.

She began stitching immediately. But I didn't have an epidural.

"Are you going to numb it?" I shrieked. My voice wasn't polite. I didn't care. They forgot that I hadn't had an epidural and quickly shot a local anesthetic, so I wouldn't feel the stitches.

The pain was excruciating. I felt every thread of that needle moving through my skin, sewing me back together.

I thought I might throw up. I was nauseous, shaking, overwhelmed. I couldn't believe I had done it. And I couldn't process it either. I didn't understand at the time, but I was dissociating. I had checked out. My body was still in the room, but the rest of me had stepped outside.

I looked up at Squirrel and frantically pleaded, "Hold him now, please, hold him now." The baby on my chest wasn't getting the calm, steady welcome the hypnobirthing lady said I should give. I wanted to be that harbor she described, but I couldn't stop shaking. My body was still in a storm, and I didn't know how to quiet it.

I clenched my fists and chewed ice and held those wooden combs in my palms like sacred objects. I didn't realize how much pressure I was putting on myself until after the baby was born. Until the pain came rushing back in, until the stitching began, and I felt every thread and wanted to come out of my body entirely. Until I looked at my son, bloody, blinking, perfect, and I still wasn't allowing myself to fully receive him because I was trying so hard to *perform stability*.

That quote had rooted itself in a part of me that had been raised to believe I should always be palatable. That my big emotions were dangerous. That if I made too much noise, I would scare people. And now here I was, in the rawest moment of my life, trying to be soft for the sake of a baby who had literally just exited my body.

What I didn't understand then, but I do now, is that I wasn't supposed to be calm. I was supposed to be real. My baby didn't need an idealized version of me. He didn't need a salve. He needed his mother. He needed the scent of my skin and the sound of my breath and the shake in my voice as I held him.

He didn't need peace. He needed presence.

The shame of that moment took time to unravel. Days later, I kept replaying the video, listening to myself moaning in the background, trying to deliver the placenta, writhing from the stitches and the pain and the shock. I sounded wild. I sounded unhinged. I sounded exactly like a woman who had just delivered a baby with no medication and was being sewn back together while still shaking from the inside out. In other words, I sounded human.

And still, I watched that video and thought, *"I was supposed to keep him on my chest for Golden Hour, and I handed him off until I could pull myself together."* Golden Hour is the sacred window, the first sixty minutes after a baby is born when everything softens. It is a time designed not for doing but for *being*. In those quiet moments, the baby is placed skin to skin on the mother's chest, still slippery with birth and blinking against the light of a world they've never seen. They are not rushed, not cleaned, not whisked away. They are simply *held*.

In this hour, their heart regulates to the beat of the one they've always known. Their temperature steadies. Their breathing finds rhythm. The scent of the mother helps them root. The voice they heard through layers of water and flesh is suddenly right there, speaking directly to them. And if all goes well, that first soft latch begins. Not just to nourish the body, but to connect everything invisible that was already tethered.

Golden Hour isn't about performance or perfection. It's about recognition. Two souls who already know each other finally meeting face to face. It's the pause before the rest of the world enters. The exhale before the paperwork and procedures and noise. It's time suspended, meant only for the two who have just traveled through something profound.

It's not something you need to earn. It's your birthright. Both of you. And I missed mine.

I've spent too much of my life trying to be composed. Trying to look good while unraveling. That quote? It didn't teach me grace. It taught me to suppress. It taught me that my baby's experience mattered more than my own. That my loudness might mark him. That my chaos might define him. But here's what I've come to understand: babies don't need a performance. They need proximity. They need love that breathes and bleeds and shakes. Not curated stillness.

Golden didn't need me to be calm. He needed me to be there.

But when he came back to me, he had already been cleaned. The vernix was gone. His skin was smooth and pink. His cheeks were flushed like a child who had already lived something. He was no longer purple and screaming. He had passed through the hardest part without me. The last time I held him, he had been raw and wild and brand new. I didn't get to be the first one to calm him. Because I was so focused on surviving the labor that I waited until I looked like a mother instead of letting myself just *be* one.

I thought I was doing the right thing. I thought I was protecting him from my pain. I thought I needed to wait until I had pulled myself back together before I could hold him again. But in doing that, I gave away something I didn't realize I would mourn.

What I know now is this: He didn't need a perfect version of me. He didn't need the blood wiped away or the shaking to stop. He didn't need a composed face or a quiet voice. He just needed me.

And it was a lasting lesson to learn in the first sixty minutes of motherhood. To realize, almost immediately, that I had already missed something I could never get back. That I had let perfectionism rob me of a moment I had spent months longing for, not because I didn't care, but because I cared so much, I got in my own way.

That regret stayed with me. Not as a wound, but as a reminder. I carried it quietly, tucked into the folds of my early days as a mother. Every time I felt the urge to get it right, to control the chaos, to wait until the dishes were done or the moment was tidy, I came back to that hour.

I didn't want to miss anything else because of my paralyzing perfectionism. I didn't want to sit out the magic just because I hadn't stopped shaking yet. I didn't want my child to grow up thinking he had to wait to be seen until he was presentable because that's what I had learned, and I was trying to unlearn it.

I let the mess in. I let the realness stay. I stopped waiting to feel ready.

And I reached for him. Every single time.

34

Postpartum Rage

"They tell you about the sleepless nights,
but no one tells you about the nights you
lie awake burning with resentment."
—Minna Dubin

Nothing bonds two people more vividly, more completely, than doing everything in their shared power to keep a baby thriving. Especially as first-time parents, navigating unfamiliar terrain, where each day demands instinct, stamina, and surrender. We were thrown into something we could not fully prepare for, yet we met it with everything we had.

We both fell in love with him immediately. There was no delay, no adjustment period. Just recognition. He was ours. And somehow, in loving him, we softened toward each other in a way that felt both ancient and entirely new. We saw each other differently. The tenderness showed up in the smallest gestures. A refill of water. A hand on a back. A long look across the room in the early dawn, half-asleep and still knowing exactly what the other needed.

There was awe in the way we were now responsible for something so breakable, so beautiful, and so entirely dependent on us. And with that awe came reverence. Not the dramatic kind, but the quiet kind that lives in the way you move slower around a sleeping baby not wanting to disturb him.

We melted at the same moments. The first time he clasped his fingers across his chest, so tiny and still somehow carrying the expression of an old man at the end of a long day. The sudden, searching flash of eye contact. The uncertain wobble of a first roll across the blanket. These were not just milestones where you feel like your baby truly sees you for the first time. They were revelations. They were proof that something miraculous was happening in real time, and we were lucky enough to witness it.

We shared those moments like oxygen. They grounded us. They reminded us who we were and why we were tired and tender and tethered. We were learning his rhythm together and our relationship as parents was growing too. That kind of rediscovery is not always smooth, but it is always real.

Even when we argued, even when we clashed over logistics or tone or the accumulation of small resentments that come from chronic sleep deprivation, it never touched how I saw him as a father. That part stayed intact. I never doubted his devotion to our son. Not once. That was not where the tension lived. That was not where the cracks formed. What we struggled with were human things. The kind of disagreements that shift when you are both stretched to your limit.

But at the core, we were simpatico. And that alignment mattered more than anything. Because even when we could not reach each other, we could always reach for him. And somehow, that was enough to keep us steady.

And for us, it was. Even when we couldn't find each other in the noise and the exhaustion, we could both find him. And for a while, that was enough. That was what tethered us. That was what reminded us of who we were and what we had chosen.

But what I hadn't anticipated was how uneven the weight of early parenthood would feel. I hadn't anticipated just how much of it would quietly fall onto my shoulders without discussion, without decision, without even realizing it was happening.

When Golden struggled to nurse, it was mine to figure out. When his weight dropped in the early weeks, it became my silent panic to carry. I was the one researching tongue ties and breast compressions. I was the one ordering herbal supplements at midnight, sterilizing pump parts between naps, logging every feed in an app that felt more like a surveillance tool than a guide. I was the one clicking through forums and obsessively comparing latch diagrams.

None of it was malicious. It wasn't that Squirrel didn't care. It just wasn't landing on him the same way. The responsibility, the urgency, the invisible math of every small decision. It wasn't that he wouldn't have helped; it's that the weight never even seemed to reach him.

Squirrel was a "chill guy." Covered head to toe in tattoos, a mop of curly brown hair, and a beard so enviable that men stopped him on the street to compliment it almost daily. He moved through life with a kind of effortless calm that people found magnetic. He had always been the steady one. Emotionally contained in a way that once felt grounding. But in those postpartum days, when my body was still bleeding, when my breasts were engorged and leaking through shirts, when I was dizzy from hunger and unable to sit without wincing, that coolness began to feel like distance.

I was wired to anticipate, to prepare, to respond before things fell apart. He was water. I was fire. And for the first time, the heat of that contrast started to burn. Because when your hormones are spiking, and your body has just been torn open, when you are both recovering and parenting at the same time, there is no room to be chill. There is no space for detachment. There is only survival. And one of us was in survival mode. The other was just inconveniently tired.

I began to notice how the emotional labor of nearly everything had quietly defaulted to me. No one said it out loud. It just happened. I was the one packing the diaper bag before we left the house. The one keeping track of how many diapers we had left. The one booking every pediatrician visit and writing down questions in advance. I monitored every rash, every feed, every possible fever. I remembered the name of the nurse at the front desk. I kept track of the co-pay receipts.

It wasn't because he didn't care. It was because someone had to do it. And I was a former producer. I knew how to manage details under pressure. I knew how to track chaos and turn it into something coherent. But this wasn't a set. This wasn't a job. This was my life. And I was drowning.

I didn't supplement with formula not because I had something to prove but because I was hanging on by a thread trying to protect what little supply I had. I knew that if I introduced a bottle too soon, my body might stop making milk. I couldn't risk that. I had read the forums. My entire feeding schedule felt like one long attempt to outrun collapse.

The nights were all mine. Squirrel took the mornings, so I could sleep in, which sounded generous, but it didn't come close to balancing things out. Living your life trying to catch up on rest is not the same as living your life rested. I wasn't recharging.

I was patching holes in a sinking boat. It was a cycle of depletion. I was always just a little too far behind. A little too close to the edge. There is no real recovery when your entire existence is reactive.

My producer years had trained me to function on fumes. I knew how to run on no sleep, how to keep everything moving when everything was on fire. But this was not the same kind of awake. This wasn't, *"If I fall asleep, the story won't make air."* This was, *"If he is left in the bassinet, how do I know he won't die from SIDS?"* The stakes weren't professional anymore. They were primal. They were life and death. And I was the only one standing guard.

It lasted eight days. On the eighth night, everything I had been holding together finally came undone. Not my worst fear, but close enough to feel its shadow. Close enough to change everything.

I remember lying in bed, already dreading the stretch ahead. I was trying to mentally brace myself for the next six to eight hours of broken sleep, painful feeds, and that low-level resentment that never quite let up. Squirrel was brushing his teeth. He walked into the room just as I was lowering into bed, and casually said, "I'm really behind on work. I need to get good rest tonight, so I can catch up on a bunch of things tomorrow."

He said it like it was nothing. Like it was reasonable.

And at that moment, I felt my blood boil. Not metaphorically. Literally. It flushed hot under my skin and surged toward my throat. I didn't even speak at first. I just stared at the ceiling, stunned, the way you do when your body knows something before your mind can catch up.

All I could think was, *The audacity.* The sheer, staggering audacity. But I was too depleted to fight. Too raw to form a full sentence. It was easier to just mumble, *"Okay,"* than to explain why his comment landed like a slap. Easier than trying to articulate to a well-rested man what it feels like to be eight days postpartum, still bleeding heavily from a retained placenta, still figuring out how to sit without wincing, still feeding a baby every two hours with a body that barely felt like mine.

I didn't have the energy to outline how offensive it was. I didn't have the clarity to put words around the fact that I was not just tired, I was in recovery. And I was doing it while being told, out loud, that his spreadsheet was more urgent than my healing.

I said nothing. And that silence cost me something too.

His work schedule was the last thing on my mind, and yet there it was. One more variable I had to account for. One more item added to the invisible checklist of the mental load that somehow only I seemed to carry. I could not sleep. I was too angry. The resentment burned beneath my skin while this innocent, perfect baby rested on my chest. He had no idea. No concept of what it meant to hold the weight of everything. No awareness of how quickly imbalance creeps into the shape of a family.

The exhaustion was unbearable. I was at the edge of what my body could carry. I was running on almost nothing. No sleep, barely any water, aching breasts, cracked nipples, hormones still in free fall. I could feel the pressure building in my chest and behind my eyes. I was living inside a body that was ringing its own alarm bell. And while I sat there barely holding myself together, Squirrel was asleep in the guest room, preparing for his so-called catch-up workday.

At some point, I must have nodded off. I didn't mean to. I was still holding him. I was still aware of the weight of him against my body. But then my eyes shut. My body gave out. It was not sleep. It was a collapse. The kind of unconsciousness that happens when every cell in you is screaming for relief.

I have no idea how long I was out. Maybe sixteen minutes. Maybe sixty. In those days, time blurred. Everything folded into everything else. But what woke me was sharp and clear.

A thud.

Low. Heavy. Immediate.

I jolted awake. My arms were empty. And in the same second, I heard it.

The scream.

It was not his usual cry. It came from some place deeper. More raw. A sound I had never heard before. It split through the room like a siren and made my skin crawl.

I turned and saw him on the floor.

My stomach flipped. My entire body flushed cold. I lunged forward and grabbed him, my hands trembling, my voice cracking into pieces as I whispered his name over and over. I could not stop apologizing. I could not breathe. I kept saying I am so sorry, I am so sorry, I am so sorry.

This was the thing I had feared more than anything. The nightmare you believe only happens to people who are not careful. The kind of mistake you tell yourself you are too vigilant to make. And then suddenly, it is happening. It is real. It is yours.

And there is no way to undo it.

I reached over and scooped him up, feeling the panic rise like a wave under my skin. His little face was bright red. I jumped out of bed and began walking him around the room, holding him tight against my chest, trying to calm him while frantically inspecting him from head to toe. I felt his back, his arms, his legs. I had no idea which part of his body had hit the floor.

And then I found it. A large knot on the right side of his head.

The realization came slowly and then all at once. This was not a low fall. The bed was high. It had not been a soft landing. He was so tiny. Too tiny for a bump that size.

By now, the screaming had stopped. He leaned his head against my chest and went quiet. I stood there in the stillness, my hand cupped around the swelling, unsure what I was supposed to do but certain that this was not normal. Not safe.

Dread threaded through me as I walked down the hallway toward the guest room. I was terrified to say the words out loud. I stood there for a moment, breathing, trying to steady myself before I gently woke Squirrel. My voice cracked as I told him what had happened, "I fell asleep, and Golden fell off the bed."

He sat up, eyes squinting in the dark. I could feel his frustration before he said anything. I had fallen asleep. I had made a mistake. I had let something happen that could not be undone.

And it was true. I had fucked up. But it wasn't neglect. It wasn't carelessness. It was exhaustion in its most dangerous form. The kind that blurs the line between intention and accident. The kind that only could have been avoided if I had never allowed myself to rest. If I had slept on the floor. If I had kept him tethered to my body every minute of every night.

But I was human. And he had fallen. And now we had to decide what to do next.

We dialed the pediatrician's emergency line and waited, breath held. When she finally answered, her voice was groggy with sleep. She asked how high the fall had been. When we told her, there was a beat of silence, and then she said the words I will never forget.

"Go to the ER now."

It is, without question, the worst experience of my life. Nothing about it is blurry. It is burned into me. Engraved. I remember every second.

When we arrived, and they saw this tiny, eight-day-old baby cradled in my arms, everything shifted. A nurse rushed over. He was taken from me without hesitation and brought back for monitoring and scans. I stood there empty-armed, vibrating with fear. I was hyperventilating. Sick with panic. My body was shaking from the inside out. I could not breathe. I could not think. I kept replaying the moment over and over again, terrified that something irreversible had happened.

They had seen me just eight days earlier when I was rushed in for labor. The same nurses. The same hallway. But everything had changed. I wasn't here to bring my baby into the world. I was here because I had fallen asleep. And he had fallen off the bed. I wasn't the new mother beaming through pain and adrenaline. I was the mother who had already failed.

They brought him back to me while we waited, and I held him closer than I ever had before, terrified of what the images might reveal. He felt even smaller in my arms. I remember counting the minutes. I think it was around fifteen minutes later when the doctor returned.

The doctor walked in with a look I will never forget and said, calmly and clearly, that there was a skull fracture. And a brain bleed. He needed to be transferred immediately to a pediatric ICU.

I wailed. My knees buckled. The sound that came out of me was not conscious. It rose from some place primal and unbearable. I was inconsolable. But even in the grief, I understood something clearly. I could fall apart during labor. I could cry and shake and be held. But not now. Not here. At this moment, I had to be composed. I had to be sharp. I had to be fully present to listen to every word, ask every question, make every decision with clarity. My heartbreak would have to wait.

We were moved to the front for an emergency transfer. An ambulance would take us to a larger hospital farther up the island to the PICU. The ambulance ride was excruciating. I was strapped into the front seat. Golden was in the back, inside what looked like an incubator on wheels. I kept craning my neck, trying to see him through the blur of flashing lights.

The sirens screamed for the entire drive. It took over an hour. When we finally pulled in, a hospital administrator met us outside the ER entrance. This place was bigger. More clinical. Not just a local community hospital. He warned me that there would be a full team waiting. Neurologists. Specialists. A trauma team. All standing by to make sure my son's brain had not suffered irreversible harm.

It felt like walking into a live episode of *Grey's Anatomy*. A voice cut through the chaos, listing my son's injuries while I stood frozen at the entryway, swallowing back the urge to be sick.

"Male. Eight days old. Fell from a bed while co-sleeping. Skull fracture. Brain bleed. Vitals steady."

It was surreal. A nightmare I could not wake from. I kept moving because I had to. Squirrel had driven behind us. There was no room in the ambulance. Without the siren, he arrived nearly half an hour later.

A social worker circled the room. I was told I would need to speak with Child Protective Services and give a full statement about what had happened. I agreed to everything without hesitation, fully understanding why they had to ask. They needed to make sure he was safe at home. And the truth was, he hadn't been safe with me. That fact sat heavy in my chest. Would they see this as an accident, or would they call it negligence? Could they decide I was unfit? Could they take him away from me?

There was no room to scream. No time to tremble. There was no space to unravel. Only to perform stability.

All of the composure I had imagined reserving for labor now had to be summoned for something much harder. Not for birth, but for the aftermath. For the fluorescent-lit stillness of the pediatric ICU. I had to show up now, not as the woman giving life, but as the woman fighting to preserve it.

My rage was not directed at Squirrel. It never really was. It was aimed straight at myself. Not the hormonal self, not the sleep-deprived new mother. The deeper self. The one I had promised would never miss a beat. I had become the mother I swore I would never be. The one who nodded instead of speaking. The one who kept quiet to keep the peace. The one who fell asleep watching the baby when she was the only one awake.

I kept replaying it. His last words. The ones about needing sleep. The casualness of them. The way I mumbled, "Okay," instead of standing in my authority. Instead of taking up space like I used to in every meeting, every set, every room I walked into before motherhood. I could have said, *"I understand you need rest, but I am at my limit. I need you to take the first shift. I need three hours of sleep, or something is going to break."* It would have taken twelve seconds. One boundary. One sentence. But I said nothing. I kept nursing, kept bleeding, kept carrying everything on a body that had nothing left to give.

And now my son had a skull fracture and a brain bleed. Not because I didn't love him. Not because I didn't care. But because I stayed quiet. And that silence did more than break me. It transformed my postpartum rage into something colder and harder to name.

An unease that settled into full postpartum anxiety, the kind that did not release its grip even after the crisis had passed. At least the rage had given me energy. It surged. It moved. The anxiety was something else entirely. It was paralyzing. It lodged itself in my chest and made everything feel fragile. I was no longer furious. I was hypervigilant. Certain that one wrong move could unravel everything. Certain that I could not afford even a moment of error.

35

Don't Panic

"Making the decision to have a child—it is momentous. It is to decide forever to have your heart go walking around outside your body."
—Elizabeth Stone

After the accident, I trusted no one. I didn't even trust myself. How could I? On my own watch, while lying right next to him, I had fallen asleep, and my precious child had endured a skull fracture and a brain bleed. From that moment forward, the floor beneath me was never solid again. Squirrel would often fall asleep with Golden resting on his chest, and I would panic. My breath would catch in my throat, my chest tight. I could not rest until the baby was back in my arms again. That kind of anxiety lives in the body. It wires itself into your system. It becomes a constant hum.

Every fleeting and silent resentment I once held about not having time for yoga or the inability to run a simple errand alone was something I eventually had to own. Because the truth was, I was the one refusing to leave. I didn't let Golden out of my sight for the first five months of his life. Not for thirty minutes. Not for a solo walk. Not even for a grocery run. I couldn't bear it. I knew I was in the thick of postpartum anxiety, but the idea of stepping away felt less like self-care and more like tempting fate. Leaving him felt potentially catastrophic.

The first time I ever left him was during a family trip to Los Angeles. We had gone together for a month to tie up loose ends after our move east. On our final night in town, John Mayer was performing the last two dates of his solo acoustic tour, and I had tickets to the finale. It felt like a quiet act of self-care, the kind the teenage version of me would have cheered for. But even an hour before the concert, I considered bringing Golden with me strapped to my chest in the BabyBjörn, his oversized noise-canceling headphones strapped over his tiny head. I knew, deep down, that I needed to try to go alone. I wasn't sure if I would stay through the encore, but I had to take that first step toward separation after the accident.

Going to Mayer shows has been one of the few constants in my life. I have seen him in nearly every era of myself, and each concert pulls a wave of nostalgia through my bones. I saw him when I was fifteen and he was twenty-seven. And now, thirty-three, I watched him at forty-five. It feels like growing up alongside a distant cousin who might not fully remember you but shares a thread of lineage that matters. That night, it felt fitting. A bookend to my time in Los Angeles, and a quiet doorway into the next version of myself. My last night in the city that raised me, and my first night leaving my baby.

The night went smoothly. I came home to find that he had only woken once, taken a bottle of pumped breast milk, and gone back to sleep. But I wouldn't leave him again for another five months, until he was ten months old, when I finally enrolled in a yoga class.

Even then, on my very first class back, I couldn't stop glancing at my phone making sure there were no urgent messages from Squirrel. Halfway through the session, the instructor reprimanded me in front of the room. I nodded quietly, rolled up my mat, and slipped out, tears already rising to the surface before I made it to the door.

The intrusive thoughts were relentless. Every time I placed him on the changing pad, I imagined him rolling over and crashing to the floor. I saw it so clearly. The hardwood, the sound of impact, the aftermath. I couldn't shake the idea that we might not be given a second chance.

Postpartum anxiety is not talked about nearly enough. It affects up to 20 percent of new mothers yet often goes undiagnosed because it doesn't always present as depression. It presents as hypervigilance, insomnia, racing thoughts, and an overwhelming sense of dread. It whispers worst-case scenarios into your ear during the most ordinary moments. It tells you that if you relax, even for a second, something unthinkable will happen.

I would occasionally watch a social media influencer that sometimes popped up on my feed. She was a mother of two boys. Her second baby was a newborn, her first a toddler. On one of her first nights out postpartum, she went to a small girls' gathering. While she was gone, her toddler wandered into their backyard and drowned in the pool. Her husband told police he had been distracted by the baby. He said he only had his back turned for three to five minutes. That was all it took.

I read the story and couldn't stop shaking. That exact fear had lived inside me since the day Golden was born. It wasn't that I didn't trust Squirrel; he was a devoted, present father from the beginning. It was that my anxiety gave me nightmares even during the daytime. What if something happened, and I wasn't there? What if my absence, even just for an hour, changed everything?

By the time Golden turned two, I still had never spent a single overnight apart from him. Not once. No girls' trips. No solo travel. I didn't even sleep in a separate room. I couldn't. Because the fear wasn't just emotional. It was physical. It lived in my breath, in my muscles, in the pacing of my thoughts.

And yet, over time, something shifted. One thing that changed dramatically was my hurricane self, the part of me that was all wind and complication. I began to calm. The sharp edges started to dull. I began thinking about the things Golden might say one day about me in therapy, and the idea of being remembered as high-strung or overbearing made me uneasy. I started letting things go. Minor friction with Squirrel. Irritations. Moments I might have once escalated.

Even in public, when a man said something snide or tried to provoke, I found myself walking away rather than taking the bait. Not because I didn't have the words, but because I needed to conserve my energy. Because making sure I stood between my child and a stranger in the subway felt more important than proving a point.

I began to ask myself: Is it dangerous or just inconvenient? I have no idea who came up with it, but it became a mantra for parents in the toddler community. That became my filter. If it wasn't dangerous, I let it go. Mud, dirt, puddles? Every day of the week. Let him run, let him roll in the grass. But sprinting through a parking lot? That was a hard no.

My son is a fireball of energy, wild and bright. Always running in the opposite direction like a streak of lightning. I see so much of myself in him. At his second birthday party, he opened the back door and took his plate of strawberries and whipped cream to sit alone on the steps. He wanted to be near us, but not inside the noise. Twenty-five people had come to celebrate him, and it was too much. I understood.

After a playdate or a class, he often walks up to me and says, "Mama, I go home now." He just knows. And every time he says it, I see myself. That quiet clarity. That intuitive knowing when enough is enough. That's me on most nights out.

Watching his personality evolve has been the most thrilling part of motherhood. Toddlerhood released me from the tight grip of postpartum anxiety. When he began to speak, to tell me how he was feeling, something in me began to breathe again. If he felt warm and could say, "I'm okay, Mama," I believed him.

I cherished his babyhood. But this stage, the expression, the emerging self, gave me something I hadn't expected. It healed me. The same way giving birth cracked me open, watching him become himself stitched me back together.

This is my birth story, too. Messy. Chaotic. Full of light and rupture and return. I will never again underestimate the weight a mother carries. Not just in her arms, but in her mind. In her memory. In the small moments where she quietly chooses to soften, to surrender, to stay.

This is where the anxiety broke, and the transformation began.

PART VII

More Will Be Revealed

Epilogue

"In the depth of winter, I finally learned that within me there lay an invincible summer."
—Albert Camus

No matter how many nuggets of wisdom you tuck into your back pocket, no matter how many self-help books line your nightstand, nothing replaces the knowing that already lives inside you. At one point, my little West Hollywood apartment looked more like a spiritual bookshop than a home, with over a hundred titles rotating like planets in my orbit. I reached for them on tender days, flipping pages like tarot cards, searching for a sentence that would reprieve my anxiety.

But the truth I kept circling was this: you cannot outsource your becoming. You can research and track and optimize, but the energy that moves your life forward lives in you. Sometimes it flickers. Sometimes it hides. It is never gone. Your gut is your lighthouse. You learn to be still enough to see it blinking through the fog.

There were seasons when my light all but vanished. Post-partum. Midwinter. After my father died. I did not cry because

I missed him. I lay in bed for days because my body finally had permission to rest.

There are moments that arrive like fate. Meeting Squirrel was one of them. I had strategized every step of my career, negotiated raises, and mapped contingencies. But I could not force love. I could not schedule a soulmate. And then one day, there he was. Not just any day, but 2/22/22 of all the days. Fate.

When I was in the depths of my depression, if an angel guide had whispered, "Two, two, two, two, two," I would have known where the light at the end of the tunnel was. But then I would have robbed myself of the growth and expansion that made me ready to meet him.

We got pregnant the first time we tried. No tests. No expectations. Just a breath and a surrender. The second time, I tried. I tracked and scheduled. Month after month, nothing. In the seventh month, we did an IUI. It worked. I tasted a fraction of what so many women shoulder when the timeline does not match the hope.

When I learned I was having a second son, I felt two seconds of wondering whether I would ever have a daughter, then a flood of gratitude. I knew what a gift another boy would be. My first son is the light of my life; he drapes his whole body over mine, exhales into my chest, and whispers, "I need my Mama." Every fear I had about raising a boy dissolved with his arrival. I felt chosen. If I am honest, the idea of raising a daughter feels heavier, because I know what the world can do to girls.

I would have the honor of two sons. To raise brothers.

His name came to us effortlessly. Indigo Wolfhart. Indy for short. Wolfhart holds a duality I love: the tension between power and tenderness, instinct and intuition. Wolf carries a wild, elemental energy—a protector and a leader who survives by courage and attunement, a creature that knows how to stand alone and how to move with a pack. Hart is an old word for deer. It is gentleness that does not retreat. It is sensitivity that stays open after bruising. Together, Wolfhart is the name of a soul who understands that fierceness and tenderness are two sides of the same divine pulse.

This time I imagined what it would mean to include Gard in his name. I avoided it with Golden. I did not want to tie him to my father's lineage, so I chose Golden Osgood. Now I am proud of Gard. I rooted it myself. It no longer belonged to my father's past. It belonged to the family I am building with Squirrel. He surprised me and suggested we hyphenate our last names to honor the pieces that make a family. At thirty-six weeks pregnant with Indigo, we stood in a courthouse signing paperwork for a name change to make it official for our firstborn too. I did not need or desire a wedding to feel committed. Our hyphenated names on our children told the story of our future.

If Golden was sunshine—warm, glowing, transcendent, and fiery—then Indigo was ocean—sparkling, restorative, expansive, and mellow. The feeling that floods your senses in a single saltwater dive, when a wave moves rhythmically over your skin, cooling the warmth left behind by the sun.

Golden and Indigo.

Six letters each. Day and dusk.

Fire and water. Radiance and reflection.

Light and gravity. Yin and Yang.

Golden watches everything. He mirrors our breathwork and whispers, *"deep breath"* right when I need it. No teacher or therapist or book has made me more present than my child's wonderment. Every night, without fail, he wants to be lifted onto our back deck to scan the sky, searching for the moon. When we're driving and he spots it above, he exclaims, "I see my moon!" like he's greeting a long-lost friend.

Motherhood rewired my nervous system. When my first son was born, the past rushed forward. My father once used my preteen image for credit card transactions. I filed the fact away and moved on. When other moms ask why I do not post my sons on social media, I smile and say I want them to build their own digital footprint. The truth is layered. My sensitivity around it feels like a landmine. What looks casual to others carries the weight of everything I have tried to protect. I keep them off the wild, ungoverned expanse of the internet. Not out of secrecy. Out of fierce protection.

From the outside, my life may have looked charmed. I was in New York when YouTube exploded, then in Los Angeles for the last golden era of morning television. Then came the implosion, newsrooms cut and budgets slashed. Friends disappeared from mastheads. The *cosmic goodness* that threads through my life is not exclusive. The universe is abundant for every soul willing to notice.

Here is the secret I learned over the years: you can be spiritually aligned and still be a hurricane woman. My sacred responsibility is to keep my storms from drowning the ones I love. Sometimes transcendence demands rupture. Sometimes going a little crazy is the only honest way forward. One of the most liberating acts for my nervous system was not breathwork or journaling. It was destruction. Sacred and unapologetic. Bottled energy breaking loose. Not to harm. To release.

After my dad died, I went back to the Florida trailer he had owned since the nineties. I expected to find my childhood boxed up and waiting. Squatters had moved in and trashed everything. Through the windows I saw no trace of us. Something in me snapped. I lifted the walkway bricks and shattered every window. Not out of hate but heartbreak. I wanted to leave a mark before the past disappeared entirely. When the trailer sold for six thousand dollars, I whispered, "Good riddance."

There were breakups too. Not just the loss of love, but the loss of a future I had built in my mind. I was not mourning a man. I was mourning the chance to rewrite the story I never got. Still, I have seen miracles arrive on their own timeline. A woman in my Topanga women circle met her partner at forty and had her first baby at forty-two. What matters more than any deadline is a vision that lives in your bones. Alcohol will not get you there. Hustling until you are hollow will not either. My generation was taught that burnout is a badge of honor. I watch the next generation choose rest and meaning and mental health. It gives me hope.

I still worry. Children dream of being influencers instead of artists or builders or poets. Who is helping them shape their values? What are we modeling?

There is a quote that changed my life. It cracked the spine of my perfectionism. In her book *Present Over Perfect,* Shauna Niequist says:

> "Picture your relationships like concentric circles: the inner circle is your spouse, your children, your very best friends. Then the next circle out is your extended family and good friends. Then people you know, but not well, colleagues, and so on, to the outer edge. Aim to disappoint the people at the center as rarely as possible. And then learn to be more and more comfortable with disappointing the people who lie at the

> edges of the circle—people you're not as close to, people who do not and should not require your unflagging dedication."

I started making circular lists. Writing names in the middle. And whenever someone from the outer rim made me question myself, I'd remind myself of where they lived in my orbit. We do not owe full access to everyone, especially not at the cost of the people closest to us.

Truthfully, I struggled in the suburbs. I did not fit the mold. There was a hum of cattiness among some "Hamptons moms" that every fiber of my being rejected. Then I found a few moms who felt like oxygen, a relief from the larger group's social scorekeeping. One of them gave me a Mother's Blessing when I was pregnant with my second son.

Time and again, you have to choose to make room for the juiciest, most nourishing dynamics, the ones that feed you instead of starve you. The sunroom in her home overflowed with flowers. We tied red threads around our wrists, an old ritual of the matriarchal line. We wore them until the baby arrived, then cut the threads as a sign of release and rebirth. For the first time since Topanga Canyon, I felt held in a sisterhood that was real, not performative.

Sometimes I read about women in their thirties discovering they are on the spectrum and I wonder about my own wiring. Two hours of small talk in a mom circle can feel like scaling a mountain. The effort to fit in with cliquish mom groups emptied me, but I showed up so my son could be included with other kids. Fulfillment returned when I invested in quality, not quantity, and let the outer edges fade.

I think a lot about culture and the environments we offer our children. I am thirty-six and I still feel most alive in motion. Thank God Squirrel is willing to be a nomadic family. You hope for a partner who truly sees you, who pulls you close at the end of the day and says, *"I have your back."* I wanted that in my late twenties. I found it. I will fight to protect it. I thank God every day for a partner who is sober, so our children never have to endure what I did.

My second labor was even faster than the first. After two hours at home, I arrived at the hospital at nine centimeters. This time I knew what I had missed before and I was determined to write a new story. I knew how to advocate for myself. I got my Golden Hour. He never left my chest. Indigo arrived calm and wide eyed, and so did I. Every ounce of ease came from what Golden taught me. He stretched me in every way, so that when Indigo came, I met motherhood feeling like a badass goddess. I was transformed.

August 17, 2025 multiplied my heart. The love for my second son was immediate and all encompassing. Unmedicated birth is the most exhilarating high. Each contraction birthed a new version of me, like Botticelli's *The Birth of Venus* rising. My body flooded with oxytocin and endorphins, a wild warmth that softened fear and sharpened focus. I moved between live versions of John Mayer singing "Wild Blue," my quiet ode to Indigo, and "Clarity." When the audience applauded, I pretended they were cheering for me. It steadied my breath and turned the dimly lit hospital room into a holy cathedral. Together those songs scored the space in a way no words could, a rhythm my body followed as my son arrived.

Seeing my sons meet for the first time will forever be one of the most surreal moments of my life. I was bursting with anticipation waiting for Golden to arrive at the hospital. He burst in with wonder and awe and proudly exclaimed, "That's my brudddddddaaa!" I was a flood of emotions, almost lifted above them, knowing I would look back on this moment for the rest of my life. It was nostalgia in real time, the urge to memorize every detail. The beginning of a brotherhood. It still gives me chills.

Life with two was admittedly more challenging than I imagined. The logistics of caring for a newborn while making sure my firstborn did not feel overlooked took every spare ounce of energy, and I was completely exhausted and blissfully happy. The second time around felt more easeful, and I soaked up my new title, "Mom of two."

And my mother. Oh God, my mother. She showed up. Patient and loving and tender with my boys. The anger I carried about what she could not give me as a child evaporated as I watched her read with Golden and hold Indigo so I could take a scalding hot shower. She held me through motherhood and healed something in both of us by supporting me when I needed it most. Grace moved through me as I realized she never had the support I now receive. She was not perfect. Neither am I. The hardest part of becoming a mother of two was losing the freedom of spontaneity. Because my mom is part of our support system, I could reclaim enough of it to feel like myself again.

In 2017, I bought the domain LastKidLeftatSummerCamp.com. The stories were already boiling. I worked quietly for two years, writing in the pockets the newsroom left me. In 2019, I announced on Instagram that I was writing a book, then archived the post a few days later. Perfectionism is a thief. It tells you to wait until you are polished.

I wanted to write about aging, about how a woman pushing a stroller becomes invisible. I used to be chased by eye contact.

Men lingered. Now they bump into me as if I am air. I posted my second pregnancy announcement and lost 517 followers in one day, most of them men. The message was clear. You are no longer our fantasy. Good riddance. Filter out.

I know women who stay in high-profile careers after kids. Some are sustained by a lattice of help and an ache at night. There is no single right way. There is always a trade-off. We cannot have it all at once. Something will give. When it does, may you choose with clarity. May you choose the path that lights you up.

The pandemic cracked something open. It gave me permission to let go. Within eighteen months, I bought two properties, one ten minutes from the beach and another in the mountains of Montana. People criticize short-term rentals. I understand. For me, it became a path to creative independence. We do not live in a system that supports mothers. We patch it together. We build the net as we walk the wire.

When I felt most untethered in New York, I did something impulsive and sacred. I painted quotes across the city's raw, ever-changing skin and signed them @cosmicgoodness. Strangers began to tag me back. Dozens a day, sharing words that met them on the street and in the soul.

> *"Instructions for living a life. Pay attention. Be astonished. Tell about it."*
>
> —Mary Oliver

> *"Live in the sunshine. Swim in the sea. Drink the wild air."*
>
> —Ralph Waldo Emerson

> *"I dwell in Possibility."*
>
> —Emily Dickinson

I did not think it through. One morning, the NYPD phoned and told me to turn myself in or face a warrant. I stood in fluorescent light, took a mugshot, and received a court date. Three weeks later a clerk called to say the case was dismissed.

Off the hook. Clean slate.

Sometimes, pushing the stroller, I look down at my sons' faces and feel heroic that I get to plan the day's adventure and watch them see the world for the first time. I pass places I once only dreamed of bringing my future children. I see a faded @cosmicgoodness tag that was once hot pink and remember the girl who sprinted through these streets scrawling quotes of literary heroes. I move slower now. I am packed to the brim with snacks and sunscreen and spare clothes. The words are still there, waiting to spark something in another woman. They remind me of the girl who needed to be heard, who turned heartbreak into scripture, who chose the bigger life even when her childhood conditioning tried to keep her small.

When I first saw *Birth of Venus* again as an adult, it felt like recognition. She stood there, vulnerable and luminous, not performing. She was simply being. Emerging. On a psychological level, her rise from the sea mirrors transformation, the passage from darkness into light. The sea is the unconscious, the emotional depths, the unknown. To step out of it is to be reborn, to embody self-knowledge and wholeness.

In modern symbolism, *The Birth of Venus* represents a reawakening of the feminine—intuition, sensuality, empathy, and creative power reclaimed after long suppression. She is the archetype of the woman who owns her becoming, who no longer performs for approval but stands in natural, unfiltered light.

For a story like *Cosmic Goodness: Surrendering the Shadows to Live in the Light,* Venus is the North Star of the feminine reawakening. She embodies everything this evolution stands for: emergence from the depths, surrender to transformation, the integration of shadow and light, and the reclamation of the feminine self. She reminds us that healing and beauty are not achievements. They are states of being that already live within us, waiting to surface when we stop resisting our truth.

Venus does not strive, and she does not hide. She arrives whole, radiant, and unashamed. She certainly does not mask to fit into mom circles. She stands in her femininity, fully grounded on the shell, her own concentric ring of armor and grace.

She mirrors what I have learned through motherhood and love and loss and change. Surrender is not a weakness. It is strength in its purest form. To live in the light, you also honor the shadows. To become yourself, you release every version that once helped you survive.

Your story matters too. The moments you weave together and the meaning you make are not random. They are sacred winks from the universe. Follow the glow that stirs something in you and trust that the spark will guide you to your very own *cosmic goodness.*

With love and gratitude,
Cassidy Rainforest Gard

Golden Osgood
June 7, 2023

Indigo Wolfhart
August 17, 2025

Acknowledgments

Writing this feels like a daydream. For nearly a decade, I pictured each detail of this book.

It did not come to life until **one person** read my proposal and saw a story worth telling.

My indelible editor, Debra Englander, responded to my inquiry, *"This is the most interesting proposal to land in my email in a long while."*

Your note gave me the most delicious burst of belief. I am grateful and indebted to you for championing my memoir to Post Hill Press.

Thank you to Lauren Campbell, Sara Ann Alexander, Brynlee Wolfe, Rachel Paul, Courtney Michaelson, Alana Mills, Anthony Ziccardi, and everyone at Post Hill Press who brought expertise and brilliant care to each page.

Mariel Hemingway, thank you for writing the foreword. Sometimes you meet a woman whose lived experience runs so close to your own that the connection feels inevitable. You told me I am cosmically good beyond measure, and the truth is, so are you. I am lucky to have a woman like you pull up a seat at the table and say, "Join us."

Mom, thank you for your renewable energy, support, devotion, and love. Now that I am a mother too, I understand in new ways all the times you have held me since birth. I love you more.

Rose, thank you for being with me on 2/22/22.

Squirrel, you were the Big Bang that changed the shape of my life and made a home of it. The morning after we met, it snowed in the Joshua Tree desert. It was rare and magical to witness, just like you. You are the love of my life. I am so glad it was you.

Golden and Indigo, your presence clarified everything in the most profound way. I prayed for you both long before you arrived. My truest vision is for you to know, always, how much I delighted in your humor, shenanigans, and heart. It is a privilege to be your mother.

I love you, infinitely. If I'm old and gray and you're reading this as an adult, call me real quick just to say "Hi, Mama." It will be the highlight of my day to hear your voices.

To my community:

Thank you to Dennis Flanagan and Joe Brondo at the East Hampton Library for being an endless resource of support, believing in me, providing children's programming through the legendary Miss Lori music class for my sons, a quiet space for a Mama to escape to write on deadline, and the many generous print jobs.

Each of you has brought magic into my life:

Jordan Snow, Christa G, Kelly J, Laura M, Lou H, LKNNAK, SWLMDSO, RGDM, Robert G, Janet W, Kathleen G, Suzanne M, Wallace M, Diana S, Sandy M, Donald V, Carolyn F, Chris B, Brent S, Jean B, Karyn D, Rebecca T, Jennifer P, Sarah Z, Alan & Mark W, Sabina G, Marci G, Duan P, Kristen B, Kelly S,

Frank E, Julie B, Olivia J, Rosette P, Bill D, Michele D, Adam S, Cesar O, Jo P, Stephanie S, Liz T, Will A, Sej S, Aviva R, Jenny B, Denise M, Mallori S, Tulsi B, Louise H, Darcy R, Adina A, Andrew V, Darwyn & Kylie M, Alise M, Dr. Nancy, Gillian C, Lauren & Doug BZ, Eva G, Rasha G, Zibby O, Elisha Z, Peiman R, Leslie S, Junot D, Drew F, Jane G, Karen L, Duha F, Cody M, Karina F, Emily G, Marianne W, Justin K, Abraham H, Michele C, Hazel G, Sage Lodge, Deuxmoi, Mariel H, S&S Corner Shop, Mel R, and my grandmothers Lucy and Shirley.

To each person who provided a blurb:

I am forever grateful for your generosity. It truly touched me. I promise to pay it forward. Thank you to Mel Robbins, Marianne Williamson, Emily Giffin, Mariel Hemingway, Mark Watts, Zibby Owens, Deuxmoi, Junot Díaz, Jo Piazza, Justin Kreutzmann, Mari Andrew, Liz Tran, Amber Rae, Carson Meyer, Jennifer Pastiloff, Aviva Romm, Mitra Manesh, Barry Barnes, Jane Green, Leslie Stephens, Drew Fortune, Will Cady, Peter Davis, Peiman Raf, and Joanna Gardner.

To my readers:

Thank you to anyone who scanned this synopsis and thought, “I have felt that way too.” Connecting through the stories that bond us is one of the most human things we do. Whether you carry pain from the shadows of alcoholism, lived through a less than picturesque childhood, joined the Dead Dads Club, endured heartbreak that felt like it might shatter you, survived a career that was both a dream and a nightmare, longed to become a mother, wondered where you fit while letting your little freak flag fly, or reached for a daily ritual to light and guide the way. A writer is nothing without readers to meet the words. My heart swells to imagine that something I wrote here might be a turning point in your life, the way so many books have changed mine.

To Cosmic Goodness:

I imagine you as a luminous current in the universe, a dash of kismet and angel guides with a divine sense of humor that exists to connect, surprise, delight, and bring the right people together at the right time. I have questioned you at times, yet I pray again and again for the highest good. Sometimes you are Venus, a multiplier that fills my heart to its fullest capacity, sometimes Jesus, sometimes nature in a spectacular sunset. On the days I seek you and find you, I witness extraordinary acts that leave me in awe of people, places, and things meant for my path. I pray every person who reads this book is inspired to seek you each day and to pay you forward to others. You are healing and miraculous. Thank you.

I WROTE A BOOK!

Home.

About the Author

Photo Credit: G M D THREE

Cassidy Gard is an Emmy Award–winning TV producer, author, and entrepreneur. A graduate of Hunter College, she rose quickly through the high-stakes world of morning television before a pandemic-era awakening led her to Paradise Valley, Montana, where she bought a cabin and named it Cosmic Goodness. Her work explores healing from childhood trauma, perfectionism, motherhood, and the quiet synchronistic winks that guide us to the miracles awaiting us. She is based in Austin, Texas, with her partner, their two sons Golden and Indigo, and fifteen-year-old Maltipoo, Hazel. Through her radical honesty and spiritual clairvoyance, Cassidy invites readers to tune to the frequency of their own inner knowing to tap into the cosmic goodness already within them.